Remembering Inflation

Remembering Inflation

Brigitte Granville

PRINCETON UNIVERSITY PRESS

PRINCETON AND OXFORD

Copyright © 2013 by Princeton University Press
Published by Princeton University Press, 41 William Street,
Princeton, New Jersey 08540
In the United Kingdom: Princeton University Press, 6 Oxford Street,
Woodstock, Oxfordshire OX20 1TW

press.princeton.edu

ISBN 978-0-691-14540-2

Library of Congress Control Number: 2013938222

British Library Cataloging-in-Publication Data is available

This book has been composed in Adobe Caslon Pro

Printed on acid-free paper. ∞

Printed in the United States of America

1 3 5 7 9 10 8 6 4 2

This book is dedicated to Emil Maria and Florence Claassen

CONTENTS

THIS BOOK TAKES a fresh look at inflation in the combined perspective of economic thought and history. It does not pretend to be an exhaustive encyclopedia-style work covering "everything you want to know about inflation." This study hinges instead on a survey of theoretical and applied work by macroeconomists starting in the last third of the twentieth century. These researchers and thinkers are the heroes of this story. They advanced the fundamental understanding of inflation by formulating sophisticated analysis and modeling that has cast the most penetrating light ever on its causes, costs, and cures.

On August 19, 2010, the *Financial Times* published an article titled "Needed: A New Economic Paradigm," by Joseph Stiglitz, co-recipient of the 2001 Nobel Memorial Prize in Economics. In that article, Stiglitz wrote,

> Bad models lead to bad policy: central banks, for instance, focused on the small economic inefficiencies arising from inflation, to the exclusion of the far, far greater inefficiencies arising from dysfunctional financial markets and asset price bubbles.

Some readers may have been impressed by this disparagement of efforts to bear down on inflation. For me it clearly signaled that the time had come for remembering inflation. For even if the successful pursuit of low inflation in many countries since the 1980s was accompanied by failures in other areas of policy that contributed to the financial and economic shocks that crystallized in the U.S. credit markets and burst upon the world in 2007–8, even worse outcomes could result in the future from forgetfulness about the costs of inflation.

The risk of amnesia has been heightened by the early-twenty-first-century experience of boom and bust. After the bust, against the background of weakened economic activity with excessive indebtedness being worked off, many observers have seen the resurgence of inflation as a remote risk, or a lesser evil than deflation, or even an inherently desirable development (as a means of reducing debt). This attitude feeds off the idea advanced by Stiglitz and others that counterinflationary policy caused distraction and complacency and must therefore bear some blame for the bust.

Worries about inflation had in any case long since subsided simply as a result of inflation being brought under reliable control. This gave rise to the temptation of "end-of-history"-type thinking—seeing inflation as yesterday's problem. The "yesterday" in question was the period centering on the 1970s, when prices rose at an average rate of 7 percent per year, leading President Ford in 1974 to call inflation "public enemy number one." Robert Samuelson (2008), recalling the unsettling and damaging effects of that time of the Great Inflation (1965–84) as American people lost confidence in their future and their leaders, observed that

> [s]table prices provide a sense of security. They help define a reliable social and political order. They are like safe streets, clean drinking water and dependable electricity. Their importance is noticed only when they go missing. (Samuelson, 2008: 4)

A descendant of what was known as "political economy" when practiced by David Hume, Adam Smith, and John Stuart Mill, macroeconomics is an easily politicized subject. This has been especially true since John Maynard Keynes, whose thought developed in the heated arena of public policy and who himself became a practicing policymaker. Macroeconomists should not complain, or at least should not be surprised, about the heat of the kitchen in which they work. Their subject has to do with the factors that affect the overall level of output and employment over time, hence general welfare. Strong opinions and emotions will always swirl around the field.

A standard defense, which I first heard as an undergraduate at the University of Dijon in a lecture by Professor Pierre Salmon, runs that "economists advise, politicians decide." The decisions of politicians often ignore the warnings they receive from economists that are regarded as inconvenient. After the financial crisis and ensuing recession of the late 2000s, the question naturally arose—in fact was posed most pointedly by the queen of England—about the foresight of experts.[1]

By way of an answer, lists of honorable Cassandras could be drawn up, among whom was Paul Volcker, who expressed his foreboding in a lecture at Stanford University in 2005:

---

[1] Andrew Pierce in the *Daily Telegraph* (November 5, 2008) reported, "During a briefing by academics at the London School of Economics on the turmoil on the international markets the Queen asked: 'Why did nobody notice it?' Professor Luis Garicano, director of research at the London School of Economics' management department, had explained the origins and effects of the credit crisis when she opened the £71 million New Academic Building" (http://www.telegraph.co.uk/news/uknews/theroyalfamily/3386353/The-Queen-asks-why-no-one-saw-the-credit-crunch-coming.html#).

Baby boomers are spending like there is no tomorrow ... and we are buying a lot of housing at rising prices.... Big adjustments will inevitably come.... And as things stand it is more likely than not that it will be financial crises rather than policy foresight that will force the change. (quoted in Silber, 2012: 10)[2]

But this defense—that economists merely advise and so cannot be held responsible for policy decisions—is not cast iron. Even academic economists whose advice is solicited by government policymakers and then offer that advice with all due caution must expect public criticism. This I know myself from experience, and it applies still more to other economists who thrust themselves into the firing line by making regular public pronouncements on policy choices, often in a way that is polemical and increasingly tendentious as they stray from their principal areas of expertise.

The spectacle of endless arguments between Keynesians and their opponents (Ricardians, say) prompts further criticism of the value and effectiveness of economists' advice to policymakers—on the fundamental grounds either that such polemic signifies a lack of any real progress in macroeconomics, or simply that economists' disputations alienate their presumed audience of policymakers and opinion formers, who end up looking elsewhere than academic research for guidance.

This question of the value of modern macroeconomic theory in the light of the financial crisis was addressed directly at a hearing held on July 20, 2010, by the U.S. House of Representatives' Committee on Science and Technology and titled "Building a Science of Economics for the Real World." Invited participants included some eminent economists such as Robert Solow, Sidney Winter, Scott Page, David Colander, and Varadarajan Chari. The main conclusion was that economists respond to incentives and that the National Science Foundation, which finances economic research, should spend more, not less, if better results are desired.

The likely return on any such investment lies beyond the scope of this book. My focus rather is on an episode in the recent history of economic, and specifically monetary, thought that does constitute a genuine breakthrough. My aim in writing this book is to give credit to all the economists who, since the 1960s, made the case for prioritizing the control of inflation and showed not only that this would improve living standards in the long

---

[2] Silber (2012: 342): "This quote and remainder of the paragraph are from a dinner speech at the Stanford Institute for Economic Policy Research Economic Summit, Stanford, CA, February 11, 2005. Personal Papers of Paul Volcker."

run but also—and perhaps most striking of all—that it need not even entail material short-term sacrifices.

These insights have been tapped by government policymakers around the world since the 1980s. As well as countering skepticism about the possibility of macroeconomics making fundamental progress and about such advances being applied for practical good, this episode also belies an assumption behind that conventional view about economists advising and politicians deciding. The assumption in question is that economists' advice will often boil down to identifying and measuring trade-offs between the costs and benefits of alternative courses of action. In this case, the economists involved demonstrated, on the contrary, that widely assumed trade-offs—in particular, between inflation and growth—can be illusory.

This whole achievement has stemmed in particular from the writings of Thomas Sargent, whose contribution was recognized by the Nobel Memorial prize committee on October 10, 2011. As a result, his work is frequently mentioned in this book.

The nature of all such breakthroughs in economics has been well summed up by Varadarajan Chari, writing in 1998 about Robert Lucas:

> Scientific progress arises from the interaction between theory and data and the desire to have one unified theory to account for the observations at hand. The search for such a theory proceeds by developing specific abstractions or models to understand specific observations. These abstractions then lead to the development of a more general theory, which in turn leads to discarding models which are inconsistent with theory and the development of better models. (Chari 1998: 171)

This account makes no spurious claim of equivalence to the natural sciences but instead evokes a process of constant and restless adaptation in a cycle of ever more sophisticated "abstractions" from new "observations." Surveying the global economic scene since the bursting of the debt bubble in 2007–8 throws up many such fresh observations. Productive reflection in a time of crisis needs detachment, despite the political demand for quick fixes. So this book also considers the contemporary relevance of the core insights of macroeconomists dating back as far as half a century. Some aspects of this potential relevance are implicit in the title of this book. In a "balance sheet" recession stemming from over-indebtedness, policymakers' immediate preoccupation is the opposite of inflation—that is, debt deflation; but the roots of inflation in chronic fiscal deficits should be recalled before it is too late. The ideas about money considered in this book—ideas that hinge on expectations and credibility—are relevant to the present-day challenges posed for monetary authorities in open economies by globalization, mercantilism, and reserve accumulation.

This book would never have been written without the initial support of Richard Baggaley at Princeton University Press, who first saw the scope for a study of this kind despite the subject being so out of line with the prevailing fashion and mood. I am also very grateful to my editors, Seth Ditchik and Jenny Wolkowicki, for their guidance, as well as to Joseph Dahm. I thank as well the referees invited by the press to review my manuscript for their valuable comments and advice.

My friends shape my thoughts, and their generosity has given me the confidence to keep writing. The list is long, and I apologize in advance for mentioning only a few: Anders Aslund, Jagdish Bhagwati, Peter Boone, Emil Maria Claassen, Simon Commander, Ned Cranborne, Padma Desai, Niall Ferguson, Roman Frydman, Christopher Granville, Carol Leonard, Ken Murphy, Peter Oppenheimer, Jeffrey Sachs, Judith Shapiro, Elif Sozen, Lina Takla, and Mai Yamani.

I am also grateful to Queen Mary University of London, which has been my academic home since 2004, and in particular to my colleagues at Queen Mary including Dick Allard, the late Alvaro Angeriz, Santonu Basu, Gerry Hanlon, Teresa Da Silva Lopes, Sushanta Mallick, Roland Miller, Philip Ogden, Pietro Panzarasa, Martha Prevezer, and Adrian Smith, as well as my PhD students including Sana Hussein, Mariusz Jarmuzek, Alex Pietrus, Shannon Sutton, Steven Telford, Eshref Trushin, and Ning Zeng.

Finally, I would like to thank Dame du Sud, Eusebio, Lily, and Gaston for keeping my spirits buoyant and free.

The conventional proviso following such thanks to friends and colleagues for their help that all remaining mistakes and shortcomings are mine alone comes not only with complete sincerity on my part but also with the happy anticipation of lively future discussions arising from their constructive criticisms—and, dear reader, yours.

BIS	Bank for International Settlements
BOE	Bank of England
CB	central bank
CBI	central bank independence
CBO	Congressional Budget Office
COFER	Currency Composition of Official Foreign Exchange Reserves
CPI	consumer price index
DM	deutschmark
ECB	European Central Bank
ERM	European exchange rate mechanism
EU	European Union
Fed	Federal Reserve
FOMC	Federal Open Market Committee
FRB	Federal Reserve Board
FT	*Financial Times*
FTPL	fiscal theory of the price level
GDP	gross domestic product
GKOs	Russian short-term treasury bills
GNP	gross national product
HICP	Harmonised Index of Consumer Price
HT	hybrid targeting
IFS	International Financial Statistics
IMF	International Monetary Fund
ISI	import substitution industrialization
IT	inflation targeting
LLR	lender of last resort
MPC	Monetary Policy Committee
NAIRU	nonaccelerating inflation rate of unemployment
NDA	net domestic assets
OECD	Organisation for Economic Co-operation and Development
OMB	Office of Management and Budget
PDCF	Primary Dealer Credit Facility
PPP	purchasing power parity
PT	price-level targeting
QE	quantitative easing

ROSSTAT	Russian Federal State Statistics Service
RPI	retail price index
SPF	Survey of Professional Forecasters
SCC	Scarce Currency Clause
SW	Sargent and Wallace
TAF	Term Auction Facility
TARP	Troubled Asset Relief Program
T-bills	Treasury bills
TSLF	Term Securities Lending Facility
UNDP	United Nations Development Programme
VAR	vector autoregression
VAT	value-added tax
VECM	vector error correction model
WEO	*World Economic Outlook*

Remembering Inflation

The End of a Mirage

More Money Increases Inflation
but Not Employment

THIS FIRST CHAPTER describes the learning trajectory that led economists and policymakers to regard controlling inflation as a priority and to pursue this goal of greater price stability more effectively. Starting from the final third of the twentieth century, the discipline of macroeconomics generated advances in the understanding of inflation that went on to have a powerful impact on the design of effective monetary policies to counter inflation.[1] At the heart of these advances was the concept of the neutrality of money over the long run as established by the classical school of economics: changes in the money supply affect nominal variables such as the general level of prices but not real variables such as unemployment or output. Yet if money is neutral in the long run, this is not always the case in the short run. Real short-term effects can be observed to result from changes in the supply of money. This duality has been well described by Robert Lucas (1996: 664):

> This tension between two incompatible ideas—that changes in money are neutral unit changes and that they induce movements in employment and production in the same direction—has been at the center of monetary theory at least since Hume wrote.

Lucas is referring here to David Hume's seminal essays *Of Money*, *Of Interest*, and *Of the Balance of Trade*, first published in *Political Discourses* (1752). The fundamental importance of Hume's contribution lies in his attack on the prevalent mercantilist school of thought and his advocacy

---

[1] The term "macroeconomics" is attributed to Ragnar Frisch (1895–1973) (Schumpeter, [1954] 1997: 278). Sandmo (2011: 330) seems to confirm it as well: "The origin of the terms micro- and macroeconomics is not quite clear, but much suggests that they are due to the Norwegian economist Ragnar Frisch who in a 1933 article used the concepts of micro- and macrodynamics. The words microeconomics and macroeconomics were later used by the research group surrounding the Dutch economist Jan Tinbergen, who in his early work was strongly influenced by Frisch."

of free trade—which had a direct influence on Adam Smith—and also because in these three essays Hume articulates the key principles of the classical school of economics. As a result, his work has been the wellspring and catalyst for most debates and controversies in monetary economics to this day. His economic ideas have been incessantly pored over by academic commentators. For our purposes, it is worth picking out from this vast literature Joseph Schumpeter's examination ([1954] 1997, 276–334) of the advances in the understanding of "value and money" during the seventeenth and eighteenth centuries. More recently Carl Wennerlind (2005) not only offered a brilliant tour of the literature but also made his own contribution by resolving one of the most contentious controversies surrounding Hume's work—namely, whether Hume misapplied the quantity theory.

In brief, in *Of Money* Hume is credited with formulating the position that money is neutral in the long run—meaning that only the price level will be affected by changes in the quantity of money—but not in the short run. As a result, there is a time lag between an increase in the quantity of money and its effects on the price level. In *Of Interest* Hume drew from his analysis of the work of his contemporaries and predecessors the conclusion that interest rates are more a symptom of wealth than its cause, and that the rate of interest is determined by the demand for loans and the supply of savings rather than solely by changes in the quantity of money (Schumpeter, [1954] 1997: 331–32). In *Of the Balance of Trade* Hume sets the framework of the monetary approach to the balance of payments by linking the money supply, trade balance, and price level. His price-specie flow adjustment mechanism describes an automatic balance of payments adjustment process: an increase (decrease) in the money supply leads to an increase (decrease) in prices, which discourages (encourages) exports and encourages (discourages) imports, resulting in an outflow (inflow) of money that eventually decreases (increases) the price level back to its original position. There is therefore a "natural balance" of trade between nations. Hume's automatic flow mechanism of international trade denied any need for governments to interfere with this "natural balance" and thus directly opposed the position of the mercantilists.

The above quotation of Lucas evokes three centuries of controversy among thinkers on political economy and practitioners of the modern discipline of economics. Successive theories have been developed to make sense of the ever-changing nature of the world economy; and ideology has never lain far below the surface of the resulting debates and disputes. Every time a "new" crisis shakes the world, the previously prevalent theories are called into question, and the old ideological battle reemerges between the partisans of laissez-faire on one side and, on the other, advocates of a "managed" economy in which fiscal and monetary policy is used to tackle economic downturns. Each cycle of controversy in economic thought generates ideas that are more or less ephemeral (depending on the timing and intensity of the next crisis) and produce illumination or obfuscation. Progress is conditional on how much economic history is remembered—while remembering also that history does not repeat itself. Most controversies can be resolved by maintaining a clear view of the distinctions between time periods—current, short, or long; or, put another way, some phenomena are valid either in the short or the long run—but not both. In this way and by keeping in mind also that the validity of new analysis is contingent on current conditions, a unified theory can be attempted.

This chapter focuses on one particular episode in the history of macroeconomic controversy—namely, how a set of economic ideas shifted the general conduct of monetary policy that had prevailed since John Hicks's interpretation (1937) of John Maynard Keynes's *The General Theory of Employment, Interest and Money* (1936). This "new" thinking about inflation and monetary policy reacted against the contemporary orthodoxy because the prevailing theory had proved to be unsatisfactory in analyzing the changing nature of the economy.

KEYNES'S REVOLUTION

Keynes's *General Theory* too had changed the way policies were conducted. It had this effect by designing a model to express "the world in which we live," and in doing so attacked the prevailing orthodoxy—the classical theory. His perception was that "classical" economics did not provide a satisfactory interpretation of the 1920s and 1930s and therefore was unable to offer policies to cure unemployment. Keynes's thinking was informed by his lifetime involvement in public policy debates—for him, economists should base policy advice on observed circumstances—and his experience of the events of the 1920s and 1930s. The perception of disorder and the high unemployment rates that characterized the British economy in the interwar years led Keynes to think that market forces alone were not enough to restore full employment and that state intervention was needed. This ran contrary to the principles of classical economists with their tradition of laissez-faire based on the idea that the economy was self-adjusting.

Keynes's prescription to actively use monetary and fiscal policies to counter the cycles of recession and booms, together with his preference for discretion rather than changes in rules, initiated a revolution in economic thinking. While corresponding with George Bernard Shaw about Marx's *Das Kapital*, Keynes announced in January 1935 (1979, 42):

> To understand my state of mind, however, you have to know that I believe myself to be writing a book on economic theory, which will largely revolutionize—not I suppose, at once but in the course of the next ten years—the way the world thinks about economic problems. When my new theory has been duly assimilated and mixed with politics and feelings and passions, I can't predict what the final upshot will be in its effects on action and affairs. But there will be a great change, and, in particular, the Ricardian foundations of Marxism will be knocked away.

Keynes's high expectations of the impact of his ideas in the *General Theory* were vindicated. Following the year of the book's publication and many years after that,

> The discussion that went on was of two kinds, the first concerned with the relationship between Keynes's theory and orthodox theory, the second with the interpretation, internal development and presentation of Keynes's own theory. The two discourses overlap, since the question of whether the *General Theory* was a revolutionary break with classical theory or a rearrangement of its pieces concerned both critics and followers. (Skidelsky, 1992: 593–94)

Even if, according to Davidson (2007), some of his most prominent followers never actually read the book nor really comprehended it, and despite what in reality was a blurred line between the classical and Keynesian camps (as Hicks [1937: 147] pointedly remarked, most of the economists classified by Keynes as "classical" "find it hard to remember that they believed in their unregenerate days the things Mr. Keynes says they believed"), there can be no doubting the revolutionary effect that Keynes himself foresaw. Keynes's "work of genius" (Samuelson, 1946: 190) was revolutionary in linking the monetary side of the economy to the real side—output and unemployment. In other words, a core message was that "money is not neutral" (Keynes, 1933: 411).

This led to a new orthodoxy called Keynesian economics developed over the two decades following WWII. As explained by Keynes's biographer Robert Skidelsky (1992: 621):

[T]he version of Keynesianism which came out of the debates following the publication of the *General Theory* was by no means wholly Keynes's. . . . Perhaps Joan Robinson was right to call it "bastard Keynesianism." But only in that form could the Keynesian Revolution survive and grow.

And for two postwar decades this new orthodoxy seemed to work in the main Western industrial countries: price stability was achieved in the 1950s, while the steady expansion of output continued into the 1960s. But then, in the late 1960s, prices began to rise. Keynesianism no longer appeared to offer all the answers, and was challenged by a new would-be orthodoxy—monetarism.

To understand the coming of the monetarist counterrevolution, it is first important to review why and how Keynes came to differ from the classical theory. One episode is of primary importance in this discussion: while Britain was slowly recovering from the First World War, Winston Churchill announced in the budget speech that he delivered as Chancellor of the Exchequer on April 28, 1925, the return of the pound sterling to the gold standard at its prewar exchange rate of $4.867. Due to the war, the gold standard had been suspended in Britain and by most other members. Members were allowed to leave the gold standard in case of shocks (war, financial crises, and terms of trade), but the assumption was that when they returned to the gold standard this would be at the preshock parity (Bordo and Kydland, 1992).

The literature on the gold standard is vast and has been beautifully surveyed by scholars such as Bordo (1981), Bordo and Schwartz (1984), and Eichengreen (1995, 1996). It will suffice here to pick out points that are particularly relevant to our subject of developments in thinking about inflation and—by extension—monetary policy. The start of the gold standard in Britain has been dated either to 1717, when silver specie disappeared from circulation, or to 1821 when the Bank Restriction Act was lifted. In other industrialized countries the demonetization of silver occurred between 1870 and 1880, marking the start of the international gold standard.

The main objective of the monetary authorities was not price stability, as in today's world, but rather to preserve the convertibility of the domestic currency into gold. The movements of the price level were regulated by the total supply of gold, which determined the money supply and price level of every country participating in the system. An increase in gold production relative to output due to new discoveries or better mining techniques led,

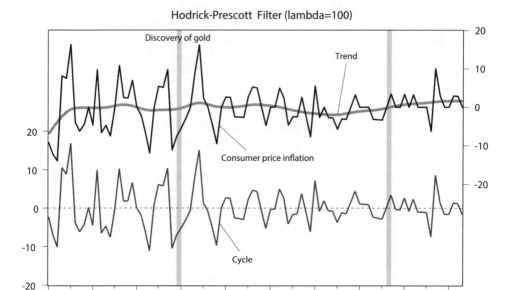

Figure 1.1. Consumer price inflation (annual percentage change), Britain, 1820–1913. *Source*: Calculated from Bank of England publications.

with a lag, to a rise in the money supply and prices, just as a slowing down or a decrease in the gold supply relative to output implied stable or even decreasing world prices. For instance, during the period 1879 to 1896, when there were only a few gold discoveries, average annual inflation rates (calculated using national product deflators) in Britain and the United States fell into negative territory (respectively –0.58 percent and –1.08 percent), while from 1897 to 1913, a time when new sources of gold were discovered in Australia, Canada, and South Africa, they rose (respectively 0.88 and 1.99 percent) (Barsky and Bradford DeLong, 1991: 816, table 1). The volatility of the price level during the period 1820–1913 is seen in figure 1.1 and in table 1.1, with high short-term volatility measured by the coefficient of variation.

To ensure convertibility, each member fixed a "rule." In Britain the rule was set by the Bank Charter Act of 1844 (Peel's Act), which guaranteed the equivalence between sterling and gold by maintaining a fixed par between gold reserves and note issue. All members' central banks pegged their local currency to a fixed quantity of gold at a fixed price using gold reserves to

TABLE 1.1

Descriptive statistics, consumer price inflation (annual percentage change), 1820–1913.

	1820–49	1850–74	1875–96	1897–1913
Mean	−0.9516	0.5387	−1.5205	1.3286
Median	−1.0870	0.0000	−2.5000	0.0000
Maximum	16.2791	16.2162	5.5556	10.0000
Minimum	−13.9535	−9.5238	−7.6923	−6.2500
Standard deviation	7.8864	5.2279	2.9231	3.2448
Coefficient of variation	−8.2876	9.7049	−1.9224	2.4423
Observations	30	25	22	17

Sources: Bank of England; author's calculations.

TABLE 1.2

Par exchange rate between the dollar and pound sterling (1870–1914; 1925–31).

	£	$	$/£
a. Quantity of grains of gold per unit of currency	113.00	23.22	4.867
b. Price of 1 ounce of gold	3 17s. 10$^{1/2}$d.	20.67	4.867
c. Number of grains in 1 ounce of gold	437.50	437.50	
Ounce per unit of currency (=(a)/(c))	0.258	0.053	4.867

Sources: Bank of England; author's calculations.

stabilize gold prices in the local currency, and it was at this fixed price that their currencies were freely converted to gold. All members' currencies were linked internationally through their tie to gold. In Britain between 1870 and 1914 (and in 1925–31), one pound sterling and one dollar were respectively fixed to 113 and 23.22 grains of gold, therefore the dollar was equal to 113/23.22, or $4.867 per pound. The price of gold was (and is) quoted in ounces, with an ounce of gold equaling 473.5 grains (table 1.2); the price of one ounce of gold was fixed respectively at £3 17s. 10$^{1/2}$d. and $20.67, this too gives the exchange rate of $4.867 per pound.

To maintain the convertibility of the pound sterling into gold at a fixed price, the Bank of England would use its discount rate (the so-called bank rate)—raising it to prevent gold outflows and decreasing it in case of inflows, with the consequences of tightening or loosening credit accordingly, affecting demand and the price level. These changes in the bank rate would also influence capital flows, with higher rates reducing capital exports from London and increasing investment in London (Williams, 1963: 514). The directors of the bank based their decision on the proportion of gold reserves to liabilities (which was monitored on a daily basis), on movements of the European exchanges (because these acted as an indicator for likely reserve changes), and on the governor's discretion—which was guided by the overall economic circumstances both at home and abroad (Ferguson, 2001: 159). For the rate to be effective it had to influence market interest rates, ensuring that the bank rate "constituted the opportunity cost of funds at the margin for market participants" (Dutton, 1984: 177). The bank rate on its own seems to have had little effect on money market interest rates, as in the 1850s the Bank of England had seen its share in the financial sector considerably reduced relative to a growing number of joint stock banks. Until the 1910s, the bank influenced market rates either by exchanging bills or by borrowing from the commercial banks (Eichengreen, 1996: 29).

At the end of WWI, the case for an immediate return to the gold standard at the prewar parity was made by the members of the "Cunliffe" committee (appointed in January 1918 under the chairmanship of the governor of the Bank of England—Lord Cunliffe). The return to gold was seen as the way to reestablish a market framework in which British industry and finance would prosper again (Booth, 1987). The Cunliffe committee was constituted mainly of bankers, apart from the Cambridge economist Arthur Pigou (1870–1957), and its report was presented in December 1919. Their conclusions—subsequently approved by the Committee on the Currency and Bank of England in 1925, and on which Churchill based his decision—were that

> [b]efore the war the country possessed a complete and effective gold standard. The provisions of the Bank Act of 1844, operated automatically to correct unfavorable exchanges and to check undue expansions of credit (Paras 2 to 7). (Sayers, 1976: 7:58, appendix)

The Cunliffe Report extended the Humeian price specie flow model. The functioning of the gold standard rested on the classical theory of automatic monetary adjustments, and such adjustments were now understood to be caused not only by the trade balance but also by fluctuations across the entire balance of payments (Eichengreen, 1995: 34–35; 1996: 26–27).

In anticipation of the return to the prewar gold parity, the Bank of England increased its discount rate from about 5 percent in 1919 to 7 percent in 1920 and 1921. Inflation fell accordingly (figure 1.2), and the exchange

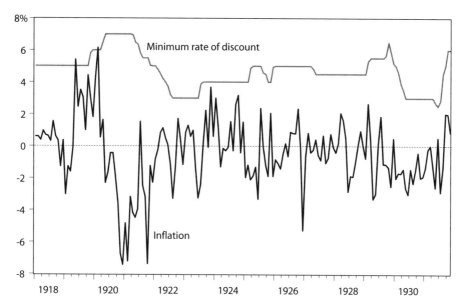

Figure 1.2. Minimum rate of discount versus inflation rate (percentage), 1918–30.

Sources: The minimum rate of discount is from the NBER series 13013, which runs from January 1836–December 1939, compiled from Bank of England publications. Data for 1836–1938: *Burdett's Official Intelligence*, 1894: 1771, 1935: 3286, and following editions (name changes to stock exchange official intelligence; then to the official *Stock Exchange Yearbook*). Data for 1939: Federal Reserve Board, Banking and Monetary Statistics, 1943. http://www.nber.org/databases/macrohistory/contents/uk.html.

Note: With regard to the minimum rate of discount, whenever rates changed within a month, NBER weighted the rates by the number of days each were in effect. The proxy for the rate of inflation is calculated as the percentage change in the wholesale price index compiled from *Journal of the Royal Statistical Society*, vol. 50: 727, *The Statist*, beginning 1913, vol. 28: 134, and the subsequent issues. *The Statist* compiled the data according to Augustus Sauerbeck's method. The base for July 1886–March 1895 is 69.0695. The base for April 1895–September 1904 is 67.2868. The base for October 1904–September 1909 is 75.1466. The base for October 1909–September 1914 is 81.960. The base for October 1914–April 1919 is 151.66. The base for May 1919–June 1921 is 220.79. The base for July 1921–July 1926 is 134.58.

rate appreciated—sharply correcting the inflation differential between the United States and Britain (figure 1.8).

Price adjustment was observed notably in the agricultural sector. Falls in the general level of agricultural prices and nominal wages were largely the result of monetary changes (Frankel, 1953: 35). These changes were greater

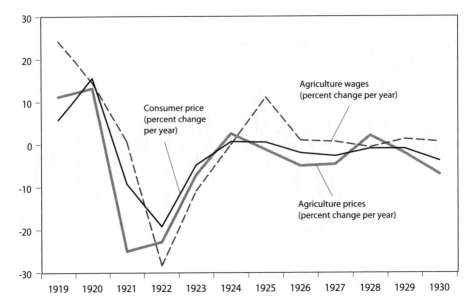

Figure 1.3. Annual changes in consumer prices compared to the changes of agricultural prices and wages, 1919–30.

Sources: Consumer prices: Bank of England. Agricultural prices: Agricultural Statistics, England and Wales; Annual Abstract and Monthly Digest of Statistics; Farm Economist quoted in Frankel (1953: 40–41). Wage rates: Abstract of Labour Statistics; Farm Economist; Ministry of Agriculture and Fisheries, Report of Proceedings under the Agricultural Wages (regulation) Act 1924 (for year ending September 30, 1925), Ministry of Agriculture, press notices quoted in Frankel (1953: 40–41).

than in the overall consumer price level and were followed by a corresponding fall in wages (figure 1.3).

The unemployment rate, according to trade union statistics, rose from about 3 percent in January 1920 to a peak of 23 percent in June 1921; a similar set of data is obtained from unemployment insurance statistics (figure 1.4).

With unemployment as a top concern, the return to the gold standard was seen as a proemployment policy restoring trade and financial patterns of the prewar period. However, resumption had to wait until 1925. But this view was by now outdated, for the war had fundamentally altered financial linkages between advanced countries: most of Europe had financed war imports with dollars borrowed from the United States (inter-allied loans);

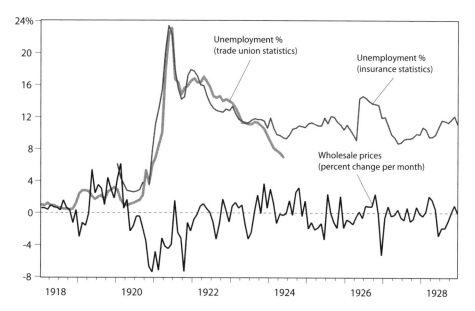

Figure 1.4. Monthly unemployment percentages derived from trade union and unemployment insurance statistics and inflation rates, 1918–28.

Sources: Unemployment percentages derived from Trade Union, NBER series 08002a, United Kingdom, percentage of total, monthly coverage: 01/1887–05/1924, Board of Trade, Labour Department (later changed to Ministry of Labour), Abstract of Labour Statistics of the United Kingdom, especially 21st abstract, 1919–33.

a. Unemployment percentages derived from Trade Union series 08002a are presented here as two variables: (1) original data, 1887–1924 and (2) original data, 1920–39. These data are based on returns collected by the Board of Trade and the Ministry of Labour from various trade unions that paid unemployment benefits; persons on strike, locked out persons, and the sick or superannuated are excluded.

b. The proxy for the rate of inflation is calculated as the percentage change in the wholesale price index compiled from the *Journal of the Royal Statistical Society*, vol. 50: 727, *The Statist*, beginning 1913, vol. 28: 134, and the subsequent issues. *The Statist* compiled the data according to Augustus Sauerbeck's method. The base for July 1886–March 1895 is 69.0695. The base for April 1895–September 1904 is 67.2868. The base for October 1904–September 1909 is 75.1466. The base for October 1909–September 1914 is 81.960. The base for October 1914–April 1919 is 151.66. The base for May 1919–June 1921 is 220.79. The base for July 1921–July 1926 is 134.58.

c. Insured workers unemployed, NBER series 08002a, area covered: United Kingdom, percentage of total, monthly coverage: 01/1920–09/1920, 11/1920–10/1939, Ministry of Labour, Abstract of Labour Statistics 18th and 21st. http://www.nber.org/databases/macrohistory/contents/uk.html.

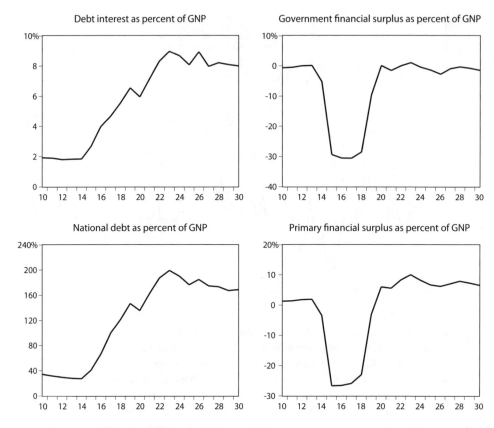

Figure 1.5. Trends in 1910–30.
Source: Bank of England.

and the issue of war reparations (transfers in gold and in kind expected from Germany by the victors) added an extra layer of complication to the reactivation of an international financial network able to release individual countries from liquidity constraints.

To finance the war Britain had ran large budget deficits, averaging 30 percent of GNP annually between 1915 and 1918 (the primary deficit averaged about 25 percent during the same period). As a result, the national debt increased from £651 million in 1914 to £7,435 million by 1919, which, as a percentage of GNP, translated into 27.3 percent and 146.4 percent, respectively, increasing the debt service from 1.85 percent of national income to 6.54 percent in 1919 and 8 percent in 1929, representing about 40 percent of the budget (these trends are shown in figure 1.5).

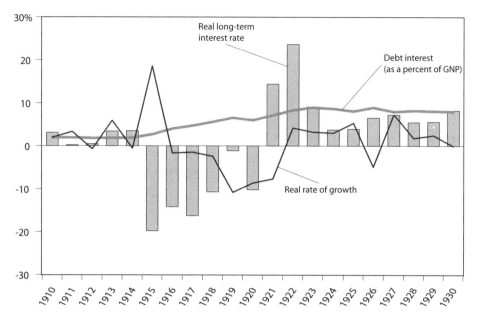

Figure 1.6. The debt burden.
Source: Bank of England.

In the 1920s the budget was kept broadly in balance—which, given the weight of post-WWI debt service entailed a substantial primary surplus. Yet the combination of deflation and low growth did not alleviate the debt burden, as seen in figure 1.6. The postwar high level of public debt made the return to the prewar parity hazardous.

Churchill did not take the decision lightly; he paid careful attention to the arguments of both advocates and critics of the move. This is demonstrated by the close consultations with his direct advisers from the Bank of England and the Treasury. He also assembled at a dinner party a group of outside experts to debate the issue, including Keynes among those opposed to the move (Sayers, 1970). Keynes was not alone in being concerned by the return to the gold standard at the prewar parity; others included the Federation of British industries and "men of influence and authority in financial matters" (Hume, 1970: 145) such as Felix Schuster, governor of the Union Bank of London, and E. H. Holden, managing director of the London, City and Midland Bank. But as many countries including the United Kingdom were faced with inflation and unemployment, and five countries—Austria,

TABLE 1.3

Inflation episodes.

Country	Dates	Average inflation rate (percentage per month)
Austria	October 1921–August 1922	47.1
Germany	August 1922–November 1923	322.0
Hungary	March 1923–February 1924	46.0
Poland	January 1923–January 1924	81.4
Russia	December 1921–January 1924	57.0

Source: Cagan (1956: 26, table 1).

Germany, Hungary, Poland and Russia—had a monthly inflation rate close to or above 50 percent (table 1.3), the return to the gold standard came to be seen as the key to price stability and economic recovery: "[W]e simply had to go back to the gold standard" (Cassel, 1932: 659).

But despite the price adjustment that took place in 1920–21, the inflation differential that had accumulated between Britain and the United States since the war made a return to the prewar parity questionable and was attacked by Keynes in "The Economic Consequences of Mr Churchill" (1970) (figure 1.7). In 1925 the British price level was still 76 percent above the 1913 value.

Not only was the U.K. inflation rate higher than the U.S. inflation rate, but it was also more volatile, as indicated by comparing the coefficients of variation (respectively 5.75 for the United Kingdom and 2.86 for the United States) measuring short-term volatility in table 1.4.

Keynes's argument was that as a result of labor becoming much more organized in the postwar period, reductions in wages would be strongly resisted. In the first instance, workers would resist any loss of salary; therefore, wages would not fall as rapidly as prices, and this would force enterprises to reduce their demand for labor, in turn causing a fall in output. Workers would start to negotiate only when unemployment reached a level sufficient to scare them into negotiation. For Keynes, restoring the gold standard at its prewar parity meant a reevaluation of about 10 percent, this "involves a reduction of 10 percent in the sterling receipts of our export industries" (Keynes, 1970: 27). As a result of tight monetary policy, aggregate demand would contract but wages were not going to fall at the same pace as prices. (There is some argument about whether the revaluation involved was 10 percent or 1.1 percent, according to the Chamberlain-Cradbury advisory

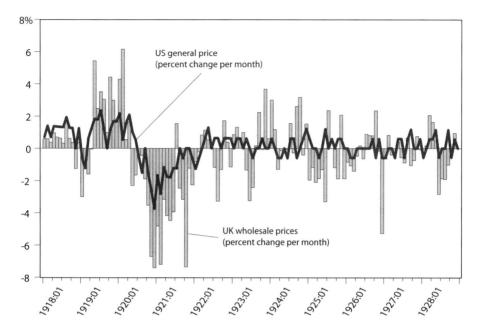

Figure 1.7. Comparison of the U.S. and U.K. inflation rates, 1918:01–1928:12.
  Sources: Bank of England and NBER.
  Note: NBER series 04051; Federal Reserve Bank of New York City, letter from reports department for 1860–1933.

TABLE 1.4

Descriptive statistics—Comparison of U.S. and U.K. inflation rates, 1914:01–1924:12.

	1914:01–1924:12	
	U.K. wholesale price (percentage change per month)	U.S. general price (percentage change per month)
Mean	0.47	0.40
Median	0.58	0.57
Maximum	6.67	3.28
Minimum	−7.42	−3.74
Standard deviation	2.68	1.15
Coefficient of variation	5.75	2.86
Observations	132	132

Sources: Bank of England; NBER; author's calculations.

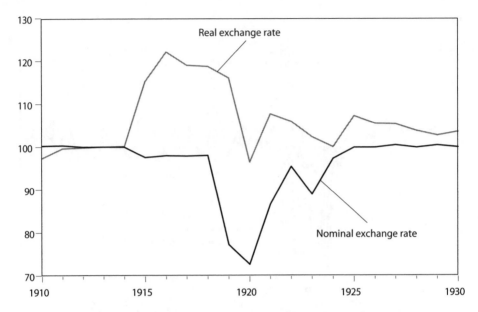

Figure 1.8. U.K. pound sterling exchange rates versus U.S. dollar, 1910–30, 1913=100. *Source*: Friedman and Schwartz (1963: 769–71, table A-4).

committee, or 3 percent as the daily exchange rates of the time seem to reveal). In fact, there is considerable discussion about the extent of the overvaluation of sterling. Depending on which index is used (see Bordo and Bayoumi, 1996), the exchange rate had started to appreciate toward parity in 1924, and in real terms the exchange rate rose by about 7 percent between 1924 and 1925 (Bordo and Bayoumi, 1996: 16) (figure 1.8).

The question of the appropriate parity at which to restore the link with gold hardly troubled most proponents. Bordo and Kydland (1992) argue that it was considered part of the gold standard normal commitment device. Moreover, and as highlighted by Bordo and Rockoff (1996), there was a strong commitment to the rule that the so-called good housekeeping seal was correlated with easier access to the capital market, facilitating the sale of bonds and therefore the financing of the large war debt. The deflationary effect of a return to the gold standard was considered minimal as "many people ... hoped that America's large gold hoard would lead to a rise of prices across the Atlantic and so bring the pound sterling back to parity without a fall of prices here" (*The Economist*, June 14, 1924: 1190, quoted by Hume, 1970: 138). This did not happen, but Hume (1970: 138) argues that the decisive factor was the "proposition that the famous gap between US and British prices was now very small," meaning that the adjustment would be small and that the gold standard could therefore be restored without any major deflation—contrary to the view of Keynes, who foresaw deflation as the direct consequence of a return to the gold standard at the prewar parity.

As Keynes had predicted, reducing nominal wages further proved difficult; wages decreased by 40 percent in 1920–21, but prices were still above U.S. prices, and British industries, especially the traditional export industries, suffered—resulting in lower output and job losses. This situation was aggravated by other countries' return to the gold standard (such as France and Belgium in 1926 and 1927, respectively) at an undervalued rate.

Real GNP fell by about 5 percent year-on-year in 1926, while the unemployment rate reached 11–12 percent by 1925–26, and a general strike ensued in May 1926. The Bank of England increased its interest rate to 5 percent on March 5, 1925, in response to the Federal Reserve Bank's rate indicating that the policy was to maintain a strong currency. But when the recession started to take effect and fearing more labor unrest, the bank rate was lowered first in August 1925 to 4.5 percent, then in October to 4 percent. Then from December 1925 to February 1930, the bank rate never decreased below 4.5 percent and much of the time was 5 percent. The recession was short-lived, confined to 1926, with real GNP picking up 7 percent in 1927, and the unemployment rate fell to about 9 percent in 1927 (figure 1.9).

For most proponents of a return to the gold standard, the problem resided in world export markets being depressed due to the lack of a stable international monetary system (Sayers, 1970: 88–91). The reasoning was that the revival of world export markets and employment would be achieved thanks to the flexibility of wages and prices; the fall in prices should have been accompanied by an equal fall in nominal wages, leaving real wages untouched as well as output and employment. The subsequent fall in aggregate demand caused prices and wages to fall by an equal amount, boosting exports and slowing down imports toward equilibrium. The former flagship export industries of the prewar period such as coal, cotton, iron, textiles, and shipbuilding failed to modernize and were continuously depressed. These sectors had already been showing signs of technological backwardness before the war. U.S. and Japanese exports had encroached into traditional British export markets in Latin America and Asia, respectively, during the war and in the postwar period of sterling overvaluation. Meanwhile, the war-induced deterioration in Britain's net external asset position had reduced its net income from abroad by a significant amount (Morgan [1952] estimated this liquidation at £285 million, or 10 percent of the total stock, which in

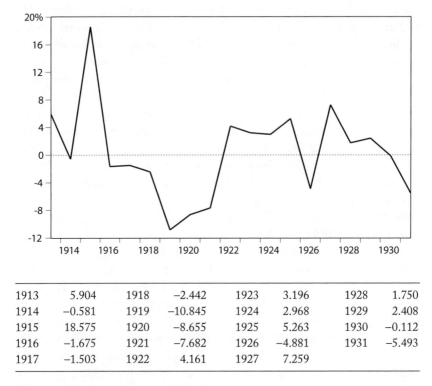

1913	5.904	1918	−2.442	1923	3.196	1928	1.750
1914	−0.581	1919	−10.845	1924	2.968	1929	2.408
1915	18.575	1920	−8.655	1925	5.263	1930	−0.112
1916	−1.675	1921	−7.682	1926	−4.881	1931	−5.493
1917	−1.503	1922	4.161	1927	7.259		

Figure 1.9. Real rate of growth, 1913–31.
Source: Bank of England.

1914 was of the same order of magnitude of British GDP), necessitating a corresponding trade improvement just to maintain current balance.

The classical gold standard of 1880 to 1914 was associated with prosperity and London's dominance; and it was therefore seen as urgent to return to this arcadia given the chaotic economic conditions of the postwar period. This consensus among bankers failed to see that cause and effect worked the other way around and that the gold standard's glory years were intrinsically linked to the major role played by the pound sterling, which underpinned an integrated international monetary system thanks to the sophistication of London (Sayers, 1970: 98; Marcuzzo and Rosselli, 1987: 370). The international gold standard was a British-managed standard (Williams, 1963). British monetary policy and the bank rate used to regulate the sterling exchange rate were central to the international monetary arrangement due to the key position held by London in world financial markets legitimized by Britain's policy of free trade. For Joan Robinson (1962: 117),

> The hard-headed Classicals made no bones about it. They were arguing against the narrow nationalism of Mercantilists in favour of a more far-sighted policy, but they were in favour of Free Trade because it was good for Great Britain, not because it was good for the world.

Britain was the "workshop of the world," exporting 7 percent of its national income just before the First World War, a level not seen in the postwar period (James, 2001: 12). Britain supplied its colonies and other countries with industrial goods while acquiring food and raw materials from them. Against this background, the City of London developed into a powerful international clearing house where transactions were cleared in pound sterling. Britain did not engage in accumulating large stocks of gold reserves, as would France and the United States after the war. Instead, surpluses were translated into more attractive investments and foreign loans.

Other countries had no equivalent of Britain's powerful private banking system oriented towards international finance and foreign investments. Most British savings were channeled into foreign investments. British banks operated all around the world, and the bill of London was used for financing not only British trade with the rest of the world, but third-country trade as well. Bills of exchange were the alternative to shipping gold; the bill on London became the favorite means of exchange in international payments after the Napoleonic Wars, a state of affairs supported by the City's well-organized foreign exchange market. Since the early nineteenth century, the discount and accepting houses had complemented the joint stock and private banks, reinforcing the key role of Britain in world trading relations. The City intermediated international claims and debts. A network of branches facilitated monetary circulation. Sterling was the international reserve currency, allowing the Bank of England to dictate its monetary policy to other central banks through its bank rate just as in any fixed exchange rate regime. Some countries held British treasury bills or bank deposits as international reserves in London. This was true not only of British colonies (especially India), but also of Japan and Russia. Therefore, part of the foreign assets held in London were monetary reserves of a large number of countries using sterling as a means of payment and reserve. These reserves and other foreign assets such as speculative capital could be converted into gold at all times on simple demand.

Therefore, far from being automatic, the entire system rested on central banks' discretion and international cooperation. By its nature the gold standard was asymmetrical, meaning that a deficit country loosing gold could be forced to reduce its money supply until total depletion of its gold reserves, while a surplus country, sterilizing gold inflows, could accumulate gold without limits and therefore exhaust the gold stock. Adjustment was complicated by short-term capital movements. Speculators gambling that a deficit country would be forced either to abandon the gold standard or to devalue its currency could take their money elsewhere, exacerbating the outflow of gold reserves from the deficit country. Before the war, this asymmetry was managed by the Bank of England using the bank rate to control the sterling exchanges and indicate to other central banks and governments the action to be taken to preserve the convertibility to gold. Through the bank rate, the City of London drew on liquidity from other countries if its own funds were stretched to finance other countries and therefore to cushion the ups and downswings of economic activity. In short, international cooperation was the key to defend currencies (Eichengreen, 1995: 65): when in trouble, a weak country's currency would be rescued thanks to other central banks discounting bills and lending gold, meaning that all countries in fact had access to the full pool of gold available to the entire gold standard system.

Because the entire system was centered on the Bank of England, it had to hold enough gold to ensure convertibility. But since the bank was a private, for-profit institution (it was not nationalized before 1946), its incentive was to hold interest-bearing assets rather than barren gold (Bernanke and James, 1990: 7). As a result, the convertibility of the pound sterling was guaranteed only by a "thin film of gold" (Sayers 1957: 18, quoted in Eichengreen 1995: 49), so thin that on three occasions—during the 1890 Baring crisis, the 1906 sterling crisis, and the 1907 American financial crisis—this very convertibility was very much in doubt. In the later nineteenth century, the ratio of the Bank of England's holding of coin and bullion against the domestic money supply comprising bank deposits and notes in circulation fell below 2 percent (Eichengreen, 1995: 49, quoting Viner, 1951: 124). In 1913 the same ratio was about 3.8 percent (Morrell, 1981: 12). This "thin film of gold" guaranteed the entire system only because all other central banks had a strong interest in assisting the Bank of England in the running of the gold standard. The heyday of the gold standard therefore rested on international integration of trade and financial linkages, the mobility of labor, and international cooperation. In the interwar period, all these were gone (Eichengreen, 1995: 49–54). With the status of Britain transformed from a position of international creditor to short-term debtor, the British managed standard was dead and the system proved unsustainable.

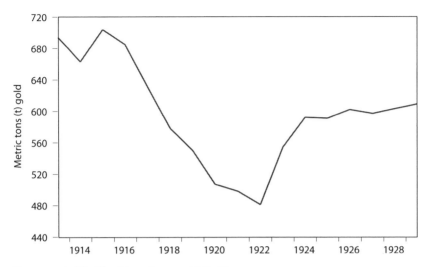

Figure 1.10. World gold production, 1913–29.

Sources: The sources of data for gold output are the mineral statistics publications of the U.S. Bureau of Mines (USBM) and the U.S. Geological Survey (USGS)—Minerals Yearbook (MYB) and its predecessor, Mineral Resources of the United States (MR), and Mineral Commodity Summaries (MCS) and its predecessor, Commodity Data Summaries (CDS). U.S. Geological Survey, Statistics, in T. D. Kelly and G. R. Matos, comps., "Historical Statistics for Mineral and Material Commodities in the United States: U.S. Geological Survey Data Series 140," http://pubs.usgs.gov/ds/2005/140/.

Note: World gold production data for the years 1900–1926 are from reported estimates by Ridgeway (1929). World gold production data for the years 1927 to the most recent are from the MYB in the "Salient Gold Statistics" and "Gold: World Production by Country" tables. Updated values for world gold production for the year 1929 reflect revised estimates by the USGS gold commodity specialist for some countries.

In the interwar period, there were concerns about gold not being produced in sufficient amount to support economic activity (figure 1.10): gold production was estimated to be about two-thirds of what was necessary to support economic activity at the current price level. The danger was that an insufficient supply of money would lead to a fall in prices and of world output, bringing about borrowers' insolvency and increasing the real value of public debt to unsustainable levels. Given such pressures, it was considered necessary to prevent government use of the printing press by discounting bills; these measures aimed at preserving price stability and the credibility

TABLE 1.5

Value of merchandise exports (in millions of dollars),
world total and for selected countries.

Year	World exports	U.K.	U.S.	France	Belgium	Germany
1924	27,185	3,538	4,498	2,169	644	1,559
1927	31,378	3,451	4,759	2,164	740	2,435
Percentage of world exports						
1924	100.0	13.0	16.5	8.0	2.4	5.7
1927	100.0	11.0	15.2	6.9	2.4	7.8

Sources: League of Nations, Review of World Trade, 1936; Memorandum on International Trade and Balance of Payments 1913–27 and 1927–29, quoted in Sayers (1970: 94, table A).

of the gold standard sometimes were so strict that they prevented gold standard members from coming to the rescue of other members.

Other measures aimed at economizing gold such as excluding gold coins from circulation and supplementing reserve holdings of gold with foreign currencies. The practice of supplementing gold reserves with reserve currencies such as sterling and U.S. dollar was reinforced by the 1922 Genoa Conference (April 10–May 19) recommending the adoption of a gold exchange standard.

The overvaluation of sterling was reflected in the difficulty of maintaining London's gold reserve and the trade balance. The share of U.K. merchandise exports by value in total world exports declined from 13 percent to 11 percent between 1927 to 1929 (table 1.5 and figure 1.11).

That 2-percentage-point decline was not large enough, however, to explain the sluggish growth and the high unemployment of the late 1920s (Bordo and Bayoumi, 1996: 19). In the prewar period there was little political resistance, leaving the central bank relatively free to use the bank rate whenever necessary to preserve the gold convertibility; this was not the case after the war. While the 1919 Cunliffe Report had still presented the traditional vision of a self-governing international economy under universal gold convertibility, the expansion of the labor movement since the legalization of trade unions in the 1870s had given rise to a tension between employment and balance of payments targets.

But while in deficit countries, wages and other prices were prevented from falling sufficiently to restore external balances, nothing prevented the rise in nominal wages in surplus countries such as France and the United

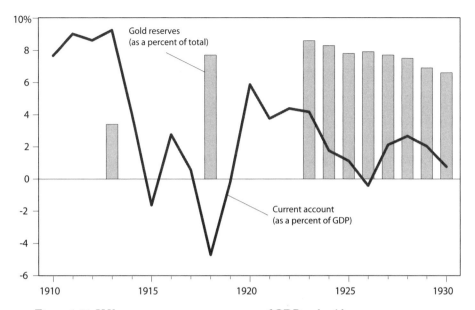

Figure 1.11. U.K. current account as percentage of GDP and gold reserves as percentage of total reserves, 1910–30.

Source: GDP and current account figures are from Jones and Obstfeld (2001), http://elsa.berkeley.edu/users/obstfeld/ftp/account_data/copyright.html.

States, and indeed they did, but despite this increase both countries remained in surplus (Eichengreen, 1995: 204–6).

Therefore while the resumption of the prewar parity played a role in the poor economic performance of Britain after 1925, the main reason lies elsewhere and has to do with fundamental flaws inherent in the gold standard system such as the distribution of gold reserves (figure 1.12). Bernanke and James (1990: 9–11) explain that both France and the United States had no incentive contrary to Britain to avoid hoarding gold. They relied on a statutory fractional reserve requirement, of at least 40 percent in the case of the Federal Reserve's gold holdings, as opposed to a fiduciary issue. The United States and other surplus countries (especially France) kept accumulating gold, and between them held about half the world's monetary gold in 1928 while reining in domestic prices. Persistent sterilization of their balance of payments surpluses transmitted deflationary pressures to the rest of the world (Bordo and Kydland, 1992: 34).

Summing up the recent literature on this subject (Temin, 1989; Bordo and Bayoumi, 1996; Eichengreen, 1995, 1996; Bernanke and James, 1990),

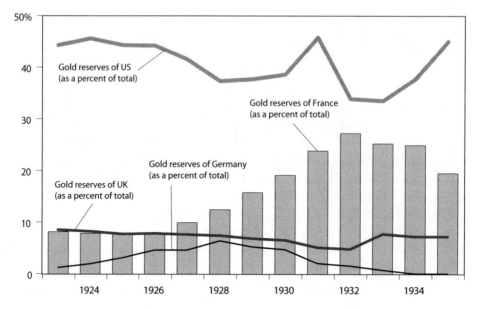

Figure 1.12. Gold reserves of central banks and governments, 1923–35, percentage of total.

Source: Hardy (1936: 93), quoted in Eichengreen (1996: 65, Table 3.1).

returning to the gold standard itself in an environment of considerable un-certainty caused by the war and of minimal international cooperation had a strong deflationary impact. With the United States and France generating balance of payments surpluses resulting from mercantilist policies of tariff protection and sterilization of current account surpluses, the distribution of gold became increasingly uneven, and this, in turn, caused inadequate money supply.

Keynes objected to the prewar parity and the monetary policy, which he judged misguided (Keynes, 1970: 29). For Keynes if credit could have been restricted by raising the bank rate further, this policy "will be, in a sense, successful" (Keynes, 1970: 39) by bringing down monetary wages and the cost of living, hence restoring real wages to their former level—albeit at the cost of strong social inequalities. Unless American prices were going to rise or the price of gold fall, his solution was to reverse the decision to restore the gold standard at the prewar parity.

For Keynes and his followers, a "drastic remedy" was needed as Keynes wrote in "Does Unemployment Need a Drastic Remedy?" The reigning orthodoxy could not provide this remedy. In this paper, as in "Can Lloyd George Do It?" (1929) in advance of the *General Theory* (1936), Keynes advocated the use of public works to reduce unemployment.

Keynes in the *General Theory* was concerned to explain the realities of the British economic situation in the 1920s and the Depression in the 1930s. The classical theory framework with its monetary neutrality and its assumption of full employment was inconsistent with these events; and this required the design of a new model in which free markets were replaced with interventionist government policies. The demand primed by the pump of public money would cushion the fall in output and resulting job losses.

In the *General Theory* Keynes formalized his theory of aggregate output and employment. His analytical framework is mainly static, as his concern was to solve the main problem of the time, which was unemployment. High rates of unemployment are due to a lack of aggregate demand, defined as the sum of consumption and investment; therefore demand had to be stimulated by increasing expenditures. Say's law does not work; supply does not create its own demand, at least not at full employment equilibrium because wages are sticky. Investment decisions are constrained by uncertainty, and this results in oversaving and thus underinvestment—a situation that could be corrected only by using public investment to fill the gap left by the lack of private investment. Fiscal policies such as cutting taxes and increasing government spending are the solution to counter a recession and a depression. Such expansionary fiscal action will expand output and therefore employment. The income of those employed in public works projects will rise—as, therefore, will their consumption expenditures, which in turn will produce a virtuous circle generating a second round of job creation.

By advocating government intervention in fiscal and more generally in monetary affairs, Keynes was breaking with the "classical" tradition. His theory was welcome because, as so beautifully put by Harry Johnson (1976), the *General Theory* offered a theory of "deep depression" (Johnson, 1976: 593) stemming from the perception of the circumstances of the depression as casting serious doubt on "the efficacy of monetary policy" (Johnson, 1976: 588). In making this pragmatic move to correct the shortcomings of accepted economic theory as laid bare by the severity of the economic crisis, Keynes drew at will on the concepts that economists had developed up to that point while at the same time upending much generally accepted economic thinking. The point that needs to be stressed in this context, however, is that what is often thought of as the Keynesian revolution in economics was a side effect of Keynes's own main pragmatic project of applying common sense—supported by the best available tools of the economist's trade—to the urgent contemporary threat not only to the material welfare of the masses but also (as Keynes saw things) to civilization itself.

This reality—that Keynes was pursuing a specific contemporary agenda more than a universal blueprint—has since been obscured from view in various ways. First, the two decades of strong growth in Western Europe and North America after the Second World War prompted a relapse into the complacency prevalent before the Great Depression that viewed actual conditions as validating economic theories (the only difference now being that the theories in question were no longer the classical framework but instead a selective formulation of Keynes's own ideas). Second, when the next big shock to the system did materialize—in the form of the "stagflation" that followed the first oil shock of the early 1970s (showing that the supposedly alternative evils of rising prices and unemployment could perfectly well be combined)—Keynes's revolution was championed as a panacea cure. But the inadequacies of would-be Keynesian cures as revealed by real life (an irony that Keynes himself would surely have cherished) led to a waning of the influence of Keynesianism as it had evolved by that stage—a development supported intellectually by Milton Friedman's critique of the project of cushioning the business cycle by using fiscal policy to stimulate demand. Yet the global financial crash of 2008 sparked a new round of the veneration of Keynes, with the authority of "The Master" invoked in support of the stimulus policies adopted by the United States, the United Kingdom, and other high-income countries to combat the effects of sharp recession.[2]

THE COMEBACK OF CLASSICAL PRINCIPLES

The "Keynesian revolution" turned "a theory designed to illuminate the role of money and monetary policy in a monetary economy into the dogmatic contention that money does not matter" (Johnson, 1976: 588). The monetarist counterattack against that "bastard" Keynesianism "established that monetary policy can do something about inflation and that central banks can reasonably be held accountable for controlling inflation" (Woodford, 2007: 3).

This result did not materialize overnight. After the Second World War and in the heyday of the new Keynesian thinking, central bankers and what might be called the economic policy community more generally took years

[2] See Skidelsky (2009).

to come around to the view that price stability was a worthy objective. Policymakers were slow in particular to learn how to conduct policy under the new monetary regime that succeeded the eras of the gold standard, which ended in 1931 when Britain left the standard, and of Bretton Woods. Arthur Burns, for example, who headed the Federal Reserve from 1970 to 1978, was skeptical about the role of monetary policy in stopping inflation (Goodfriend, 2007: 50). On this view, higher output and employment were associated with expansionary monetary policy and moderate inflation was merely a price to be paid for higher employment.

The United States emerged from Second World War as the preeminent world power, and the dollar became the main international reserve currency—formally linked to gold until 1971. The shift at that point to fully fiat money and floating exchange rates was accompanied by high inflation and economic dislocation. Four periods can be distinguished between 1948 and 2009 (figure 1.13):

- 1948–64: the period of postwar prosperity when the average annual rates of inflation, output, and unemployment were, respectively, 1.9 percent, 4.3 percent, and 4.9 percent.
- 1965–84: what became known as the Great Inflation when annual inflation, output growth, and unemployment rates averaged about 6.1 percent, 2.9 percent, and 6.1 percent. This is the period that interests us most as the high inflation rates resulted in the reduction of inflation becoming policymakers' primary concern.
- 1985–2007—the Great Moderation when annual inflation, output growth, and the unemployment rate averaged 2.9 percent, 2.2 percent, and 5.8 percent, respectively.
- The contrast with the most recent period since the financial crash of 2008 is startling. In 2008–9, the rates of inflation and unemployment averaged 1.7 percent and 7.5 percent, respectively, while output contracted in real terms by 6.3 percent. This raises the question of whether this shock could presage for the dollar's global reserve asset role what the shock of the First World War set in train for sterling.

Keynes (1919) wrote of debauching the currency (with specific reference to Bolshevik state-sponsored inflation) as the key to destroying a market economy. But there was a time when economists, including many who identified themselves strongly with Keynes, saw inflation as a necessary evil (or perhaps not even an evil at all) in the pursuit of social welfare and justice. The dominant doctrine was that inflation needed to be "traded off" against employment.

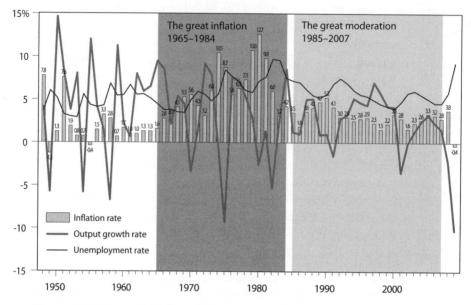

Figure 1.13. U.S. annual inflation, CPI, output growth rate, industrial production index (IPI), and unemployment rate, 1948–2009.

Sources: The Federal Reserve System and the Bureau of Labor Statistics.

Note: Inflation is calculated as $\pi_t = 100^*(\log CPI_t - \log CPI_{t-1})$

This doctrine was rooted in the empirical relation between the rate of inflation and unemployment observed by Alban Phillips (1958)—a relation that became known as the "Phillips curve." Favoring employment, Samuelson and Solow in "Analytical Aspects of Anti-Inflation Policy" (1960) famously suggested that the Phillips curve showed clearly a trade-off between output and price stability and that this result should be taken into account when implementing monetary policy. Their view was reflected in policymakers' standard perception during the 1960s and 1970s that there was a trade-off between inflation and unemployment (DeLong, 1997; Meltzer, 2005; Sargent, 1999; Taylor, 1997, 1998). But then inflation rose and employment on average did not increase; high inflation set in motion high wage demands and expected inflation, which in turn led to high inflation and high unemployment. These ideas contributed to the Great Inflation, where annual inflation rates rose above 10 percent in the United States and other industrialized countries in the 1970s. That experience directly supported Friedman's conclusions by showing that, beyond the short run, any trade-off is deceptive. The way for the monetarist counterrevolution was opened.

Independently at around the same time, Milton Friedman (1966, 1968) and Edmund Phelps (1967, 1968) contested the reasoning of Samuelson and Solow and argued that the Phillips curve was a short-term relation. In the long run there is a natural rate of unemployment defined as the rate "which has the property that it is consistent with equilibrium in the structure of real wage rates" (Friedman, 1968: 8). In other words the natural rate of unemployment is determined by supply and demand of labor at an equilibrium real wage. At that natural rate of unemployment, the so called nonaccelerating inflation rate of unemployment (NAIRU), inflation is stable. In other words, the monetary authorities can target the inflation rate at a level satisfying the price stability goal; there will be no trade-off between inflation and unemployment, and the Phillips curve is vertical. Divergences between the actual and natural rates of unemployment condition whether inflation accelerates or decelerates.

In his Presidential Address to the American Economic Association in December 1967, Friedman focused on the role of monetary policy and reached the conclusion that monetary policy does not influence real variables in the long run but may exert an influence in the short run, at the cost of accelerated inflation. This line of argument led to Friedman's famous formulation that in the long run monetary policy determines inflation—which is essentially a monetary phenomenon.

In the short run the data show a trade-off between inflation and unemployment because the money illusion is at work. For a short time consumers take inflation as a rise in purchasing power and therefore adjust their consumption; firms that take inflation as a rise in their real returns will increase their production and hire more workers. In other words unemployment can be traded off against inflation only if higher absolute prices are mistaken for higher relative prices; this trade-off is temporary as over time economic agents realize their mistake, and when they do cut back on their consumption and production, the trade-off is revealed to be an illusion. As a result of rising inflationary expectations, policymakers hoping to exploit the temporary trade-off to reduce the actual unemployment rate below the natural rate through expansionary policy will achieve only a temporary reduction in unemployment at the risk of higher inflation in the long run.

One of the most important developments to stem from Friedman's address and Phelps's paper—in particular, Friedman's insight about the possibility of a short-run economic stimulus as a result of an *unanticipated* increase in inflation—was the growing importance of the concept of expectations in economists' thinking about inflation. For both Phelps and Friedman, people take time to anticipate inflation and to adjust their behavior accordingly, and this allows the monetary authorities to trade off inflation against unemployment in the short term. The introduction of the expected rate of inflation in the relationship describing the links between inflation and unemployment led to the name of "expectations-augmented Phillips curve" (Friedman, 1970b). Accordingly unemployment varies with unanticipated inflation. If inflation is not fully anticipated, meaning that actual inflation is above or below expected inflation, workers will take the increase or decrease in nominal wages as real and will be tempted to take on or refuse job offers, leading to the actual unemployment rate falling below or increasing above the natural rate. However, once workers realize that real wages have not increased or decreased, unemployment will return to the natural rate, demonstrating that there is no permanent effect of inflation on unemployment. But if people can be fooled by the monetary authorities not once but twice, this means that they are not rational since they are not learning from the past. By using the concept of rational expectations as reformulated by John Muth in 1961, both Lucas (1972) and Sargent (1973) incorporated rational expectations into the natural rate theory. This led them to conclude that monetary authorities should not try to exploit any short-run trade-off between unemployment and inflation. For since manipulating the inflation rate will now be expected, the monetary authorities' action will be ineffective—leading to more inflation but not to more employment. Hoover (2008) quotes Abraham Lincoln's adage to explain this result, which led to warning monetary authorities against using policies exploiting people's misunderstanding:

> You can fool some of the people all the time, and all of the people some of the time, but you cannot fool all of the people all of the time.

To be sure, adaptive expectations is not always a straightforward mechanism. Adapting requires many turns as learning from past mistakes can take some time. This is certainly the case with governments' developing inflation policy in the 1980s and '90s. Thomas Sargent (1999) in *The Conquest of American Inflation* tells the story of inflation policy with a model using adaptive expectations.

This study considers monetary authorities' trajectory in learning from past policies aimed at exploiting the Phillips curve. The experience of the 1970s clearly left an impression on Paul Volcker and Alan Greenspan, whose respective tenures at the head of the U.S. Federal Reserve reflect a clear intellectual commitment to the natural rate hypothesis—leading them to pursue the lowest rate of unemployment compatible with price stability. Developments of this kind informed Timothy Cogley and Thomas

Sargent's (2005) interpretation of the history of inflation in the United States since World War II as an interactive government learning process. The outcome of that process—as we will see in more detail in chapter 3— was that by the 1990s many central banks from high- and middle-income countries were committing themselves more strongly to the goal of price stability and adopted explicit inflation targets (Bernanke, Laubach, Mishkin, and Posen, 1999).

But if the experience in the decades since 1980 has borne out the notion that monetary policy determines inflation in the long run and influences unemployment only temporarily, the "dynamic relationship between inflation and unemployment remains a mystery" (Mankiw, 2001a: C59). For a start, although the NAIRU concept is powerful, and inflation forecasts using the empirical Phillips curve tend to be more accurate than those using other variables such as interest rates or monetary aggregates or commodity prices (Stock and Watson, 1999), estimates of the natural rate of unemployment are imprecise. Economists still have to agree on the reasons why the 1990s were characterized by low and stable unemployment and inflation rates compared to the 1970s and 1980s. In the 1980s, the U.S. natural rate of unemployment was believed to be in the range of 6–7 percent, while in the 1990s it seems to have fallen to 5 percent. There is no firm understanding of what the actual level of NAIRU is or should be at any particular time, how stable or unstable that level will be and what have been the main drivers for changing that level. The list of factors that have been propounded is long—ranging from changes in demography and labor market regulations to productivity growth. The only certainty is that these factors are outside the control of monetary policy. This uncertainty as regards the natural rate of unemployment (and also the level of potential output and hence the output gap) can lead to seriously misguided policies (Orphanides, 2003). For instance, reexamining the reasons for the 1970s stagflation, Orphanides (2004) reached the conclusion that the natural rate of unemployment was underestimated (at around 4 percent), leading to monetary policy being excessively stimulatory and therefore generating increasing inflation. However, if inflation expectations had been stable as during the 1960s, these errors would have had relatively small consequences; but in a world of "perpetual learning," the public learned and integrated these errors into their inflation expectations and in doing so "unpegged" inflation expectations from the monetary authorities' objectives, leading to the 1970s stagflation (Orphanides and Williams, 2005).

Taylor (1998) warned against the danger that as inflation becomes lower and more stable, econometric-based questioning of the natural rate hypothesis will strengthen—in turn undermining support for low inflation. Cogley and Sargent (2001) back up Taylor in cautioning policymakers to not be tempted by the mirage once again of the Phillips curve trade-off between inflation and unemployment.

The pragmatic response to the objective uncertainties in estimating NAIRU and the output gap has been for central banks to focus primarily on price stability (Mishkin, 2008a) and to communicate this paramount goal of monetary policy—and the chosen methods of pursuing that goal—as transparently and clearly as possible to the public.

Origins of Inflation
Monetary, Fiscal, and Financial Links

> D'ailleurs ce roi est un grand magicien: il exerce son empire
> sur l'esprit même de ses sujets; il les fait penser comme il
> veut. S'il n'a qu'un million d'écus dans son trésor et qu'il
> en ait besoin de deux, il n'a qu'à leur persuader qu'un écu
> en vaut deux, et ils le croient. S'il a une guerre difficile à
> soutenir, et qu'il n'ait point d'argent, il n'a qu'à leur mettre
> dans la tête qu'un morceau de papier est de l'argent, et ils en
> sont aussitôt convaincus.
>
> Moreover, this king is a great magician: he holds sway
> even over his subjects' minds; he makes them think as he
> pleases. If he has only a million crowns in his treasury and
> needs two million, he has only to impress on them that one
> crown is worth two and they will believe him. If a war is
> proving difficult to prosecute with the treasury exhausted,
> he has only to put it into their heads that a piece of paper is
> money, and they will be immediately convinced.
> —Montesquieu ("Lettres Persanes," Lettre XXIV, 1721)

THE PREVIOUS CHAPTER reviewed the journey that, starting in the aftermath of the First World War and ending with the Great Inflation of the 1970s, led many central bankers—supported by government policymakers—to view price stability as their main goal rather than as merely one side of a trade-off between inflation and unemployment. The control of money creation—the source of inflation—is the sine qua non for stabilizing inflation. This is the traditional view endorsed by John Maynard Keynes in 1923 and developed in particular by Phillip Cagan in 1956 in his study of hyperinflations. Milton Friedman (1968: 12) observed that "every major inflation has been produced by monetary expansion—mostly to meet the overriding demands of war which has forced the creation of money to supplement explicit taxation." But the story does not end there. This second chapter turns to subsequent important developments in economists' thinking on the origins of inflation. These new ideas, which first emerged in the early 1980s and were elaborated during the following two decades, demonstrated that tighter monetary policy is not a sufficient condition for controlling the rate of inflation.

For this purpose of examining the roots of inflation, one-off price increases may be ignored. Such increases may be due to an external shock such as an increase in the price of oil or other commodities, and which for a limited period may have an effect on the price index depending on the weight of these commodities in the domestic basket used for the calculation of the percentage change in the price level. An increase in VAT is an example of the several other kinds of shocks that can have a material short-term effect on "inflation" in the sense of the price index.

Throughout history since the invention of money, inflation has been an elusive phenomenon. Money improved on barter both by making trading exchanges more efficient and by creating a means of savings. It also allowed exchange and saving to be easily accounted for. These attributes and the utility of money are impaired by inflation, which reduces the quantity of goods or services that can be bought with the same amount of money over a certain period of time. When money was a commodity itself, such as gold, silver, or copper, discovery of new deposits led to inflation. The monetary coinage was often debased to finance spending when taxes proved insufficient to finance wars, monuments, or other projects. Such has been the immemorial practice of spendthrift rulers and regimes of all kinds and times.

History has seen inflationary episodes occupying all points on a scale of magnitudes—from low to moderate, from high to very high (culminating in hyperinflation), and lasting for a wide variety of periods. Although there are no hard-and-fast conventions on the definition of these different magnitudes, "very high inflation" is generally taken to mean an annual inflation rate above 100 percent.

In the second half of the twentieth century, episodes of very high inflation were relatively frequent, as can be seen by the examples given in table 2.1. Such episodes in recent decades include Argentina, Bolivia, Brazil, Israel, Mexico, and Peru in the 1980s; former Soviet bloc countries such as Poland and Russia in the 1990s; and Zimbabwe in the first decade of the twenty-first century.

The study of these episodes as well as others in the more distant past—France of 1795–96 (Sargent and Velde, 1995), Austria, Germany, Hungary, Poland, and Russia in the 1920s (Sargent, 1993)—underlay the latest

TABLE 2.1
Episodes of very high inflation (above 100 percent annually).

Country	Date of episode	Country	Year(s)
Afghanistan	1985–86	Kyrgyzstan	1992–94
Afghanistan	1988–89	Lebanon	1990–92
Angola	1991–97	Mexico	1985–88
Argentina	1974–91	Mozambique	1986–91
Armenia	1993–94	Nicaragua	1984–92
Austria	1921–22	Peru	1982–92
Azerbaijan	1992–94	Poland	1923–24
Belarus	1994–2002	Poland	1989–90
Bolivia	1981–86	Romania	1991–94
Bosnia-Herzegovina	1992–93	Russia	1992–94
Brazil	1980–95	Serbia	1993–94
Bulgaria	1996	Sierra Leone	1989–91
Chile	1971–77	Somalia	1987–89
China	1948–49	Soviet Union	1921–24
Congo (Zaire)	1989–96	Sudan	1990–94
Costa Rica	1981–82	Suriname	1992–95
Georgia	1993–94	Taiwan	1945–49
Germany	1922–23	Tajikistan	1993–95
Ghana	1982–84	Turkey	1993–95
Greece	1942–45	Turkmenistan	1993–96
Guinea-Bissau	1986–88	Uganda	1984–88
Hungary	1923–24	Ukraine	1991–94
Hungary	1945–46	Uruguay	1989–91
Israel	1978–86	Venezuela	1988–89
Jamaica	1991–92	Yugoslavia	1990–94
Japan	1948–51	Zambia	1988–94
Kazakhstan	1993–95	Zimbabwe	2001–09

Sources: Fischer, Sahay, and Vegh (2002: 59, table 14, appendix 1); IMF, International Financial Statistics, various editions.

developments in understanding the origins of inflation. One of the most powerful and recurrent reasons for the frequency and intensity of high inflation is that governments need to generate revenue. Faced with inadequate tax revenues, governments can borrow either explicitly by issuing bonds or implicitly by expanding the monetary base. Until the second half of the twentieth century, most instances of large budget deficits and government debt were related to the financing of war (whereas recessions have become a more frequent cause since the second half of the twentieth century).

These historical examples—and also from the more recent if somewhat less drastic experience of inflation in the United States during the 1970s—shaped the thinking of economists about the importance for effective monetary policy of understanding the link between inflation and public debt. The threat to monetary policy from high levels of government indebtedness stems from the temptation to use monetary policy to erode or eliminate public debt (Dornbusch, 1998). This chapter examines this area of thinking with particular reference to the episode of very high inflation in Russia in the 1990s, since that episode demonstrates well the linkages between fiscal and financial conditions and monetary factors in bringing about high inflation.

ORIGINS OF INFLATION

While there is no reason in principle why money should not be issued by competing private providers, the state's monopoly of legitimate violence in practice ensures its monopoly of money issuance—something that in any case has come to be regarded as a public good, or at any rate the natural order of things. But, as monopolists, governments have proven vulnerable to the temptation of extracting a profit. In the case of metallic commodity currencies, this was done through debasement. In the case of fiat money, whose creation involves negligible real resources, there is no need for debasement. Instead of being initially given to individuals, fiat money is simply spent by the government on the acquisition of resources. A problem arises because of the difference between the near-zero cost of money production and the value of the resources acquired by that money—therefore making it profitable to produce more and more of it. The profit motive that operates in allocating resources in private free markets fails as an efficient regulator of the supply of money (Klein, 1974). This phenomenon of profiting from the issuance of money goes by the name of either government seigniorage, in the case of money creation (i.e., the change in monetary base defined as currency and reserves) in a stable price environment, or inflation tax when governments resort to inflation as a source of supplementary revenue (Marty, 1973: 1143).

Bernholz (2003) analyzes twelve episodes of very high inflation and observes that all these episodes were caused by the financing of budget deficits through money creation. He reaches the conclusion that when the budget deficit reaches 40 percent of government expenditures, hyperinflation will

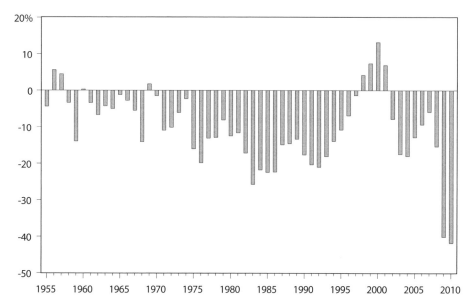

Figure 2.1. U.S. federal government outlays as a percentage of unified budget deficit.
Source: Office of Management and Budget.

Note: The unified budget surplus or deficit is the difference between total federal spending and receipts (from taxation and all other sources) in a given year.

not be far away. Applying this "rule" to the United States leads to some interesting conjecture given that, according to the Office of Management and Budget (OMB), the United States hit the 40 percent mark in 2009 (figure 2.1). The United States ran deficits equal to 40.16 percent and 41.81 percent of expenditures in 2009 and 2010, respectively. This means that the U.S. government has to borrow 40 percent of what it spends. As a result, much hinges on the ability of the U.S. government to continue to inspire confidence in its ultimate creditworthiness—a point we will return to in chapter 3.

The explanation for Bernholz's finding lies in the way that fiscal and monetary policies are connected through the government budget constraint.

$$D + iB + Ei^*B^* = \Delta B + E\Delta B^* + \Delta CBR \qquad (1)$$

All variables are expressed at the period end and in nominal terms. The left side of equation (1) includes the primary balance $D = G - T$ (D stands for primary deficit, that is, the difference between public spending on goods and services G and the revenue net of transfer T); the interest payments on the domestic outstanding public debt iB; and the interest payments on the foreign currency denominated public debt, Ei^*B^*, with E being the nominal exchange rate. The right side of this equation includes the new issues of debt both domestic (ΔB) and foreign $E\Delta B^*$ as well as any revenue made by the central bank (CBR) that is transferred to the Treasury. In 2009, for instance, the Federal Reserve transferred to the Treasury \$46.1 billion earned on securities acquired through open market operations.[1] That sum represented 2.3 percent of total U.S. government budget receipts in that year.[2] Central bank revenue also includes the sale of gold.

Equation (1) describes the fiscal balance in nominal terms. Expressing this balance in real terms with P standing for the deflator produces equation (2), with $d = D/P$ and using the lowercase letters notation for deflated variables and the difference operator Δ for both domestic and foreign debts written explicitly:

$$d + i\frac{B_{-1}}{P_{-1}}\frac{P_{-1}}{P} + Ei^*\frac{B^*_{-1}}{P_{-1}}\frac{P_{-1}}{P} = b - \frac{B_{-1}}{P_{-1}}\frac{P_{-1}}{P} + Eb^* + E\frac{B^*_{-1}}{P_{-1}}\frac{P_{-1}}{P} + \frac{\Delta CBR}{P} \quad (2)$$

Replacing $\frac{P_{-1}}{P}$ by $\frac{1}{1+\pi}$ with π being the inflation rate and $\frac{i+1}{1+\pi} = 1 + r$, r being the real interest rate, leads to

$$d + rb_{-1} + Er^*b^*_{-1} = \Delta b + E\Delta b^* + \frac{\Delta CBR}{P} \quad (3)$$

On the left side, in calculating the real deficit, the decrease of the nominal debt due to inflation has to be taken into account to not overestimate the deficit by $\frac{\pi}{1+\pi}b_{-1} + E\frac{\pi}{1+\pi}b^*_{-1}$; only "surprise" inflation will reduce the burden of government interest-bearing debt. If inflation is anticipated, the public will require higher nominal interest rate on government debt.

Introducing the central bank balance into the fiscal balance gives

$$d + rb_{-1} + Er^*b^*_{-1} = \Delta b + E\Delta b^* + \frac{\Delta MB}{P} \quad (4)$$

with MB standing for base money composed of currency and bank reserves. In the United States in June 2010, this consisted of about \$1,099 billion of bank reserves and \$899 billion of currency in circulation. Currency is

---

[1] See http://www.federalreserve.gov/newsevents/press/other/20100112a.htm.

[2] Source: Office of Management and Budget, "Budget of the US Government FY 2011, Historical Tables, Table 2.1," http://www.gpoaccess.gov/usbudget/fy11/sheets/hist02z1.xls (last accessed May 3, 2010).

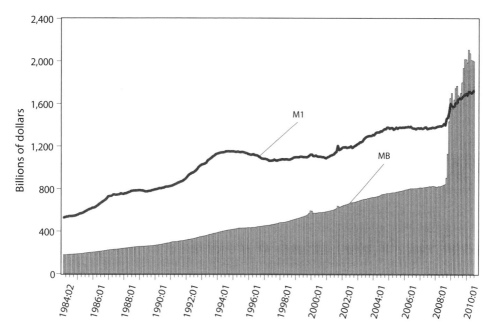

Figure 2.2. U.S. M1 and monetary base (February 1984–June 2010).
Source: U.S. Federal Reserve.

mainly held by households; reserves are held by the banking industry and
are composed of required reserves and excess reserves. Required reserves
are the minimum amount of checkable deposits that banks are obliged
to keep in the central bank (figure 2.2). Cecchetti (2008a: 8) provides a
useful clear description of the formation of the reserves portion of base
money in the United States: the Federal Reserve Board "sets the minimum level of reserves commercial banks must hold either as cash in their
vault or on deposit at the Fed" and the "requirement is graduated, with
the first few million dollars in deposits exempt, then 3 percent on the next
$45 million or so, and 10 percent on amounts above that." The figure of
10 percent means that for every dollar a bank receives in deposits, it can
lend out $0.90.

When minimum reserves are required on bank deposits of commercial
banks, they can be used both as a monetary instrument to raise money demand and as a tax to extract seigniorage revenues from bank reserves.

As a monetary instrument, an increase (decrease) in the required reserve
ratio expressed as a percentage of deposits decreases (increases) the share

of the currency component of the monetary base relative to bank reserves. Immobilizing (releasing) in this way a larger portion of bank deposits has the effect of decreasing (increasing) the money multiplier, hence contracting (expanding) the money supply.

If reserves do not bear interest or bear it at a rate below the market rate, reserve requirements constitute a form of taxation as the affected portion of deposits could have earned interest (Black, 1970; Brock, 1984; Fama, 1980; Romer, 1985). Deposit takers pass the cost on to their customers, and those who pay the tax include depositors via a lower, or negative, real interest rate on deposits and recipients of bank loans via a higher interest rate on loans. This distortion affects the efficiency of intermediation between savers and investors, which takes place via the financial system. Such distortions are classified in the literature under the heading of "financial repression" (McKinnon, 1973; Roubini and Sala-i-Martin, 1992, 1995). Moreover banks have designed sophisticated schemes to limit the amount of reserves they hold in order to avoid the tax. Cecchetti (2008b: 420, quoted in Cecchetti, 2008a: 8) mentions that

> banks use complex algorithms to shift funds in and out of accounts with limited withdrawal privileges that do not attract a reserve requirement. They do this in such a way as to make the reserve requirement irrelevant.

In many mature economies (e.g., in Australia, Canada, Sweden, and the United Kingdom), the use of the reserve requirement ratio has been eliminated or, as in the case of the United States, reduced. While it has the advantage of being a powerful monetary management instrument that affects all commercial banks equally, reserve requirement changes run the risk of causing liquidity problems for banks with low excess reserves. Therefore in most developed financial systems, open market operations are the preferred tool for tuning the interest rate or the money supply. When compulsory reserve requirements are in use, the way to eliminate the tax on reserves is to pay a market interest rate on required reserves. The advantage is to eliminate the tax on reserves with all its negative externalities such as tax avoidance, but also to allow the monetary authorities to use changes in required reserve ratios to smooth money market volatility.

The central bank balance in equation (4) expressed in real terms leads to

$$\frac{\Delta MB}{P} = \frac{MB}{P} - \frac{MB_{-1}}{P_{-1}} \frac{P_{-1}}{P}$$

with $mb = \frac{MB}{P}$

$$\frac{\Delta MB}{P} = mb - \frac{mb_{-1}}{1 + \pi} = \Delta mb + \frac{\pi}{1 + \pi} mb_{-1}$$

Δmb, the change in the monetary base, measures the goods and services the government can acquire by creating more money and/or by raising the reserve requirement. Seigniorage, or the tax on money creation, can be computed as the change in the narrow (without excess reserves) or broad monetary base (including excess reserves). $\frac{\pi}{1 + \pi} mb_{-1}$ refers to the inflation tax—the tax implied by a positive rate of price change. It is calculated on the total amount of base money, including excess reserves. Inflation erodes the real value of a given quantity of nominal balances and thereby compels or induces the public to save additional amounts of current income in order to maintain the real value of their money balances.

$$d + rb_{-1} + Er^*b^*_{-1} = \Delta b + E\Delta b^* + \Delta mb + \frac{\pi}{1 + \pi} mb_{-1} \qquad (5)$$

Equation (5) shows that even if the rate of inflation is negligible the government still receives revenue from the issuance of base money, which is non–interest bearing. The private sector (households, enterprises, and banks) suffers from inflation, whether inflation is anticipated or not, because of the costs attached to holding money in the form of currency (cash) and reserves if they are non-interest-bearing assets (Granville, 2003). Thus equation (5) is useful above all for showing the various options at the disposal of a government in financing its expenditures: direct and indirect taxation, domestic and foreign debt, seigniorage and inflation tax. It therefore highlights that the financing of government spending through the creation of base money is an alternative to explicit taxation or a second-best tax system (Phelps, 1973). If the rate of return on money differs from the rate of expected inflation, holders of cash balances incur a cost, inflation acts as a tax, and consumer preferences are distorted.

Phelps (1973) accordingly proposed that inflation should, like all other taxes, be part of the decision-making process of fiscal policy. The government should resort to deficit financing as long as the ratio of the welfare cost of inflation to the inflation tax is less than the ratio of the collection costs of other taxes to the amount collected. Indeed, if the government is to adopt some alternative method of financing such as issuing bonds or increasing taxes, any such alternative to inflation has its own costs. Since, on this view, the costs and benefits of the inflation tax option should be weighed in comparison with other sources of budget revenues, such an assessment might conclude that a positive rate of inflation could be optimal.

For Phelps, all taxes are distortionary; therefore any excess burden across all taxes should be minimized. When taxes imply excessive inefficiency and/ or when the collection costs of taxes are too high, governments should use a mix of both conventional taxation and inflation to minimize the overall distortionary effect of the entire tax burden. Barro (1979) adds that marginal deadweight losses (that is excess burden) should be equalized not only across all available taxes but also over time.

Various authors such as Calvo and Leiderman (1992), Mankiw (1987), Poterba and Rotemberg (1990), and Trehan and Walsh (1990) have carried out empirical tests of whether monetary policy has in practice been conducted in line with these precepts. In mature economies Phelps's recommended approach does not seem to have been followed. The main reasons are that the proceeds of seigniorage

Account for a small share of total government revenue; and
Do not appear to move in line with other tax revenues.

The significant exception to that second observation occurs in wartime. During WWII, seigniorage revenues seem to have been much more closely correlated with the government budget deficit than with other taxes (Walsh, 1998: 161). This highlights the impact of surprise inflation arising from a temporary shock such as war. In contrast to expected inflation, surprise inflation does not affect cash balance holding or generate distortionary costs; but it does have a wealth effect equivalent to a lump sum tax. It should be noted in this context that preventing such instances of monetary policy being dictated by fiscal imperatives was a key motive underlying the trend that began in the 1980s to make central banks independent from their countries' governments for the very purpose of isolating monetary policy from fiscal exigencies. Other commentators on the ideas of Friedman and Phelps (such as Kimborough, 1986) have argued that the validity of their conclusions depends on whether money is considered an intermediate or a final good. As an intermediate good, money reduces transaction costs and should not be taxed.

The effect of seigniorage on the fiscal balance and the private sector is not the only way in which they resemble other sources of government revenue. As with other taxes, there is a limit to the revenue-raising potential of the inflation tax. Above a certain threshold tax rate (i.e., inflation rate), the net government proceeds will be negative. This Laffer curve effect results from the reality that an increase in the inflation rate raises not only the proceeds from the inflation tax but also the opportunity costs of holding money, discouraging money demand and therefore lowering the base on which the tax is levied. In other words, the relation between the inflation rate and the inflation tax is not one to one. Cagan's (1956) study of the monetary dynamics of hyperinflation, while investigating the inflation rate that will maximize government revenue, shows that the demand for real cash balances is a function of the expected inflation rate, which is in turn dependent on the actual inflation rate. While the existence of a Laffer curve for this inflation tax makes sense intuitively, Heymann and Leijonhufvud (1995: 20) highlighted the difficulties that researchers have encountered in identifying a definite maximum in the curve.

The above-mentioned effect of inflation in discouraging money demand (because the cost of holding nominal balances rises) plays out in practice in the form of various strategies for economizing on money holdings. People reduce their currency holdings and banks reduce their excess reserves, thereby decreasing the monetary, hence the tax, base. With regard to bank reserves, if reserve requirements imposed are perceived as too high, either depositors reduce their deposits or banks evade the relevant regulations, as was the case in Russia in the 1990s (Granville, 1995). Of course the government can always issue more currency, but only at the risk of higher and higher inflation. Monetary innovations develop accordingly to reduce money holdings. For example, payment periods are shortened. Also bank demand deposits begin to carry interest. Eventually the monetary base falls so much that the government's inflation tax revenue decreases.

Another difficulty of using inflation to bolster government revenue is the way that long collection lags of conventional taxes erode the real value of explicit ordinary fiscal revenues (Tanzi, 1978). When considering optimal inflation, the issue of tax collection lags has to be taken into account. In our study comparing 1990s inflation in Russia with 1920s inflation in Germany, we saw as predicted by the Tanzi-Olivera effect that increased inflation tends to aggravate tax arrears, allowing "tax payers to exploit time lags between the calculation and payment of tax liabilities which in turn reduced real tax revenues, hence increasing monetary financing requirements" (Ferguson and Granville, 2000: 1075). The factors underlying tax evasion are best shown by Albert Fishlow and Jorge Friedman (1994: 110). In addition, the inflation tax reduces the overall tax base and weakens compliance by reducing available private income.

This has important consequences for the financing of budget deficits and the related monetary dynamics. If a government needs to finance a higher budget deficit while the inflation tax is already at its maximum (even allowing for the above-mentioned difficulty of determining the precise level of that maximum efficient tax rate), this higher deficit will be financed only at a higher rate of inflation; ultimately if the government cannot sort out its finances, hyperinflation will result.

Therefore in a stable environment banks hold only the minimum required reserves because any excess reserves could be lent out at a profit. This is not true of an unstable environment, as illustrated by the U.S. monetary policy in the aftermath of the 2007–8 financial crisis when the Fed resorted to inflationary strategies to counter the slump in demand and economic activity. Since the peak of the financial crisis precipitated by the collapse of Lehman Brothers, the United States has been accumulating excess reserves. Excess reserves or working balances (also non–interest bearing) are funds held in the Central Bank over and above the compulsory minimum as a cushion against uncertainties. Figure 2.3 shows that excess bank reserves increased from about $1.875 billion in August 2008 to a peak of $1 trillion in August 2010, returning to $972 billion in November 2010. An increase in excess reserves on this scale has never been seen before.

These excess reserves are a threat to the money supply in case the banking system decides to lend them out. If this large quantity of reserves were to be unleashed, this could lead to an increase in the inflation rate. Historically

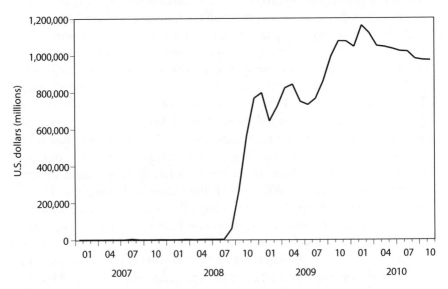

Figure 2.3. U.S. excess reserves (January 2007–November 2010) (millions of U.S. dollars).

Source: U.S. Federal Reserve.

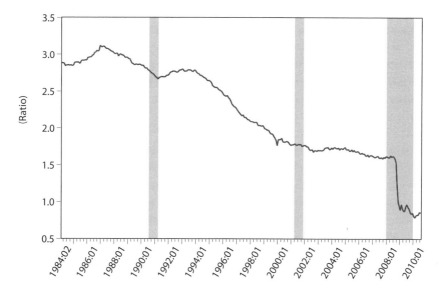

Figure 2.4. M1 multiplier, February 1984–July 2010.
Source: Federal Reserve Bank of St. Louis.
Note: The M1 multiplier is the ratio of M1 to the St. Louis Adjusted Monetary Base. For further information on monetary aggregates, refer to definitions, notes, and sources at http://research.stlouisfed.org/publications/mt/. Shaded areas indicate U.S. recessions.

the M1 multiplier oscillated between 3 and 2 but fell to 0.85 in July 2010 (figure 2.4).

The reason for this increase in excess reserves was that the Fed since October 2008 had started paying interest on excess reserves (at the time of writing, set at the rate of 0.25 percent), severing the tie between the quantity of reserves and banks' readiness to lend. This approach allows the Fed to raise market interest rates to slow any revival in bank lending activity without affecting the level of excess reserves, therefore guarding against inflationary pressures. Cochrane (2011: 18) describes the mechanism as follows:

> By creating such reserves the Fed can rapidly expand the supply of short-term, floating rate debt, without needing any cooperation from the Treasury or a rise in the Congressional debt limit. It also can execute massive open-market operations at the stroke of a pen. With a trillion dollars of

excess reserves, changing the interest on reserves from 0 to the overnight rate is exactly the same thing as a trillion-dollar open market operation.

If there is a limit on how much revenue a government can extract through printing money, there is also a limit on how much debt it can issue. This further limit is the subject of the next section of this chapter.

Money Issuance Involves Seigniorage, but the "Seigneur" Should Not Put His Hands in the Till

The metaphor of the "till" in this part of the thinking of the "new classical" economists is applied to fiscal policy as the practical framework in which governments use the proceeds of the inflation tax to acquire more resources. This phenomenon is clearest when budget deficits (i.e., spending in excess of ordinary tax revenues) are financed straightforwardly by printing money. But the "new classicals" showed that the same result may apply when budget deficits are financed by the issuance of bonds. And in doing so, they came up with a paradoxical breakthrough, in effect qualifying the principle that reducing inflation depends on limiting money creation. They showed rather that when governments pile up bond debt, tighter monetary policy (higher interest rates) designed to entice borrowers with higher returns will raise the nominal interest payments on the national debt that must be made by the government. When that expedient has been exhausted, the only recourse will be printing money. The resulting inflation will reduce the real value of tax payments and increase nominal interest rates—which for the government means a higher nominal debt service burden, hence, an increase in the size of the budget deficit that needs financing. Above all, success here will depend on for how long the government can print money faster than the public anticipates. Eventually the process will break down as the real money base becomes smaller and smaller.

In 1981, Thomas Sargent and Neil Wallace in "Some Unpleasant Monetarist Arithmetic" argued that the capability of the monetary authority to fight inflation by means of conventional monetary policy instruments was limited, and that, in the long run, tight monetary policy may lead to current and future higher inflation. In doing so, Sargent and Wallace (SW) were qualifying Milton Friedman's statement (1970a: 24): "Inflation is always and everywhere a monetary phenomenon." Their analysis emphasized the importance of budget stabilization for controlling inflation rather than limiting money growth per se. SW concluded that permanently higher government deficits must eventually be accommodated by increases in the monetary base. Financing the budget deficit through bonds (as opposed to printing money) may stave off inflation but cannot prevent it in the long run.

The government sector's budget constraint connects fiscal and monetary policies. A budget deficit needs to be covered either by monetary issue or by debt. If the monetary authorities decide to tackle inflation by contracting the money growth rate or the money stock, the budget deficit will have to be decreased either by increasing taxes or decreasing expenditures or by increasing borrowing.

For instance we saw in the previous section that it does not seem that the monetary and banking effects of the 2008 crisis—a massive expansion of the central bank balance sheets and increase in "high-powered money"—in themselves threaten inflation. The same cannot be said, however, about the fiscal effects of the crisis.

Governments just like individuals are limited in their ability to spend. A feckless government will sooner or later have to face its creditors. Put another way, deficit financing either by debt issuance or by seigniorage and the inflation tax has a limit. This limit is measured by the decreasing capability to finance budget deficits perceived to be increasingly unsustainable. This is the so-called intertemporal budget constraint. This constraint can be simply written as

$$\Delta b = (r - n)b_{-1} + d - \Delta m \qquad (6)$$

with b being the debt-to-GDP ratio, r the real rate of interest on government bonds, n the rate of real GDP growth, d the primary budget balance (i.e., revenues versus expenditure not including debt service) as a share of GDP. A primary deficit implies $d > 0$ and a primary surplus $d < 0$; Δm stands for seigniorage, that is, the rate of base money growth as a share of GDP.

The identity captures the "unpleasant monetarist arithmetic" flowing from real interest rates exceeding real growth rates,

> thus increasing government deficits just at a time when recession is already pushing the budget in the same direction. In this situation, attempts to fight inflation by reducing money creation add further to the necessary increase in debt financing, and give rise to expectations that the government will be forced to repudiate its debt either explicitly or through inflation. (Basevi and Giavazzi, 1986: 43)

The only antidote to this trap—where financing the budget deficit leads to the expansion of the deficit—is to improve the primary balance. But increasing the primary surplus means reducing government demand;

and since such adjustments are often attempted only in crisis conditions (governments generally avoiding such tough decisions until they have no choice), the foregone demand will not be easily substituted from other sources, resulting in still lower growth, hence lower tax revenues and no progress after all in reducing the budget deficit. This vicious cycle is exemplified by the Eurozone crisis. In short, even the most heroic attempts to restore the public finances to health can end up reinforcing creditor perceptions that the debt path is unsustainable. And when creditors consequently start selling off their holdings of a troubled government's debts, this will precipitate the outcome that they (the creditors) fear—namely, that the unsustainable debt burden is lightened or removed either by default (perhaps dressed up as a "restructuring") or by means of inflation.

Recent economic and financial history provides plenty of examples of this ruthless chain of cause and effect in action. In emerging markets, government debt has been associated with major financial crises. Until the aftermath of the 2007–8 global financial crash, mature economies were relatively immune in the sense that a high public debt burden was not their immediate constraint. Still, the way they managed their monetary policies had huge consequences for the rest of the world. For example, at the end of the Great Inflation decade of the 1970s, the main industrialized countries tightened their monetary policy in order to fight inflation. As a consequence, their interest rates reached very high levels, which in turn increased the cost of external debt priced to Libor rates of developing countries to such an extent they lost any kind of credit worthiness. Refinancing had become unaffordable, let alone raising net new debt to finance the servicing of previously contracted debt. Inflation picked up as a result, further increasing the budget deficits. By the end of 1982, forty countries were in arrears in their interest payments. Mexico defaulted in August 1983, followed by many other countries including Argentina, Brazil, and Turkey (Reinhart and Rogoff, 2009: 18).

The preceding discussion of the intertemporal budget constraint highlights the danger of public debt increasing faster than the real rate of economic growth over a period of time. In the 1990s several countries learned the hard way about this "unpleasant monetarist arithmetic." One such country was Russia, on which I have written extensively (Granville, 1995, 2001; Ferguson and Granville, 2000; Granville and Mallick, 2010).

The collapse of the Soviet Union in December 1991 led to a high inflation episode after the suppressed inflation built up in the preceding years of monetary expansion combined with continuing price controls burst into the open as most prices were freed. But the reason that high inflation persisted after this initial shock was monetary financing of deficits (aggravated

TABLE 2.2

Russian inflation, 1992–2009: Summary statistics, monthly percentage change in CPI.

Sample	Jan 1992– July 1995	Aug 1995– July 1998	Aug 1998– Dec 1999	Jan 2000– July 2009
Mean	21.6	1.6	5.6	1.1
Median	15.2	4.7	2.8	1.0
Maximum	296.0	4.7	38.4	3.1
Minimum	4.6	−0.3	1.2	−0.4
Standard deviation	43.5	1.5	8.9	0.7
Observations	43	36	17	115

Source: Calculated with data from ROSSTAT.

by the continuing Soviet practice of the central bank directly financing enterprises as well as the government).

Table 2.2 shows the mean, median, and standard deviation of the inflation rate divided into four subperiods: from January 1992 to July 1995, from August 1995 to July 1998 (August 17, 1998, marked clearly the end of the second period with the announcement by the government of the domestic debt default), from August 1998 to December 1999 (which was the last phase of the Yeltsin administration), and finally from January 2000 to July 2009.

By 1995, the government finally launched a full stabilization program supported by the International Monetary Fund (IMF). The Central Bank Law enacted in April that year provided the basis for the end to monetary financing envisaged under that program, and with the central bank no longer lending "printed" rubles to the government, ruble-denominated short-term treasury bills (Russian acronym: GKOs) became the favored budget deficit financing instrument.[3]

In July 1995 a crawling peg of the ruble to the dollar became the key de facto anchor helping to drive down inflation from 131 percent in 1995 to 10.5 percent in 1997. The exchange rate played an important role in the conduct of monetary policy, providing a clear nominal anchor for expectations. But even after the stabilization program was launched and, thanks largely to the exchange rate peg, began to produce apparently satisfactory results, high budget deficits persisted. In other words, the exchange rate peg helped camouflage the reality that the underlying stabilization process

[3] The 1995 Federal Budget Law.

was incomplete. The deficit was too large to be financed by issuing bonds to domestic savers, especially since the experience of successive monetary confiscations and the recent experience of very high inflation had discouraged domestic savers from holding what remained of their savings in ruble deposits or similar instruments. So the bond financing of the budget deficit required a stable exchange rate and capital account liberalization to attract foreign savers into the domestic T-bill market, which, apart from the limited funds available from international financial institutions, was the only additional financing source.

The initial success of this approach amid the benign external conditions of 1996–97 compounded the effect of the exchange rate peg in causing complacency about the urgency of fiscal adjustment. The government in any case lacked the political capital to face down the resistance to any such adjustment, and instead preferred to increase its reliance on the capital market.

Russia was now caught in what has become known as the "open economy trilemma": with the exchange rate pegged and the capital account liberalized, the outside world will determine domestic interest rates.

The 1997–98 "Asian crisis" triggered risk aversion and capital outflows from all emerging markets including Russia. The central bank decided to increase the refinance rate, which acted as an effective cap on the T-bill yield (Granville, 2001: 120) to whatever level necessary to stem capital outflows and preserve both the exchange rate peg and the bond financing of the budget deficit by foreign savers:

> The calculation was that inflows would be attracted by the huge real returns available from the combination of high nominal yields on ruble-denominated debt and the promise of a stable exchange rate. (Granville, 1999: 723)

But the attractiveness of this trade rapidly paled. The rewards of triple-digit yields on short-term GKOs were offset by the reality that declining growth was making that debt increasingly unsustainable. And the reason for that growth slowdown—namely, the effect of the Asian crisis in driving down the price of oil and other commodities exported by Russia—not only undermined the fiscal position but also pointed to the need for a devaluation, which would undermine foreign investors' returns on their GKO holdings. "So it was that this perceived devaluation risk completed the vicious circle that led in the end to both insolvency (default) and a massive devaluation" (Granville, 2001: 124).

The oil price correction was much more a trigger than a cause of Russia's financial collapse and the dramatic ensuing declines in output and real incomes. The root cause was the failure to make the necessary fiscal adjustment earlier—that is, in calmer times, while it might still have been practicable to achieve the primary surplus required to ensure a sustainable debt path. Here again, we see in action our key theme: sustainable fiscal positions are an essential condition for achieving and maintaining low inflation.

Put another way, even if budget deficits are financed by the more "virtuous" method of bond market borrowing as opposed to money creation, in the end those deficits must still be brought under control.

The condition for bringing budget deficits under control is a primary surplus equivalent to the initial public debt multiplied by the difference between the real interest rate and real GDP growth. If that condition is not met, the government will have no choice but to rely increasingly on money creation. As money grows, so does the price level. And accelerating inflation caps government revenue from seigniorage. As the public progressively abandons the domestic currency, the government finds it harder to finance the budget deficit through seigniorage revenue, making conventional fiscal adjustment measures (lower spending and/or higher taxes) the only possible solution. The political window for such harsh adjustment typically opens only after the crisis has reached a climax in some combination of default, devaluation, and inflation. Once again, the case history of Russia exemplifies the point. The 1998 debacle forced the Russian authorities to adopt a policy of fiscal discipline. Together with high oil prices, fiscal discipline led to fiscal surpluses averaging about 4 percent of GDP during the period 2000–2008, average annual real GDP growth rates reached around 7 percent, and the average current account surplus for the period was about 10 percent of GDP (Granville and Mallick, 2010: 434). As for annual inflation itself, the average for the period remained at the somewhat elevated level of around 14 percent. This was the result of a failure to complement the new fiscal rule with a rule-based framework for monetary policy—which is the theme of the next chapter.

Mature Economies Are Different: Are They?

This close examination of the Russian experience raises the question of whether the SW analysis is equally well validated by the experience of mature economies. King (1995: 171) argues that the SW analysis does not apply to mature economies characterized by low inflation and with seigniorage constituting only a small part of overall government revenues.

For King and others, fiscal deficits and the public debt stock in mature markets have no effect on price stability because of Ricardian equivalence (Barro, 1974) and central bank independence. Ricardian equivalence is the observation that issuing bonds and taxation are equivalent. In case of a tax cut, if the public expects current government deficits to have to be repaid in the future by increased taxes (to cover the interest and principal repayment of the increased stock of bonds), they will save the incremental income arising from the tax cut, so leaving aggregate demand and the price level unchanged. In other words the public assumes that the present value of their tax liabilities has not changed. And even if the budget deficit had aggregate demand implications, it is argued that the central bank will be able to control inflation by offsetting the fiscal policy effects by adjusting the nominal interest rate. Meltzer (2005: 170) remarked that in the United States

> [t]he much smaller budget deficits of the 1960s occurred with rising inflation rates, and the larger deficits of the 1980s accompanied falling inflation rates. A major difference was that the Federal Reserve did not believe it was obliged to finance the 1980s deficits, and it did not do so.

Dornbusch (1998) explained that one of the reasons why the link between debt and monetary policy in mature economies was not investigated further in the 1990s was that the literature such as Jones (1985) on the United States did not provide enough empirical evidence. Walsh (1998: 141) however argues that one of the problems with some of these empirical papers, such as Demopoulos, Katsimbris, and Miller (1987), which examined this link for eight OECD countries, is that they "ignore information about the long run behaviour of taxes, debt and seigniorage that is implied by the intertemporal budget balance." In other words, wrong econometric techniques lead to wrong conclusions; these authors used simple regressions of money growth on deficits, while they should have used a vector error correction model (VECM).

But even if empirically it has been difficult to demonstrate a correlation between inflation and the size of budget deficits, the threat that public debt can pose to price stability should not be underestimated. After the crash of 2008, the reduction of government deficits and the control of the rate of growth of the outstanding debt moved once more to the forefront of discussion about debt sustainability and its implications for the price level.

A burdensome public debt in the worst case is either inflated away or repudiated; in the best case the resulting high interest rate complicates monetary policy. Any further increase in interest rates worsens the budget deficit precisely at a time when its financing is causing concern. Whether the central bank is independent or not, tough or not, budget deficits and public debt have to be financed by taxation, inflation, or repudiation. The Eurozone crisis again provides the most graphic contemporary illustration of these realities. But while in the 1930s surprise inflation was seen as providing a solution for starting afresh from a clean slate, today's public (mainly via financial markets) anticipates the authorities' move to inflate the short-term debt away by building inflationary expectations into the interest rates demanded on that debt. "Debt leads to inflation even though inflation does not help reduce indebtedness" (Dornbusch, 1998: 15).

While central bank independence, as we will see in the next chapter, has come to be seen as guarding against the risk of inflationary pressures emanating from profligate governments, it may be doubted whether this protection is adequate when monetary policy, whether or not conducted by an independent central bank, is hostage to the budget deficit and the public debt, meaning that an increase in real interest rates would immediately worsen an already fraught fiscal position.

Ending Inflation Without Prolonged Recession
Introducing Credibility

> Three morals: You cannot end inflation (i) if you don't agree
> on how to do it, (ii) if you and the public think it is less
> costly to let it continue, and (iii) if you are overly influenced
> by politics. The Federal Reserve was better able to control
> inflation when the President was named Eisenhower or
> Reagan instead of Johnson, Carter, or Nixon.
> —Meltzer (2005: 172)

A PROMISE IS a promise—in other words, a contract, whose benefits in terms of credibility policymakers seem to have understood by committing fully in the conduct of monetary policy to the primary objective of low inflation. Various means have been developed to enhance the credibility of this promise, such as developing rules and communicating as transparently as possible with the public. Monetary policy credibility has also been built on the strength of track records of inflation control and of adhering to anti-inflation commitments.

Following the Great Inflation in the late 1960s and 1970s in mature economies and high inflation episodes in the 1980s and 1990s in emerging economies, by the end of the 1990s, high inflation had disappeared from the OECD area and also from most emerging economies. In the ten years from 1991 to 2001, U.S. inflation fell from 5.26 percent in 1990 to 2.1 percent in 1999, while real annual GDP growth accelerated from 0.9 percent to 4.22 percent. The same trend was observed in most mature economies.

Economists of course do not agree on a single explanation for these positive results of combining low inflation with positive growth. Some argue that it was just good luck, others that economies responded more flexibly to external shocks, others, last, that central bankers were better at doing their job in part because of advances in macroeconomic thinking over the past three decades (Cecchetti, Flores-Lagunes, and Krause, 2006; Chari and Kehoe, 2006). This chapter investigates the latter view.

Some authors argue that the relationship between current and past inflation has declined since the Great Inflation, such as, for instance, Cogley, Primiceri, and Sargent (2008), others that it has remained stable, such as, for instance, Sims (2001), Stock (2001), Pivetta and Reis (2007), and O'Reilly and Whelan (2005) for the Eurozone. This relationship is called persistence and has immediate consequences for the conduct of monetary policy, because "the more stationary inflation is perceived to be, the sooner it is expected to revert to its mean and the less urgent is the need for anti-inflationary action" (Primiceri, 2006: 871). Policymakers therefore need to understand the patterns and determinants of inflation persistence. For the IMF (2006) the decline in inflation persistence is linked to better conduct of monetary policy and monetary policy credibility. This result is confirmed by Cogley, Primiceri, and Sargent (2008: 33), who found that inflation had become substantially less volatile, persistent, and unpredictable, a change attributable mainly to monetary policy while, "better luck—in the form of a less volatile and persistent cost-push shock" accounts for "about half the magnitude of the effect of monetary policy."

Starting from the premise that social welfare should be the ultimate aim of monetary policy as of economic policy more generally, a consensus has built over the years that monetary policy is optimal from the social welfare point of view when both nominal interest rates and inflation are low. We saw the rationale for this view in chapter 2—namely, that money is beneficial to economic agents in lowering transaction costs, but it is also costly as instead of holding cash the money could be invested and therefore earn some interest. The foregone nominal interest rate is the price of money or opportunity cost. Since fiat money is costless to produce, Friedman (1969: 21) concluded in what became known as the Friedman rule that monetary policy should aim at zero or very low nominal interest rates. The Friedman rule has generated a vast literature debating whether zero nominal interest rate or positive nominal interest rate are optimal (see Schmitt-Grohé and Uribe, 2005; Chari and Kehoe, 2006). One of the main conclusions is that the rate of inflation and nominal interest should be kept low, and while there has never been more than a vague consensus about what this should mean in practice, "low" has come to be seen by most central banks as an inflation rate in the region of 2 percent.

This chapter describes how, since the 1980s, policymakers have managed to reduce and control inflation without unacceptably adverse welfare impacts by changing the monetary policy regime in a way that subjects policy to an external rule. The record in this period suggests that policymakers and economists have arrived at a better understanding of monetary policy and on how to keep the price level low and stable while at the same time keeping real growth high and stable. This understanding

> incorporates three key beliefs. First, there is a natural rate of unemployment at which inflation is stable. Second, there is a transmission mechanism through which monetary policy actions affect the economy. Third monetary policymakers face trade-offs. (Ellison and Sargent, 2009: 5)

While price stability has become the long run target of monetary policy, central bankers focus day to day on a particular level of interest rates. Kahn (2009) remarks that the interpretation of price stability by central bankers is varied among them and is not literal; they do not target a constant price level. Instead price stability is interpreted either as inflation not being factored into economic agents' decisions (Volker, Greenspan) or as a low and stable variable or as a numerical target such as the Bank of England's target of 2 percent annual inflation in the CPI.

Modern macroeconomics began with Keynes's *General Theory*. Before that, its classical ancestor was the economics of money and the price level. And the basic wisdom derived from that ancestor was that rules (e.g., the gold standard) could ensure stability. Rules set bounds on behavior, while Keynesian economics substituted discretion. Advances in macroeconomic understanding in the later twentieth century were largely a discovery—or rediscovery—of the function of those old rules.

The shift from a discretionary to a more rule-based framework for policy emphasizing credibility, transparency, and accountability appears to flow directly from the work of Lucas (1976) on expectations and the time inconsistency problem identified by Finn Kydland and Edward Prescott in 1977. That work was developed by Barro and Gordon (1983), leading to the conclusion that price stability will be more easily achieved with independent central banks. The common thread running through such economists' work in this area is that monetary policy should follow a clear transparent program rather than be determined by calculations of short-term trade-offs between unemployment and inflation. The reasons for this are that an economy cannot indefinitely exceed either its natural rate of unemployment or its potential gross domestic product (GDP). For in either case, economic agents will anticipate the result.

The concepts of expectations and credibility lead to the thinking that there are no lasting welfare benefits from inflation and that the purported output losses (negative welfare impacts) of reducing inflation can either be avoided altogether or at least remain negligible. A credible policy can reduce inflation without causing a recession. Some of these principles of macroeconomics have been especially influential in gearing monetary policy toward low and stable inflation and have had a direct influence on the trend toward central bank independence and inflation targeting.

We saw in the previous chapter how debt, public deficits, and inflation are linked through the intertemporal budget constraint. This leads to focusing on the incentives faced by central banks when setting their goals and wielding selected policy instruments—hence the strategy of confining their role to maintaining price stability. The establishment of central bank independence (CBI) from the government meant introducing rules and institutional constraints—above all, to limit budget deficit financing by monetary authorities. The belief was that a degree of independence from political influence would equip central banks to deliver lower average inflation.

The validity of this assumption is not self-evident. There is not enough evidence to conclude that institutional reforms are the causes of disinflation either in the 1980s in the United States where no institutional change occurred (Christiano and Fitzgerald, 2003) or in the 1990s and 2000s globally where low inflation was observed independent of the institutional setting (Ball and Sheridan, 2005). Therefore while CBI may provide a useful guard against government profligacy, the explanation for the low inflation rates seen in the past two decades may have more to do with the overall credibility or commitment of the monetary authorities toward a nominal target than with CBI as such.

Moreover while some countries have high debt but no inflation, for some economists such as Cochrane (2011) debt and deficits do not need to be huge to lead to inflation. Monetary policy credibility can be undermined by the burden of debt and fiscal deficits even if the authorities are fully committed to low inflation. Economic agents may perceive such a burden as increasing the risk of high inflation in the future. If economic agents expect fiscal trouble, they will also expect higher inflation and will hedge against it by dumping money and government debt, leading to a vicious circle where the government will have to pay ever higher interest rates reflecting both expected inflation and a higher risk premium on its debt. This is what happened in Russia in the 1990s as we saw in the previous chapter. The event that will unleash this vicious circle is not predictable. Many emerging market countries have been through this experience, for instance, during the financial crisis of 1997–98 that began in Asia, or in Argentina in 2001. It is not sure that in such situations an independent central bank can make any difference. In short, although central bankers in the past two decades seem to have mastered how to manage and to anchor inflation expectations, and while institutional reforms may in several cases have been a necessary precondition for such progress, such reforms do not appear to be a sufficient condition. All that can be said with confidence is that central bankers have no choice but to adjust to whatever new dynamics and challenges the world economy throws at them. In the words of Frederic Mishkin (2007b: 1),

> ... there remains, and will likely always remain, elements of art in the conduct of monetary policy, in other words, substantial judgement will always be needed to achieve desirable outcomes on both the inflation and employment fronts.

A CREDIBLE POLICY CAN REDUCE INFLATION WITHOUT CAUSING A RECESSION

In 1975, Sargent and Wallace introduced the main results of the "new classical" school of thought, which can be traced directly back to the rational expectations revolution reintroduced by John Muth in 1961. Any anticipated monetary policy is not effective in the short run. Only "surprises" can exert an influence over the level of real income. The reasoning here is that if an increase in inflation is expected, no real effects will be observed; nominal interest rates will adjust upward, leaving the real interest rate unchanged.

In "Econometric Policy Evaluation: A Critique" Lucas (1976: 41) declared,

> Given that the structure of an econometric model consists of optimal decision rules of economic agents, and that optimal decision rules vary systematically with changes in the structure of series relevant to the decision maker, it follows that any change in policy will systematically alter the structure of econometric models.

His "critique" of the evaluation of policy changes on the basis of past data had major implications for the understanding of the formation of expectations and for evaluating monetary policy changes. In questioning the relevance of these traditional econometric models, Lucas showed that the formation of expectations was molded in the present, responding to changes in policy. An anticipated shift in monetary policy such as a reduction in inflation did not need to cause a recession as long as the change in monetary policy was credible.

As already noted, for much of this period in the history of macroeconomics, the conventional wisdom was that stabilization policies aimed at lowering inflation cause recession and aggravate poverty. The prevalence of this view may have been due to the difficulty highlighted by Stanley Fischer and Franco Modigliani in 1978 of quantifying the social and individual costs of inflation in both the short and long run. The social and individual costs of unemployment, by contrast, are usually quite visible. The analogous damage from inflation is not so transparent. The difference between these perceived burdens can be an important cause of bias in the outcome of macroeconomic policy choices confronting policymakers when they are faced with alternatives that seem to pose a trade-off between the two.

Meltzer (2005), in his account of the Great Inflation, highlights that inflation persisted because disinflation was perceived by both the public and policymakers as too costly in terms of unemployment. Lacking political support, the Fed had little appetite to tame the inflation dragon. The public did not see inflation as a major problem: polling data from the 1970s showed that fewer than 14 percent of respondents regarded inflation as "the most important problem facing the country" (Meltzer, 2005: 147). Attempts at reining in inflation were aborted as soon as unemployment started to rise, making it harder to convince the public that the next attempt would be serious. This stop-and-go policy, oblivious of public expectations, led to the worst of all worlds—a combination of high inflation and high unemployment (stagflation).

The standard view was that the cost of reducing inflation is measured by the so-called sacrifice ratio, which posits a quantum of annual output that must be foregone to reduce inflation by one percentage point. Arthur Okun's (1978: 348) survey of Phillips curves led to the famous conclusion that "the average estimate of the cost of a 1 percentage point reduction in the basic inflation rate is 10 percent of a year's GNP, with a range of 6 to 18 percent." Policymakers at that time concluded therefore that "it might be better to accept a permanent modest rate of inflation than to pay the costs of reducing inflation to an even lower rate" (Briault 1995: 41). Okun in 1971 questioned whether inflation could be maintained for long at a modest level, portraying this as the "mirage" of steady inflation. As things turned out, this mirage would induce monetary authorities to inflate more and more.

In 1982, Thomas Sargent responded by showing that the cost of reducing inflation can be much smaller than standard estimates of the sacrifice ratio. If a disinflationary policy is announced in advance and is credible, people will adjust their expectations quickly so the disinflation need not cause a recession:

[I]nflation can be stopped much more quickly than advocates of the "momentum" [a view that sees an inherent momentum in the process of inflation] view have indicated and that their estimates of the length of time and the costs of stopping inflation in terms of foregone output ($220 billion of GNP for one percentage point in the inflation rate) are erroneous. This is not to say that it would be easy to eradicate inflation. On the contrary, it would require far more than a few temporary restrictive fiscal and monetary actions. It would require a change in the policy *regime*: there must be an abrupt change in the continuing government *policy, or strategy,* for setting deficits now and in the future that is sufficiently binding as to be widely believed. (Sargent, 1982: 42)

Sargent's support for his argument was to analyze how high inflation in the 1920s experienced by Austria, Germany, Hungary, and Poland was brought to an end. Looking at the graphs of the respective price indexes, Sargent found that "inflation stopped abruptly rather than gradually" (p. 43) with little output cost thanks each time to a change in the policy regime:

The essential measures that ended hyperinflation in each of Germany, Austria, Hungary, and Poland were, first, the creation of an independent central bank that was legally committed to refuse the government's demand for additional unsecured credit and, second, a simultaneous alteration in the fiscal policy regime. These measures were interrelated and coordinated. (Sargent, 1982: 89)

Vegh (1992) supported this conclusion by developing a model showing that a credible stabilization program ends inflation with no effect on real output. Low inflation is shown to be achieved through the use of a nominal variable—the money supply, the exchange rate, the price level, or the inflation rate—to anchor inflation expectations. These lessons were reinforced by inflation stabilization experiences in Israel and Latin America in the 1980s and in postcommunist transition economies in the 1990s. This key step of altering the basic macroeconomic policy stance was labeled "regime change" (long before that same phrase took on a different connotation in U.S. foreign policy).

The effectiveness of this approach was further demonstrated by the stabilization policy applied in Bolivia in 1985. Jeffrey Sachs (1987: 279) relates that from August 1984 to August 1985, Bolivia's inflation rate was running at 20,000 percent and that from May 1985 to August 1985, the annualized rate jumped to 60,000 percent. A new government took office in August 1995 and set about stabilizing prices by controlling money growth. Credibility was established through balancing the budget on a day-to-day basis. Mishkin (2004: 674) assessed this effort in the context of preexisting notions of the economic and welfare costs of stabilization:

If the rule of thumb that a reduction of 1 percentage point in the inflation rate requires a 4 percent loss of a year's aggregate output had been applied to the Bolivian case, it would have meant that ending the Bolivian hyperinflation would have required halving that country's aggregate output for 1,600 years. Instead the Bolivian inflation was stopped in its tracks within one month, and the output loss was minor (less than 5 percent of GDP).

In "What Determines the Sacrifice Ratio?" Laurence Ball (1994: 155) tested empirically the supposition of "an iron law that disinflation produces large output losses," whether the speed at which disinflation occurs has an impact on its output cost, and finally whether the outcome is affected by the economic environment such as the initial level of inflation or the openness of the economy. His comparison of the costs of disinflation was based on data from a sample of countries belonging to the Organisation for Economic Co-operation and Development (OECD) during the period 1960 to 1991 on a quarterly and annual frequency. The sacrifice ratio is proxied by "the ratio of the total output loss to the change in trend inflation," with trend inflation being defined as a moving average of actual inflation (Ball 1994: 156). Ball's main results support those of Sargent:

> There are two main results. First, the sacrifice ratio is decreasing in the speed of disinflation (the ratio of the change in trend inflation in the length of the episode). That is, as suggested by Sargent, gradualism makes disinflation more expensive. Second, the ratio is lower in countries with more flexible labor contracts. The most important feature of contracts is their duration. (Ball, 1994: 156)

The view—as first argued by Fellner (1976, 1979)—that a credible disinflation can entail a relatively low cost in terms of output was at first contested by various authors such as Perry (1983), Gordon and King (1982), Clarida and Friedman (1983), and Friedman (1984). Their contention, based on 1982–83 U.S. data, was that the "credibility hypothesis" (the idea being "that the foregone-output costs of a disinflationary episode will be smaller if the public correctly believes that the attempt will not be abandoned"; McCallum, 1985: 106) was factually incorrect. They argued that disinflation was taking place but at the cost of high unemployment. Perry (1983) highlighted the fact that unemployment reached 10 percent in the fourth quarter of 1982.

McCallum (1985: 124) however reworked some of these authors' attempts to contradict the credibility hypothesis, that is, "the importance of expectations for output-inflation tradeoffs" and found these results unconvincing. Fischer (1984b) used the same data assuming a natural rate of unemployment of 6.5 percent and a 5 percent drop in inflation; the sacrifice ratio was found to reach about 5 to 6 percent (i.e., a 1 percentage point reduction in the rate of inflation costs about 5 to 6 percent of annual output). More to the point, the reason for disinflation proving costly in terms of output during the early 1980s—the Volker disinflation period—was that credibility at that stage was not yet established. Paul Volcker was appointed Fed chairman in August 1979 (holding the office until August 1987), but the process of containing inflation started in earnest only in late 1980 and early 1981 (Goodfriend and King, 2005). The public had imperfect knowledge (Fellner, 1982) and no certainty that the Fed would continue to rein in inflation. Backus and Driffill (1985) noted that attempts to stabilize the inflation rate during the 1970s were often aborted soon after they were announced, explaining why any new attempt was met with disbelief—worsening the effects on employment and output. In other words the public needed convincing that the monetary authorities were serious about tackling inflation. Faced with the need to fill a credibility gap, monetary authorities may be induced to adopt more drastic measures than required to persuade the public that a new stabilization initiative is for real (Backus and Driffill, 1985). One lesson of Volcker's tenure at the Fed, when credibility was built up gradually through the 1980s (Hardouvelis and Barnhart, 1989), is that it takes time to establish the monetary authorities' credibility (Cagan and Fellner, 1983).

The question of course is how to measure credibility. Marvin Goodfriend (2007: 65) depicted this as a lacuna in the work of the "new classicals": "no fully satisfactory theory exists to explain the loss or acquisition of credibility for low inflation or similarly, how inflation scares occur." Sargent (1983) suggested that a good measure of credibility is how fast disinflation is achieved. In other words, the speed and effectiveness with which disinflation is achieved may be taken as a sign of the degree of commitment by the monetary authorities.

Credibility is usually measured by inflation expectations. Various surveys exist. The oldest one with a quarterly frequency is the Survey of Professional Forecasters (SPF), begun in 1968 by the American Statistical Association and the National Bureau of Economic Research and conducted since 1990 by the Federal Reserve Bank of Philadelphia (which also conducts the Livingston Survey, with data going back to 1946). Others include the Federal Reserve Board (FRB) expectations series, the University of Michigan's Survey of Consumers, and the Federal Reserve Bank of Cleveland. All these surveys, while using different methods, have confirmed broadly that,

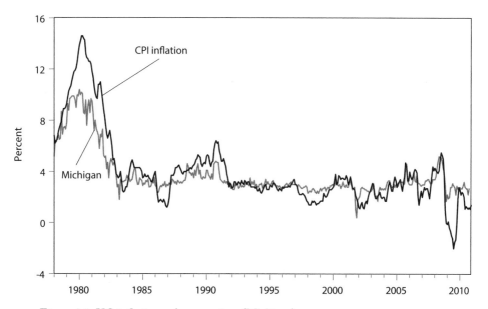

Figure 3.1. U.S. inflation and expectations (Michigan).
Sources: Survey Research Center, University of Michigan and Federal Reserve Bank of St. Louis.

in the early 1980s, the credibility of anti-inflationary monetary policy was low. Demertzis, Marcellino, and Viegi (2008: 9) compared the FRB, the SPF, and consensus forecasts and found that the differences among these measures of expectations are small and tend to move together. Likewise, the Michigan Survey showed that inflation expectations were systematically below actual inflation at the beginning of the 1980s (figure 3.1).

This period is characterized in the literature as of low credibility. Demertzis, Marcellino, and Viegi (2008), modeling inflation and inflation expectations in a general vector autoregression (VAR) model, derived a measure of credibility. This measure assesses the degree to which expectations are anchored. During the Great Inflation from 1965 to the early 1980s it declined from 1, meaning that the anchor matches the target of the central bank, to a value of 0.75, while at the same time long-term inflation expectations increased. Moreover these authors point out that while inflation reached its peak during the first quarter of 1981, it took another four quarters before credibility started to rise. In 1984 the Demertzis, Marcellino, and Viegi measure of credibility increased to 0.9 when for the first time the Fed managed to use the interest rate to keep inflation under control at 4 percent without causing a recession (Goodfriend, 2007). In short, announcing a target and acting upon this announcement ensures credibility for the monetary authorities, in turn allowing them to progress toward low inflation at a lower cost than would have been incurred in the absence of credibility (Bomfim and Rudebusch, 2000).

From Credibility to Institutional Monetary Economics

If a credible policy can reduce inflation without causing a recession, what makes a policy credible? The most effective practical advance in this area of institutional underpinning for a rules-based framework has concerned central banks.

As state entities, central banks naturally fall under the influence of their governments' desire to stimulate the economy, leading over time to inflation (Kydland and Prescott, 1977). The only effective way to counter this tendency is by means of a set of measures pledged by a credible monetary authority (Barro and Gordon, 1983). The economists at the center of this story argued that the best way to attain such credibility is to put the monetary authorities (i.e., central banks) at arm's length from governments, hence sheltered from government improvidence (Rogoff, 1985), and to submit the monetary authorities to a rule, putting in place a strong nominal anchor to constrain the price level and therefore support low and stable inflation expectations.

The thinking here had to do with the time or dynamic inconsistency problem, whereby the public understands that the central bank may be inconsistent over time and therefore distrusts declarations by the monetary authorities. The best answer to this problem is a rules-based framework for policy, minimizing discretionary decisions. The benefits of such a rules-based framework also stem from the way this can compensate for institutional shortcomings. In developing countries especially, long-lasting stabilization can prove elusive, despite repeated efforts by the authorities to initiate anti-inflationary policies. Typically, the democratic structures of developing countries are weakened by powerful lobbies, fiscal capacities are stretched to fulfill promises of populist politicians, and financial sector infrastructure remains underdeveloped. Thus many of these countries, but also many other countries besides, have experienced difficulty stabilizing inflation.

In the 1990s this shift to a rule-based framework was most often achieved in the context of one or both of the following two institutional changes in the practice of monetary policy: central banks were made more independent from governments and price stability was given pride of place in the charters of many central banks.

Central Bank Independence (CBI)

When a country's legislature confers independence on its central bank, the resulting dividend hinges on credibility. The public will be more inclined to believe that an independent monetary authority, by dint of its autonomy and detachment from the tactical play of current politics, will be capable of implementing its mandate (which typically comprises a price stability objective) year after year and without fear or favor. Moreover, in a virtuous circle, that very public expectation will in turn facilitate the central bank's efforts to lower inflation. CBI is seen as contributing to lower inflation by increasing the monetary authority's credibility—which may be defined as the public believing that policies announced by the monetary authorities have actually been carried out (McCallum, 1985; Rudd and Whelan, 2003) and, accordingly, expecting that they will continue to be carried out in the future.

At the same time, this proven dividend can all too easily engender the illusion of CBI as a panacea or some ineffable higher state, when in reality it is merely a contingent arrangement that does not differ materially from any other political expedient. For the very same legitimate political authority that grants independence to the central bank can decide later to rescind that independence.

Coleman (2001: 729) recalls Friedman's (1960, 1984) doubts about the feasibility of genuine CBI and, in support of those doubts, cites the case of the Australian Notes Issue Board from 1920 to 1924. Upon its creation in 1920, this board was granted the discretionary monetary policy competence previously vested in the treasury. The independence of the new board was designed to ensure the integrity of monetary policy. But the board's decisions proved unpopular, and it was disbanded after four years and its powers passed on to a more pliable entity. And even if CBI is enshrined in a country's basic law, this is ultimately no defense: for despite the difficulties of amending a written constitution, those difficulties can always be overcome by sufficient political will.

In short, pragmatic arrangements for CBI should not be mistaken for the foundations of a political culture. Such arrangements reflect an aspiration that the general interest should prevail over vested interest. But if that aspiration is not rooted in the culture of a national political community and in the overall design and functioning of its institutions, CBI will be like a castle built on sand. It is a strong political culture that creates effective and lasting CBI, not the other way round.

Various benchmarks have been suggested to assess the degree of a central bank's independence. A distinction is usually made between economic and political independence (Grilli, Masciandaro, and Tabellini, 1991). Political independence means that the central bank is left to fix its own objective without interference from the political authorities; in the case of economic independence, the objective can be fixed by the government or legislature, but the task of how best to pursue that objective will be left to the discretion of the central bank. Crowe and Meade (2007) list four standard legal criteria for ascertaining the independence of a country's central bank from its government: whether the central bank's management is appointed independently of the government, the scope for interference in the central bank's policy decisions, the inclusion of a mandate on price stability in the central bank's constitution, and the existence of clear safeguards on central bank lending to the government.

As already noted, the empirical evidence on whether CBI is beneficial to price stability is inconclusive. Some research focusing on the link between political pressures exerted on the central bank and the level of the inflation rate in mature economies concluded that independent central banks were more likely to deliver low inflation rates (Alesina, 1988; Grilli, Masciandaro, and Tabellini, 1991; Alesina and Summers, 1993). But Cukierman, Webb, and Neyapti's (1992) extensive study covering seventy-two countries and sixteen legal variables to construct a CBI index failed to reach any positive conclusion with regard to a causal role played by CBI, whether actual or formal, in inflation outcomes.

This lack of evidence seems to be confirmed by Crowe and Meade (2007: 73) in their survey of central bank governance that includes indices for independence and transparency. As regards the United States, which required no institutional change to its central banking arrangements either to get out of the Great Inflation in the 1980s or since, these authors explain that if the Federal Reserve's score of 0.48 is the same as in the 1980s and below the mean for the advanced countries in 2003, this is "because the underlying central bank law has not been amended." To resolve the doubts sown by this empirical evidence, they offer the following interpretation:

The Fed is historically a very independent central bank whose policies are credible around the world. It is less important to amend the Fed's legal statutes (if it ain't broke, don't fix it!) than it is to rewrite those of central banks that have not enjoyed actual independence or credibility.

Despite some appearance of circularity ("credibility is defined as credibility"), the sense is clear. Regardless of how anti-inflationary credibility originates, in countries like the United States where it happens to have been well established, then—as Jonas and Mishkin (2003) remarked—the "just-do-it" approach (see Bernanke et al., 1999) can suffice. It may be another matter in countries like Russia or Brazil, for instance, where effective counterinflationary action will require a more exacting rules-based framework.

But such frameworks depend first and foremost on the existence of at least some rudimentary form of the rule of law. This point was made by the Duke of Saint-Simon in his famous warning to the Duke of Orleans in 1716 against John Law's Royal Bank proposal. He relates in his memoirs (1716, in Saint-Simon 1985: 5:884) the discussion he had with the duke (who was ruling France in that period of the infancy of Louis XV in the capacity of Regent). He told the duke that while he was not an expert in finance, in his view, such a bank might be excellent in a republic or a monarchy like England where high finance is subject to some accountability, but disastrous in an absolute monarchy like France where expensive wars are fought, where the greed of a prime minister, a favorite, or a mistress is accommodated, where money is spent luxuriously and extravagantly. The prodigality of a king will exhaust and ruin the bank and with it all its depositors, resulting in the overthrow of the kingdom of France.[1]

Closer to our time Acemoglu, Johnson, Querubin, and Robinson (2008: 3) have drawn some more subtle distinctions between the effectiveness of institutional constraints on interference with central banks in various political contexts. They show that a move to CBI brings the greatest benefits in countries with an intermediate level of legal constraints on politicians such as Argentina and Chile rather than countries either with a highly developed rule of law (such as the United Kingdom, where inflation was already low when the BOE was made independent) or none at all, such as Zimbabwe and Sudan:

> [F]ew people would expect privatization, financial liberalization or central bank independence . . . to have fundamental effects in Zimbabwe

---

[1] Saint-Simon ([1716] 1985: 5:884: "que ce qui était excellent dans une république ou dans une monarchie où la finance est entièrement populaire comme est l'Angleterre, était d'un pernicieux usage dans une monarchie absolue telle que la France, où la nécessité d'une guerre mal entreprise et mal soutenue, l'avidité d'un premier ministre, d'un favori, d'une maîtresse, le luxe, les folles dépenses, la prodigalité d'un roi ont bientôt épuisé une banque et ruiné tous les porteurs de billets, c'est-à-dire culbuté le Royaume."

as long as Robert Mugabe is in power or in Sudan as long as Omar al-Bashir's kleptocratic and genocidal regime remains in place.

Cukierman, Miller, and Neyapti (2002), in their study of CBI in transition economies, remarked that for CBI to be instrumental in lowering inflation, the economy's structural features have to be sufficiently close to those of mature economies. Countries also vary in their citizens' aversion to inflation, with Japan, the United States, and Germany having greater inflation aversion compared to Italy and France (Cukierman, Webb, and Neyapti, 1992; Scheve, 2004). In other words CBI may be an endogenous variable embedded into history as in Germany, where the inflationary experiences of Weimar Germany left a strong mark.

The irony is that granting CBI to ensure less discretion by the government can backfire in making central bankers more powerful and less accountable to the legislature, turning them into absolute supremo authorities assuming total discretionary power over the monetary and financial institutions instead of being rule based. Indeed "an independent central bank is not the same as a rule-bound central bank" (Mankiw, 2006: 40).

CBI tends to assume implicitly that central bankers carry out "good" monetary policy, ignoring that "not all wisdom lies with central banks." The risk is that if central banks are given not merely operational independence but also goal independence, then the chosen goal may be misconceived. This point is well illustrated by the Australian Notes Issue Board, which was conducting some "foolish" policies such as "the Board's attempt to eliminate any seasonal fluctuations in the currency" (Coleman, 2001: 747).

Crowe and Meade remarked (2007: 78),

> Greater independence for a central bank must be reconciled with the requirements of institutional and personal accountability in a democratic society.

According to the arrangements put in place in the United Kingdom by Gordon Brown in 1997, the inflation target is set by Parliament, while the Monetary Policy Committee (MPC) is guaranteed the right to be able to pursue that target as its sees fit (while being obliged to give account of itself if the target is missed). This strikes a good balance between the benefits of operational CBI and underlying democratic legitimacy. By contrast, under the terms of the Maastricht Treaty, the independence of the ECB extends to the ECB itself having the right to define its price stability goal. Despite the existence of certain accountability mechanisms to the European

Parliament, questioning the goal that the ECB sets for itself would be an illegal challenge to its independence.

Proponents of free banking such as Lawrence H. White (2010) would happily abolish central bankers, arguing that the monetary policy carried out by the Fed since 2001 was harmfully discretionary:

> The independence of Federal Reserve policy in 2001–07, . . . did not deliver stability but fueled an unsustainable path in mortgage volumes and housing prices. The key to stability is not the independence but the *restraint* of central bank money and credit creation. Because the incentives facing central bankers do not produce self-restraint, external restraint is needed. (White, 2010: 460)

While CBI is held to guard central banks against capture by vested interests, it can also been argued that their actions lack accountability. After all, central bankers, unlike members of parliaments, are not elected. Clearly, central bank operations cannot be totally transparent, especially in times of financial crisis for fear of panicking financial markets; but there is an issue if central bank actions commit the taxpayer to rescue insolvent financial institutions. For White (2010: 459) a rule-bound central bank should be "limited to the functions of serving as bankers' banks for clearing and settlement and enforcing known rules regarding the solvency and liquidity of banks in its jurisdiction."

There can be no better illustration than the measures taken by the Fed, the BOE and the ECB in response to the 2007–8 financial crisis of the view that emergencies will have the practical effect of eroding central banks' independent pursuit of a price stability mandate—in particular by blurring the line between fiscal and monetary policy. The Fed, for instance, from mid-2008 undertook what to all intents and purposes were fiscal operations and bailed out bankrupt financial firms using the "emergency provisions of section 13(3) of the Federal Reserve Act" (White, 2010: 457). Most of the extraordinary measures taken by the Fed could not be described as monetary policy actions but rather fiscal, credit allocation (Goodfriend, 2009) or industrial policy (Taylor, 2009b). Policymakers are always

> in danger of assigning to monetary policy a larger role than it can perform, in danger of asking it to accomplish tasks that it cannot achieve, and as a result, in danger of preventing it from making the contribution that it is capable of making. (Friedman, 1968: 5)

Regardless of variations in political context and their implications for the form and effectiveness of CBI, it seems to be a fair generalization that the desired benefits of CBI depend on the central bank being accountable to the public. In this regard, the imposition of rules such as inflation targeting along the lines introduced in the United Kingdom and Eurozone has been widely seen as a fruitful advance in framing monetary policy. A word of caution expressed by Sims (2005: 283) leads to the next question that needs examining—namely, the use of one or another anchor for the purpose of ending high inflation:

> A cynical view might be that inflation targeting has become attractive less because of advances in our discipline than because of the demand for a replacement for the gold standard, monetarism, and exchange rate anchors.

In other words, the establishment of a credibly independent status for a country's central bank may be a necessary condition for the credibility of a monetary stabilization program, but is not a sufficient one. For the choice of aids—that is, nominal anchors—to support a stabilization program raises a whole further set of credibility challenges.

A History of Nominal Anchors

Economists have a long record of designing alternative monetary policy anchors with varied success—and, in some instances, clearly counterproductive results.[2] Historical examples of disastrous anchors are plentiful, one of the most vivid examples being the 1997–98 emerging markets financial crisis that began in Asia, spread to Russia, and culminated in the Argentina crisis in 2001. We saw in the previous chapter that the hazards of using an exchange rate peg to anchor anti-inflationary policies are exemplified by the experience of Russia in the period between the beginning of that country's first serious stabilization program in January 1995 and the financial debacle of August 1998 (which entailed a remarkable combination of both a huge devaluation and an outright default on domestic currency-denominated government debt).

These episodes marked the end of widespread use of the exchange rate as a nominal anchor for stabilization programs. Nevertheless, and as we will

---

[2] This section draws on materials originally published in Granville (1999).

see later, the global financial crash of 2007–8 had many of its roots in the earlier phase of crises that began in 1997.

Whatever the nominal anchor—the quantity of money, exchange rate, or an inflation target—monetary policy will always find its limit in fiscal policy. In the absence of a credible fiscal policy, the monetary policy anchor on its own will fail.

Exchange Rate Anchor

[T]he exchange rate is the most important price in any economy. Being the price of one national currency in terms of another, it is the link between all prices quoted in that currency and their counterparts in other countries' currencies—not only the prices of goods and services but also those of real and financial assets. (Kenen, 1988: 7)

The attraction of pegging the exchange rate to a low-inflation foreign currency was seen as an easy way to achieve low inflation in the domestic country as it provided "an immediate focal point for co-ordinating price expectations and price setting" (Bruno, 1990: 7; see also Dornbusch, Sturzenegger, and Wolf, 1990: 57). This was especially true for countries lacking credibility in terms of both political will and institutional arrangements. The credibility of the country issuing the currency to which the stabilizing country's currency was pegged could be imported instantly. Vegh (1992: 637), examining various hyper inflation episodes from the post–World War I European hyperinflations to the Bolivian hyperinflation (April 1984–September 1985), notes that during high inflation virtually all prices are indexed to a "hard" credible currency; hence stabilizing the exchange rate is tantamount to achieving price stability. The dollar has been the most frequent choice of currency to peg to; but some other inflation-free currencies have filled this role, such as the deutschmark or, more recently, the euro in Europe and the yen in Asia.

The risk of course is that, although the country of the anchor currency will, by definition, have a track record of stability, shocks are always possible—and any such shocks will be immediately transmitted to the inherently more fragile pegging country. A good example is the fiscal-inflationary shock of German unification being felt in various and often—as in the case of the United Kingdom on "Black Wednesday" in September 1992—quite dramatic ways in other European countries that were pegging their currencies to the deutschmark.

Exchange rate targeting was seen as an improvement to quantity-of-money targets in achieving a reduction in inflation. The link between domestic and international prices—the exchange rate—can be a more or less perfect transmitter of price signals from the rest of the world depending on the regulations attached to dampen the effects on the domestic economy. These regulations depend in turn on whether the domestic economy is inward or outward looking. Bruno (1990) observed that to achieve the best results in inflation reduction, the choice between exchange-rate versus money-based stabilization programs should depend on the strength of the link between the anchor used and the price level: that is, the exchange rate link to the price level or the money link to the price level.

The exchange rate anchors the price level through its impact on tradable prices, while the relationship between monetary growth and inflation is affected by changes in the velocity of money. In other words, if money demand and velocity are unstable, the effectiveness of money as an anchor is reduced. Rising velocity is a frequent consequence of rapid inflation as the public seeks to rid itself of a rapidly depreciating asset. This reduces the seigniorage that the government can obtain through creation of central bank money. At the same time the availability of alternative assets influences the dynamics of inflation through increased velocity, or partial abandonment, of the local currency.

Another advantage of an exchange-rate-based stabilization is that simpler tools are used than with money-based programs. When the central bank pegs the exchange rate by selling (buying) foreign exchange, it reduces (increases) base money and therefore the money stock. However, access to foreign exchange reserves (either generated by trade surpluses or borrowed) sufficient to maintain the peg and to give confidence is necessary.

Monetary policy cannot be loose, that is, financing the assets on the left-hand side of the central bank balance sheet, such as credit to the government—budget deficit financing—and/or commercial banks, is limited by the amount of foreign reserves and external debt. A too accommodative monetary policy will quickly put at risk the exchange rate anchor as foreign reserves will be depleted. This will erode the confidence and credibility in the authorities to defend the parity, risking devaluation and the abandonment of the peg. It follows that exchange-rate-based stabilization is effective in reducing inflation only if combined with fiscal tightening and proper regulation of the financial system.

Those conditions were softened in practice—and the effectiveness of using the exchange rate as the nominal anchor accordingly impaired—by increases in capital flows. In the 1980s most advanced countries went from limited to relatively full convertibility, while the 1990s saw a global easing of restrictions on cross-border capital flows. Limited convertibility as defined in Article VIII of the IMF statutes means that there are some exchange restrictions on specific types of transactions (capital account in this case) depending on the origin of the agent—foreigner or domestic—while full convertibility means the total absence of any such restrictions. Capital mobility has been encouraged by the unprecedented financial liberalization since the 1980s both at the domestic and international levels as well as by the development of information technology. These two factors led in turn to surges in competition and innovation in the financial sector.

The practical result most relevant to this discussion was that increasingly easy access to foreign funding of domestic government (and corporate) debt resulted in efforts to control inflation by tighter monetary policy (see table 3.1) being accompanied by rising budget deficits (see table 3.2, showing how OECD countries' budget deficits rose from zero in the 1960s to an average of 3.3 percent of nominal GDP by the mid-1990s). In the case of emerging market countries, Fischer (1998) highlighted the importance of foreign-financed debt expansion for understanding the series of financial crises in these countries (from the Mexican crisis of 1994, via the Asian and Russian crises of 1997–98, to the Argentinean default of 2001). Foreign demand for emerging market credit boiled down to the hunt for yield in a period of falling interest rates in the developed world (see table 3.3). From the point of view of the governments of many of these emerging markets, such portfolio inflows heightened the attraction of pegging the exchange rate. In that way, foreign lenders would be encouraged (their

TABLE 3.1

Inflation: Percentage changes in consumer prices, year on year.[a]

	1970–79[b]	1980–89[b]	1990–95[b]	1996	1997	1998
United States	7.2	5.6	3.5	2.9	2.3	1.6
Japan	9.1	2.5	1.7	0.1	1.7	0.6
European Union	10.1	7.1	4.0	2.4	1.9	1.6
Total OECD	9.2	8.8	5.6	5.2	4.5	3.8

Source: OECD (1999: 242, annex, table 16).

a. Aggregates are computed using weights based on 1997 consumer expenditure expressed in private consumption purchasing power parities.

b. Average over the period.

TABLE 3.2

General government financial balances: Surplus (+) or deficit (–)
as a percentage of nominal GDP.

	1960–69[b]	1970–79[b]	1980–89[b]	1990–95[b]	1996	1997	1998
United States	–0.1	–1.0	–2.5	–3.0	–0.9	+0.4	+1.7
Japan[a]	+1.0	–1.7	–1.5	0.0	–4.2	–3.4	–6.0
European Union			–4.3	–4.8	–4.1	–2.5	–2.1
Total OECD	0.0	–1.6	–2.9	–3.3	–2.6	–1.2	–0.9

Sources: OECD, Economic Outlook, various issues, quoted in Warburton (1999); OECD (1999: 254, annex, table 30).

a. The 1998 outlays would have risen by 5.4 percentage points of GDP if account was taken of the assumption by the central government of the debt of the Japan Railway Settlement Corporation and the National Forest Special Account.

b. Average over the period.

TABLE 3.3

Short-term interest rates (percentage).

	1981–89[a]	1990–95[a]	1996	1997	1998
United States	8.5	4.9	5.0	5.1	4.8
Japan	6.0	4.3	0.6	0.6	0.7
European Union	10.5	9.0	4.7	4.2	3.9
Korea[b]	N/A	15.0	12.7	13.4	15.2
Mexico	61.1	24.9	32.9	21.3	26.1

Source: OECD (1999: 260, annex, table 36).

a. Average over the period.

b. The average for Korea is between 1991 and 1995.

riskier exposures hedged by portfolio insurance or derivatives), and the effect of the peg in bearing down on inflation, far from entailing any pain, would thus be accompanied by stimulatory effect of a credit expansion.

In short, the use of an exchange peg provided the appearance of more credibility than was warranted by the actual conduct of monetary policy. For example, the confidence in a peg on the part of markets and all economic agents concerned may persist for a period in which monetary policy is in fact being subordinated to other policy priorities such as fiscal stimulus. A floating exchange rate would react quickly to any such weakness in monetary policy, forcing a timely correction. By contrast, under the veil of an exchange rate peg, monetary policy can easily deteriorate to the extent that when markets finally begin to doubt the credibility of the peg, it has become politically and practically very difficult to implement the necessary corrective measures. In such episodes, the typical outcome is the abandonment of the peg, denoting the final failure of the anti-inflationary policy.

The agreeable effects of lower inflation and faster growth brought about by the combination of an exchange rate peg with unrestricted and powerful cross-border capital flows were usually short-lived. That combination soon enough resulted in high volatility of output and employment. The transmission mechanism here is domestic interest rates. As already noted in the previous chapter, the root problem here is the following "trilemma":

> An open capital market, however, deprives a country's government of the ability *simultaneously* to target its exchange rate and to use monetary policy in pursuit of other economic objectives. (Obstfeld, 1998: 6)

If the authorities are determined to defend an exchange rate peg, domestic interest rates will fall or rise in response to, respectively, capital inflows (i.e., foreign demand for the local currency, which, in order to keep the parity stable, the domestic central bank will absorb into its reserves, thereby increasing the monetary base and driving down interest rates) or outflows (with the symmetrically opposite effects). In short, the monetary authorities are pulled between

> a desire to control inflation (that is, to provide a nominal anchor) and a wish to limit fluctuations in competitiveness or to minimise output losses. (Eichengreen, Masson, Savastano, and Sharma, 1999: 5–6)

The crisis and breakdown of anti-inflationary regimes based on an exchange rate anchor typically comes when foreign capital flows out of the country. We have seen in the case of Russia how an exchange rate-based stabilization program can be undermined by inadequate macroeconomic policies and poor bank regulation. Inadequate bank regulation has been an even stronger harbinger of crises in countries where the private sector rather than the government was the recipient of most of the credit resources flowing in from outside the country (Otker and Pazarbasioglu, 1995). This was the case in the Asian countries that, despite sound fiscal positions (Radelet and Sachs, 1998), were hit by the emerging market crises of the late 1990s: confidence in the exchange rate peg led many companies to take out cheap short-term loans provided by foreign lenders and denominated in foreign currency. The outstanding face value of short-duration loans from developed market banks to emerging market banks (mostly in

TABLE 3.4

Foreign reserves as a percentage of short-term foreign debt.[a]

	End 1990	Mid-1994	End 1996	End 1997	Mid-1998
Indonesia	55	58	53	47	65
Korea	73	62	50	142	123
Malaysia	475	397	241	34	176
Thailand	151	101	83	67	93
Russia	N/A	N/A	43	40	32

Source: IMF, Bank for International Settlements, quoted in OECD (1999: 189, table VI.3).

a. Foreign reserves equal total reserves minus gold; short-term debt is defined as claims of all BIS reporting banks vis-à-vis the countries, at maturities up to and including one year.

Asia) peaked in 1996 at $240 billion (IMF, 1998b: 40). The authorities' response of raising interest rates to defend the exchange rate and stem outflows foundered not only because of weak financial sector regulation but for two other reasons besides. First, similar to the Russian case, higher interest rates triggered worries about solvency, with the cost of servicing debt (whether public or private) surging as a percentage of GDP. Second, the short duration of foreign liabilities increased the likelihood of default as foreign reserves declined relative to GDP (table 3.4 illustrates this in the main affected countries)—and the reward of higher yields was insufficient to offset this risk.

In addition, interest rate hikes proved counterproductive against the background of the foreign lenders' currency hedging strategies. In the typical case where lenders insure themselves against devaluation risk by buying forward currency sale contracts with domestic banks, those same banks will be forced to finance their obligations under those contracts by buying the foreign currency sold by the central bank in its attempt to stave off devaluation. Central banks thus in effect financed the attacks on their own reserves (Garber and Spencer, 1995: 513).

On this phenomenon of the medicine of higher interest rates failing to avert the collapse of exchange rate-anchored stabilization programs, van Wijnbergen (1991: 91) comments,

This ultimately inflationary effect of tight credit policies under an unsustainable fixed exchange rate regime is related to the Sargent-Wallace result of high inflation in response to temporary tight money policies in a closed economy context.

Various intermediate policy responses were suggested to deal with phenomenon of capital flows putting fixed exchange rates under strain. The existence of the relatively high degree of convertibility associated with increased capital mobility and increased sophistication of financial instruments led first to the recommendation that countries should move to a more flexible exchange rate regime such as crawling pegs. Dornbusch, Sturzenegger, and Wolf (1990: 58) advocated shifting to a crawling peg exchange rate even though this might create additional difficulties for price stabilization:

> Exchange rates should be fixed at the outset, but soon after should switch to a crawling peg in order to maintain the real exchange rate. This measure increases inflationary pressures in the economy and therefore shifts more weight to the budget as the central stabilising force. Overvaluation notwithstanding, to advocate a fixed exchange rate, with the idea that the resulting recession would teach price setters a lesson, is risky. It may fail on political grounds.

But during the 1990s financial crises, "crawling peg" regimes were swept away. The distinction between a peg and a band is not black and white. The convention is that a peg has become "understood as a band in which the margins on either side of the central parity are less than or equal to 2.25 percent" (Mussa, Masson, Swoboda, Jadresic, Mauro, and Berg, 2000: 48). And the band or the peg can be qualified by various adjectives such as "crawling" or "galloping," but the point is that in one way or another there is a certain degree of fluctuation that is limited and is publicly announced or worked out by the market. Under crawling pegs, the central bank has two targets: the monetary base and the band of the crawling peg. Capital flows create a conflict between these two targets and force the central bank to choose whether to prioritize the interest rate or exchange rate.

For a while following violent exchange and payment crises of the 1990s, it was thought that any exchange rate arrangements in the middle ground between hard peg and relatively free float were not sustainable (Obstfeld and Rogoff, 1995). But preference for an absolutely fixed exchange rate can be equally risky, as demonstrated by the collapse of Argentina's currency board system.

Until the Argentina crisis (2001), the credibility of currency boards was highly rated owing to the fact that the monetary authorities' loss of freedom to print money is set by law, so the political cost of altering such an exchange rate regime is high. For sure, the Argentinean currency board was successful in reducing inflation, but similar to all other fixed exchange rate regimes, if the fiscal position including debt service was not credibly sustainable, and the banking sector poorly regulated, there was little chance for such a system to survive a speculative attack. Unsustainable fiscal policy tends to undermine credibility whatever the exchange rate regime adopted. Kehoe (2003: 628) stresses that "unpleasant monetarist arithmetic doomed the [Argentinean] Convertibility Plan to failure." Credibility is better built at home rather than borrowed.

The exchange rate is part of the overall economic strategy: countries are successful not because of their exchange rate policy but because they follow economic policy that is consistent with the exchange rate strategy given greater capital mobility. Emerging countries were slow to move to free-floating exchange rates, with early examples being Indonesia (1999), Korea (1999), and South Africa (1995). Most emerging countries opted for more flexible—but still managed—exchange rate regimes (i.e., crawling pegs with varying sizes of permitted fluctuation bands around a central rate). This reluctance to abandon exchange rate management in favor of the most accessible alternative method of fixing inflationary expectations—namely, inflation targeting (precociously adopted by advanced transition countries like Poland and the Czech Republic)—was rationalized by the BIS (2000: 62) on the grounds that the necessary framework for inflation targeting, such as modeling the transmission mechanism of monetary policy, estimating the impact of exchange rate volatility on inflation and inflation expectations, and calculating the output gap, may prove difficult in the medium term to achieve. Also the share of imports in consumption makes "it difficult to meet a narrow inflation target given volatile exchange rates or commodity prices" (BIS, 2000: 45). The danger, however, is that if both inflation and the exchange rate are targeted, at one point or other tensions will arise, and when this occurs, it will be already too late to change the strategy in a smooth manner. It took the further shock of foreign capital outflows triggered by the crisis of 2008 to induce Russia to shift at last to a floating exchange rate as the basis for a new monetary policy framework of "pure" inflation targeting.

In any case, it will be clear from this discussion that exchange rate anchors will not have the desired anti-inflationary effect unless accompanied by a range of other appropriate policies. As we have seen, fiscal discipline is a necessary condition for the stability of any exchange rate system, and the danger of fixed exchange rate regimes is that the peg may act as a veil hiding or delaying the necessary fiscal adjustment as in the Argentinean or Russian cases. And even in cases where exchange rate management makes a successful contribution to lowering inflation, it will be important to prepare an exit strategy and not wait until capital inflows are such that the potential of that same capital to flow out again could jeopardize the whole stabilization process. Eichengreen and Masson (1998) recommend that the move to more "flexible" exchange rates should take place during calm period.

But if such a statement makes sense in principle, in practice it is more difficult to apply: why should a country abandon an exchange rate arrangement when it seems to be performing well, incurring the risk of destabilization and volatility?

The conclusion must be that in a globalized world most countries should stay away from exchange rate pegs given the high costs when such pegs collapse. We come back once again to the "open economy trilemma" (Obstfeld and Taylor, 1998). It is a trilemma because it is possible to combine only two of the following three features: independent monetary policies, fixed exchange rates, and an open capital account. If a government chooses fixed exchange rates and capital mobility, it has to give up monetary autonomy. If a country wants monetary autonomy and capital mobility, it has to go with floating exchange rates. If it wants to combine fixed exchange rates with monetary autonomy, it has to restrict capital mobility.

Obstfeld, Shambaugh, and Taylor (2003) tested empirically the constraint of the open economy trilemma, reinforcing the conclusion that only a relatively free-floating exchange rate regime or capital controls allow an independent monetary policy free to pursue domestic aims. This conclusion is buttressed by the findings of Husain, Mody, and Rogoff (2004) that fixed exchange rate regimes perform relatively well in relatively closed capital markets characteristic of poor developing countries but not so well for more open emerging countries.

Inflation Targeting

Since the 1990s many countries have adopted the rate of inflation as a nominal anchor. This approach involves an "interest rate feedback" rule whereby the central bank uses the nominal short-term interest rate to target a preannounced level of inflation (usually measured by the retail price index [RPI] or the consumer price index [CPI]). While some authors advocate focusing strictly on a numerical point or an interval, others favor adjusting interest rates in response to both inflation and output. Taylor (1993) developed a guideline or nonmechanical "rule" (the so-called Taylor rule), which prescribed that in order to control inflation, central bankers should set the short-term interest rate according to the inflation and output gaps, the inflation gap being the difference between the actual and the targeted inflation rate and the output gap the difference between actual output and potential output from existing capacity. In practice, however, the output gap is not easy to calculate (Orphanides, 2000).

There is a distinction between strict inflation targeting, where the central bank concentrates on maintaining and achieving an inflation outcome as close as possible to the targeted rate, and flexible inflation targeting, which takes account of other factors such as exchange rates and employment. Most central bankers practice inflation targeting (IT) not as an "ironclad rule" but as a framework absorbing as much information as possible to reach the medium- to long-term inflation targets (Bernanke and Mishkin, 2007: 215).

After the breakup of the Bretton Woods system in 1971 and the abandonment of fixed exchange rates, increased inflationary pressures led many countries, such as Germany (1974), the United States, Canada, and Switzerland (1975), the United Kingdom (1976), and France (1977), to move to monetary targets. We saw earlier that inflation reached high levels in most mature markets in the 1970s, for instance in 1975 the inflation rate in the United Kingdom reached 25 percent. The move to monetary targets whereby the money supply was targeted to grow at a constant rate, however, did not prove as reliable as expected as money demand became less predictable with financial innovations and deregulations occurring in the 1980s and 1990s. In other words for money targeting to work the relationship between money and inflation has to be stable, and in the United Kingdom this was not the case. As shown in table 3.5, the preferred money supply target (which was the broad "M3" aggregate) was systematically missed. This approach therefore had little success in stabilizing the inflation rate.

Starting in March 1987 the United Kingdom pursued an informal exchange rate target by shadowing the movements of the deutschmark; this policy was then formalized with the United Kingdom joining the European exchange rate mechanism (ERM) in 1990. The timing was unfortunate as it coincided with German unification and with the United Kingdom being in recession. The tension between the desire to keep domestic interest rates low while at the same time keeping sterling pegged to the deutschmark resulted in speculative attacks against the pound and ended with the decision to leave the ERM.

Having tried exchange rate targeting (Bretton Woods, ERM) and monetary targeting, the search for a strong nominal anchor led many countries to move in the late 1980s and 1990s to IT. The pioneers were, among others, the Reserve Bank of New Zealand in 1990, the Bank of Canada in 1991, and the Bank of England in 1992. The 1990s saw this shift being expressed most clearly with a price stability mandate anchored by an inflation target

TABLE 3.5
Intermediate targets, United Kingdom, 1976–87, percentage.

Year		Money aggregate	Target	Outcome
1976–77	Apr–Apr	StM3	9–13	8.0
1977–78	Apr–Apr	StM3	9–13	15.1
1978–79	Apr–Apr	StM3	8–12	11.4
1978–79	Oct–Oct	StM3	8–12	13.7
1979–80	Jun–Oct	StM3	7–11	17.2
1980–81	Feb–Apr	StM3	7–11	19.4
1981–82	Feb–Apr	StM3	6–10	12.8
1982–83	Feb–Apr	StM3	8–12	11.2
1983–84	Feb–Apr	StM3	7–11	9.5
1984–85	Feb–Apr	StM3	6–10	11.9
		M0	4–8	5.4
1985–86	Mar–Mar	StM3	5–9	16.7
		M0	3–7	3.4
1986–87	Mar–Mar	StM3	11–15	19.0
		M0	2–6	4.4

Source: Reproduced with permission of Dave Smant, http://sites.google.com/site/davesmant/monetary-policy/mpol-uk-boe.

Note: StM3 was renamed M3 and formally abandoned in 1987.

(rather than a monetary, exchange rate, or price-level target) included in the central bank constitution as for instance in the case of the ECB, where the final target is defined in article 105(1) of the Maastricht Treaty. In its stability-oriented monetary policy strategy, the ECB has given the following definition of its inflation target:

> Price stability shall be defined as a year-on-year increase in the Harmonised Index of Consumer Prices (HICP) of the Euro area of below 2%.... Price stability is to be maintained over the medium term.

While IT includes many elements that were parts of monetary targeting such as communicating to the public in order to build a credibility rapport to anchor firmly inflationary expectations, IT also has distinguishing characteristics such as announcing a target for inflation rather than a monetary aggregate target. Contrary to monetary targets that involved targeting the growth of a monetary aggregate (M0, M1, M2, etc.) as a policy instrument, under IT the instrument or operating target is the interest rate, usually the rate at which the central bank provides short-term funds to the banking system. McCallum's (1981) work provided an early systematic account of the advantages of using short-term interest rates as the primary instrument of monetary policy—with the level of the short-term rate being decided by the monetary authorities and adjusted using open market operations.

Communication is a crucial element of IT. The public has to be convinced that the monetary authorities will keep to their word and respect the inflation target, which can be set as a point—for instance 2 percent as in the United Kingdom and the EU—or as a range—for instance between 1 and 4 percent in the United Kingdom before 1997 (table 3.6). Communication is enhanced through the publication of regular Inflation Reports. In the case of the Bank of England which has had operational independence since May 1997, Inflation Reports are published each quarter, setting out "the detailed economic analysis and inflation projections on which the Bank's Monetary Policy Committee bases its interest rate decisions, and presents an assessment of the prospects for UK inflation."[3]

The United Kingdom adopted IT in October 1992 following sterling's chaotic exit from the ERM. The Bank of England Act of 1998 constituted the enabling legislation for the operational independence of the BOE. Decisions on interest rates are made by the Monetary Policy Committee (MPC) consisting of nine members: the governor of the BOE, the two deputy governors, the bank's chief economist, the executive director for markets, and four external members appointed by the Chancellor of the Exchequer for fixed terms. These "independent" MPC members have for the most part been academic and professional economists. Meetings of the MPC take place monthly to discuss and decide the interest rate, currently the BOE repo rate, which applies to open market operations (figure 3.2). As noted above, the inflation target itself is set by the parliament.

The inflation target was initially set at 2.5 percent, and based on the RPI (excluding mortgage interest payments). This was changed in 2003 with the move to the CPI, while the target itself was reduced to 2 percent (table 3.6).

To take account of output and unemployment, the target is symmetrical. That is, as explained by William Allen (1999: 6), it is considered as much of a policy error to undershoot as to overshoot the target. "If inflation is expected to be below target, it is the BOE's duty to ease monetary policy. Moreover the BOE is required by law to support the government's economic policy, including its objectives for growth and employment, subject to the overriding objective of maintaining price stability." The governor of

---

[3] See http://www.bankofengland.co.uk/publications/inflationreport/index.htm.

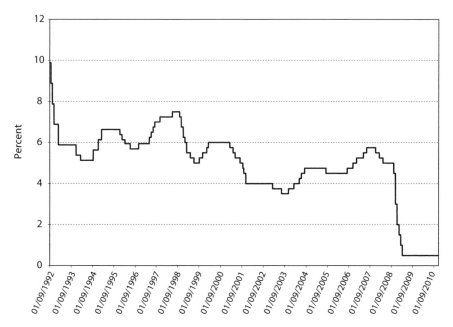

Figure 3.2. U.K. official bank rate.
Source: Bank of England.

the Bank of England has to write an open letter to the Chancellor of the Exchequer if the target is missed by more than 1 percentage point on either side, that is, if the annual rate of CPI is more than 3 percent or less than 1 percent, explaining the reasons for the over/undershoot of the actual inflation rate compared to the targeted one.

In this U.K. version of IT, the essential accountability and public communication elements comprise, in addition to the above-mentioned inflation reports and the letter of the BOE governor, regular testimony of MPC members before the Treasury Select Committee of the House of Commons, and the minutes of those meetings are published. The way each member of the MPC voted is published two weeks after each meeting, with the respective arguments of the "doves" (favoring lower interest rates) and "hawks" (favoring higher interest rates) being followed in the press and discussed widely. Important as this is for enhancing credibility, such transparency also runs the risk of creating occasional confusion.

In their regular public remarks, MPC members tend to hold different views feeding healthy and positive debates. For example external member

TABLE 3.6
Inflation target, United Kingdom, 1993–2011, percentage.

Year	Index	Target	Outcome
1993	RPIX	1–4	3.0
1994	RPIX	1–4	2.3
1995	RPIX	1–4	2.9
1996	RPIX	1–4	3.0
1997	RPIX	2.5	2.8
1998	RPIX	2.5	2.6
1999	RPIX	2.5	2.3
2000	RPIX	2.5	2.1
2001	RPIX	2.5	2.1
2002	RPIX	2.5	2.2
2003	CPI	2	1.4
2004	CPI	2	1.3
2005	CPI	2	2.1
2006	CPI	2	2.3
2007	CPI	2	2.3
2008	CPI	2	3.6
2009	CPI	2	2.2
2010	CPI	2	3.3
2011	CPI	2	4.5

Source: Office for National Statistics, http://www.statistics.gov.uk/.

Adam Posen (appointed until September 2012) in his speech to the Hull and Humber Chamber of Commerce, Industry and Shipping on September 28, 2010, titled "The Case for Doing More," preached a case for more quantitative easing (QE) on top of the £200 billion pounds worth of gilts that the BOE bought between March 2009 and January 2010, while one of the internal (BOE) MPC members, Spencer Dale, in his remarks titled "Inflation, Inflation, Inflation" made on September 22, 2010, to the Cardiff Business School, reminded his audience that the MPC's job is to achieve the inflation target and warned against the risk of the CPI inflation being consistently above target inflation (CPI inflation at that point had been above target for forty-one out of the previous fifty months—see figure 3.3 below).

[T]he fact that inflation has been higher than expected; and that it is likely to remain above target until the end of next year all contribute to

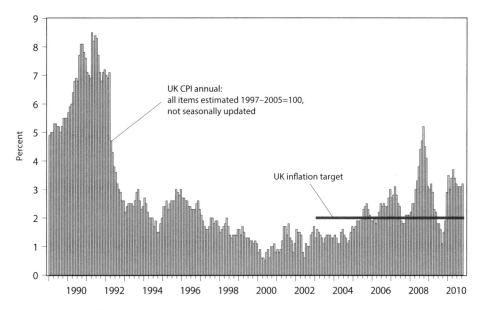

Figure 3.3. U.K. annual CPI inflation rates and inflation target.
Source: Office for National Statistics.

the risk that credibility and confidence in the MPC may start to waver. (Dale, 2010: 11)

While remaining judiciously cautious in his assessment of inflation risk, Dale simply noted the risks to the inflation target were there and recalled that the role of monetary policy and therefore of the MPC is a "balancing act" (Dale, 2010: 12).

The question is, while debates are healthy, whether too much dissent can be counterproductive if it undermines the smoothness of the monetary policymaking process in an IT regime given that financial markets are easily unsettled. The composition of the MPC with insiders and outsiders may enhance or damage the credibility of the monetary policy process—the publicly aired differences of opinion between MPC members are not trivial—and thus have a potentially major bearing on the performance of the economy. If these differences of opinion become too loud, they risk undermining the very credibility of monetary policymaking, which the mixed composition of the committee is designed to enhance. As Dale (2010: 11) remarks,

We lose our credibility at our peril—once the genie of inflation credibility escapes, it is costly to put back.

Bean (2003: 12) is aware of this problem but dismisses it and argues that

this willingness to disagree has, I believe, turned out to be a strength in that it reinforces the point that the future—not to mention the past—is uncertain and it is reasonable for there to be (usually slight) differences in interpretation.

The new burgeoning literature on the MPC and the way its members vote—mirroring the literature on the Federal Reserve's Federal Open Market Committee (FOMC) decision making modeled on members' career backgrounds—tends to confirm that overall the MPC composed as it is has a positive impact. For instance Petra Gerlach-Kristen (2009) found that dissent brought by external members has a positive impact on the predictability of monetary policy and therefore on anchoring inflation expectations. One issue was whether the career background of the external members explained their dissent. In an early paper, Gerlach-Kristen (2003) showed that outsiders tended to be "doves" and to dissent more than insiders reflecting various motivations such as raising their profile, career concerns, or not having access to as much information or many opportunities as insiders to discuss their views. These results are not supported by Mark Harris and Christopher Spencer (2008: 19), who found that "career experience plays a very weak role in determining a member's decision to dissent." Moreover Berk, Bierut, and Meade (2011) show that if externals dissent they do so but only in their third year, when they become "experienced"; the first two years of their term, externals tend to vote as the internal members.

The importance of such a committee as the MPC composed of both insiders and outsiders should not be underestimated. The MPC debates contribute to interpreting and identifying the reasons for the variations in the CPI and in doing so help to follow the "right" course of action. Art and judgment are essential for any kind of IT (explicit or implicit) to work properly, and the contribution of outsiders has proved broadly positive (Hansen and McMahon, 2010).

None of these monetary policy decision-making bodies are beyond criticism. For instance the FOMC is exclusively composed of internal members, with the seven governors of the Federal Board and the twelve presidents of the Federal Reserve Banks (of whom only five vote in rotation). Romer and Romer (2008) attacked the forecasting performance of the FOMC, while Ellison and Sargent (2009) built a convincing counterattack in defense of the FOMC "as a robust policymaker." They conclude (2009: 20) by quoting from a report in *Forbes* magazine (January 4, 2008) on a discussion of Romer and Romer (2008) by former Federal Reserve Monetary Affairs Director Vincent Reinhart at the American Economic Association meetings in New Orleans:

> However, former Fed staffer Vincent Reinhart said while it may look as if "the FOMC's contribution to the monetary policy process is to reduce forecast accuracy," they are not there primarily to be forecasters. Instead, they exist in a political system and have to be held accountable for the outcomes of their decisions. "They can be bad forecasters and good policymakers," Reinhart said, "if the diversity of views about the outlook informs their policy choice."

This debate usefully highlights one central problem with IT—namely, the accuracy of forecasting. Given that monetary policy is directed to hit an inflation target through the interest rate instrument, accurate forecasts of future inflation are important but difficult to achieve even with a very short-term horizon. This is because the relationship between leading inflation indicators (as for instance commodity prices) and short-term interest rates (such as the federal funds rate) is neither strong nor stable. For Cecchetti (1995), the solution is to incorporate these imprecisions into the monetary policy rule. Alternatively, and as mentioned above, art and judgment by monetary policy committees should compensate for this lack of precision.

In the United Kingdom the inflation forecast is drafted by the BOE staff before being discussed and revised by the MPC in advance of publication in the form of quarterly *Inflation Reports*. This ensures constant monitoring of the inflation rate through an inflation forecast based on different assumptions about the interest rate. Members of the MPC base their interest rate decisions on various forecasts on inflation and GDP.

Despite these difficulties, low inflation and good economic performance in general have coincided with IT (Roger and Stone, 2005), but the causal relationship between the two has not been definitively demonstrated (Mishkin and Schmidt-Hebbel, 2007).

Lawrence Ball and Niamh Sheridan (2005) pointed out that inflation fell both in countries that have adopted inflation targets and in other countries that have not. The specific contribution of institutional arrangements to this positive outcome is therefore unclear. Ball and Sheridan compare seven OECD countries that adopted IT in the early 1990s, with thirteen that, according to the authors, did not. They conclude that some of the improvements in macroeconomic stability in the IT countries may have been unrelated to the adoption of IT. Mark Gertler (2005: 276) commented that one reason for Ball and Sheridan's results is to be found in the fact that most if not all of the nontargeters adopted monetary policy frameworks "very similar in practice to formal inflation targeting." Among the thirteen nontargeters surveyed, eight countries belong to the European Union, and it is doubtful that these eight countries should have been included in the control group; the remaining five countries include Denmark (which is strange since Denmark has been part of the EU since 1973), Japan, Norway, Switzerland, and the United States. Gertler remarks that both Denmark and Switzerland have followed a monetary policy very similar to that of the EU, while Norway seems to have pegged its monetary policy to that of Sweden, one of the sample inflation targeters. Japan experienced deflation, so could arguably distort this sample. As regards the United States, Marvin Goodfriend (2005: 324) argued that the improvement in U.S. macroeconomic performance since the early 1980s could be attributed in part to inflation-targeting policy procedures that the Fed adopted gradually and implicitly over that period of two decades, showing that the Fed has achieved price stability and arrived at monetary policy procedures that resemble IT by "just doing it."

Perhaps the more important conclusion is that targeting need not be explicit to be effective. For example, there is nothing in the data up to 2001 to suggest that covert targeters like the United States would have benefited from adopting explicit targets. The Federal Reserve Act defines the goals of U.S. monetary policy as "maximum employment, stable prices, and moderate long term interest rates." Contrary to the ECB, in the case of the United States price stability is not prescribed, as the final target, section 2A of the Federal Reserve Act, states,

> The Board of Governors of the Federal Reserve System and the Federal Open Market Committee shall maintain long run growth of the monetary and credit aggregates commensurate with the economy's long run potential to increase production, so as to promote effectively the goals of maximum employment, stable prices, and moderate long term interest rates.

This suggests that what is important to successful monetary policy is the existence of a strong nominal anchor, and in the United States the anchor became personified for a period in the long-serving Fed Chairman Alan Greenspan (Mishkin, 2007b). However that may be, experience with previously fashionable nominal anchors such as fixed exchange rates suggests that inflation was never stopped for long by the use of one anchor alone.

We have already seen how this proved especially true of exchange rate pegs, as exemplified by the Argentina's financial crisis of 2001 (Kehoe, 2003); but the same rule must also apply to star central bankers. Their status as sources of confidence will always be vulnerable to shocks. To be sure, the anchor can take any form but has to inspire trust and confidence for expectations to form in a way that fits the monetary authorities' goal of price stability.

IT as an anchor has proved resilient over a lengthy period. Rose (2006: 4) remarks that while the international financial system of Bretton Woods with its fixed exchange rates and capital controls lasted from 1959 (the date at which European currencies were made convertible on the current account of the balance of payments) to 1971—that is, about thirteen years, by contrast, IT had at the time of writing become the dominant trend in monetary policy in the decades following its adoption by New Zealand in 1990.

Yet any such anchor can be only one element in overall macroeconomic policy. If a strong inflation target is set to contain inflation expectations while at the same time the budget deficit is growing, various banks are failing, and unemployment is rising, this will damage the credibility of the monetary authorities' commitment to the target and inflationary expectations will build up. While IT is the most comprehensive institutional and policy management package evolved to date, any such package is not a sufficient condition in itself for efficient inflation control, but still requires the underpinning of political will on which the all-important factor of credibility ultimately depends.

Price-Level Targeting

Under price-level targeting (PT), which has only ever been attempted in practice by Sweden in the 1930s (see Berg and Jonung, 1999), any medium-term deviations of the chosen price index from the target path (the path usually being defined inside a band) must be corrected, usually by means of altering the short-term interest rate. The difference from IT—which, as we have seen, targets a defined rate of change in the price level over the medium term—is that if the central bank misses the target, it may have to give account of itself (as in the United Kingdom), but there is no correction: the CB has just to do its best to hit the target during the next period. IT introduces a random walk element into the price level; the base for the next period IT is the actual price level. Put another way, PT differs from IT in having a memory. The risk with IT is that the long-term variance of the price level is higher than with PT and therefore may introduce a high level of uncertainty with regard to decisions involving long-term savings and investments such as long-term fixed bonds and retirement plans. In other words the price level path drifts under IT.

The issue really is the meaning of price stability—whether it refers to the rate of change in prices or the absolute price level. Obviously if it means low inflation and if an inflation target is used, price level stability is not guaranteed since the price level drifts over the years with the above-mentioned long-term risks for savings and investments. This does not imply that proponents of PT focus on targeting a constant price level. For the same reasons as with IT where the target is set above zero, the price level target will increase over time, allowing a low but still positive inflation rate, the main reason being that at very low inflation rates nominal short-term interest rates may be close to zero, rendering monetary policy ineffective. Moreover measures of inflation being imperfect, a positive inflation rate ensures that the economy is not actually in deflation and facilitates reduction of real wages to maintain employment in an economic downturn. The benefits of PT would be that economic agents would be able to predict over the next thirty years or so where the price level would be.

That benefit of PT must be weighed against its costs—namely, increased volatility of both inflation and output. The risk is that if the target is overshot because of some supply shock such as the oil price, the consequences can be painful: contracting monetary policy, driving down short-term output performance. Fischer (1994) condemned PT altogether, arguing that such an arrangement was too costly for output in the short term and introduced a high level of inflation volatility (see also Haldane and Salmon, 1995). Gaspar and Smets (2000: 68) however argue that the reason for this negative view is that it is rooted in the disinflation experience of the 1980s responding to a one-off price jump. Assessed inside the framework of the new Keynesian Phillips curve macroeconomic models with forward-looking behavior, PT has been regarded in a more positive light than IT (see for instance Ball, Mankiw, and Reiss, 2005; Clarida, Gali, and Gertler, 1999; Woodford, 1999a). Current inflation depends on expected inflation and on the output gap. The output loss related to a jump in the inflation rate is milder, cushioning current expectations of future inflation and therefore inflation persistence and variability (the variance of changes in inflation).

The literature on PT argues that PT will help policymakers to manage long-term inflation expectations by reducing uncertainty about the long-term level of prices. On this view, the commitment of the central bank to limit the drift of the price level improves the trade-off between inflation and output, stabilizes inflation expectations, and in turn results in a more stable economy (Gaspar and Smets, 2000). Svensson (1999) and Vestin (2006) argue that PT compares favorably with IT on this same criterion of producing a better trade-off between inflation and output variability. If economic agents are forward looking and base their inflation expectations on PT, fluctuations in output and inflation could be reduced. This conclusion is supported by Coletti, Lalonde, and Muir (2008) and reinforced in the presence of terms of trade shocks: the authors find that for Canada, PT will perform slightly better than IT.

PT is also seen as potentially decreasing deflation risk when short-term interest rates approach to zero (the so-called zero bound) in times of recession (Eggertsson and Woodford, 2003; Wolman, 2005). Berg and Jonung (1999) showed that fears of deflation were successfully alleviated by raising inflation expectations.

At the zero bound traditional monetary policy tools are ineffective because nominal interest rates cannot go below zero. The task of the monetary authorities is further complicated if economic agents expect deflation, as real interest rates will then rise, further depressing economic activity.

This is well illustrated by the situation in the United States where the FOMC sets a target for the interest rate on overnight loans (the "federal funds rate") in order to achieve its above-mentioned twin mandate of promoting employment and stable prices. After the federal funds rate fell to zero in 2008 the Fed was unable to use further interest rate cuts and expanded its balance sheet by relying on "nonstandard" monetary tools to prevent the risk of depression. These instruments involved exchanging central bank liquidity for private assets via various facilities such as the Term Auction Facility (TAF) and the Primary Dealer Credit Facility (PDCF) (Del Negro, Eggertsson, Ferrero, and Kiyotaki, 2010).

Other nominal anchors discussed in the literature are average IT and hybrid targeting (HT). Average IT is closely linked to PT as average IT involves setting an inflation rate over a certain period, for instance, 2 percent over three or four years. If the inflation rate reaches 2 percent the first year but overshoots the next year, for instance, by one percentage point, this overshoot will have to be corrected the following year to meet the average target. Nessén and Vestin (2005) argue that just like PT, average IT through inflation expectations acts as an automatic stabilizer, decreasing output and inflation fluctuations. Average IT may also facilitate communication with the public as inflation as a point of focus is very embedded and easier to comprehend than a price target. Economic agents are used to thinking in terms of inflation; thus trying to change it to PT may take time and prove difficult. The inflation target is essentially a number, a point, or a range of points that has to be reached in a certain period, while the price level target involves communicating not only the price-level target over a certain period over a long time but also the rate of variation of the price level to achieve this target over time. Communication, as we saw before, is an essential part of anchoring inflation expectations under IT and is relatively easier to accomplish than it is under PT.

So while PT seems theoretically appealing it is not clear that central bankers will gain by switching to PT since it has not been empirically tested. The fact that this framework has not been tried since the 1930s while IT has been practiced with success, reducing inflation volatility and persistence in many countries since 1990 gives little incentive to central bankers to experiment with this alternative framework, especially at the risk of increasing output volatility. At a time of uncertainty and when most mature economies are trying to revive economic growth after the financial crisis and recession of 2007–9, the time does not seem ripe to test new schemes. For this could add to uncertainty about the meaning of a new target and undermine the credibility of the monetary authorities, especially to the extent that economic agents needed reeducating. It is true however that if suddenly these same economies were facing deflation, central bankers would perhaps reconsider their position. However, it may be wiser to first try HT as an alternative to strict PT.

The Coordination of Monetary and Fiscal Policy

> In recent years, the greater public acceptance of the goal
> of price stability has been, to use a favorite central banking
> word, welcome. But it has led to unpleasant fiscal arithme-
> tic. This has compounded the existing fiscal problems. And
> since soundness in two dimensions has been rare, it raises
> the fear that the commitment to price stability will, in the
> future, come under threat as unexpected inflation looks to
> be an attractive expedient for reducing the debt burden.
> Historical experience would reinforce that concern. It is
> vital therefore, that unpleasant fiscal arithmetic not lead us
> back to unpleasant monetary arithmetic.
> —King (1995: 179–80)

So FAR IN considering the components of effective monetary policies to control inflation we have highlighted the decisive role that is played by cred- ibility and seen how credibility can be established and enhanced through rules-based policy frameworks and independent agencies to implement such regimes. This chapter examines how the same test of credibility, hence supportive public expectations, must also be passed by fiscal policy. For if this fiscal test is failed, even the best designed monetary policy efforts will be unavailing. This chapter also shows how transparent rule-based inflation targets can facilitate resolution of the most intractable fiscal problems.

At the time of writing, such problems were most apparent in several of the countries that use the euro. Attempts to address concerns about their solvency by fiscal tightening were having the counterproductive effect of damaging growth hence further increasing their debt-to-GDP ratios, and all the while raising the likelihood of a social and political backlash against higher taxes and spending cuts. As a result, inflating away the debt may end up having an irresistible appeal.

The central question is well formulated by Canzoneri, Cumby, and Diba (2011: 936):

What coordination of monetary and fiscal policy is necessary to provide a stable nominal anchor?

The coordination of monetary and fiscal policy in support of price stability lies at the heart of the fiscal theory of the price level (FTPL). While this theory is not without its critics, such as for instance Buiter (2002) and McCallum (2001) and others thoroughly reviewed in Canzoneri, Cumby, and Diba (2011), it provides a warning to central banks and governments that efforts at conducting tight monetary policies with an interest rate rule, but without creating expectations of a Ricardian fiscal policy, not only may prove unsuccessful as total government liabilities play a role in price determination, but may counterproductively end up in an inflation spiral. The FTPL posits fiscal policy as the prime determinant of the price level, with monetary policy taking second place.[1] The assumption is that if governments are not committed to the Ricardian rule whereby real debt service flows are adjusted to satisfy the intertemporal budget constraint—in other words, if fiscal policies are "non-Ricardian," it is the aggregate price level that will adjust for any shifts in discounted future government surpluses (Woodford, 1994).

We saw in chapter 3 that the pursuit of price stability can be helped by making central banks independent and having them act within clear and firm frameworks such as a Taylor rule. For three decades from 1980, this approach gave credibility to monetary policy by sheltering policymaking from politicians' propensity to make decisions motivated by short-term calculations on how to win or retain power. This separation, however, is a bit like the Maginot Line. It can work when dealing with expected challenges but is liable to be outflanked by a shock—i.e., when major financial crises strike. In such crisis conditions, the proper role of central banks becomes a source of tension. As Sargent (2011: 199) remarks with his usual wit, opinions on this matter tend to shift not only among politicians, voters, and leading economists but also "sometimes even within the mind of a single economist." At such times, rapid actions are needed, short-term priorities prevail over medium- and long-term ones, and the consequences of these actions are often understood only afterward.

This applies equally strongly to fiscal policy. We saw in chapter 2 how large budget deficits can lie at the origins of high inflation. But fiscal rules and targets tend to be quickly jettisoned in a crisis. One traditional view

---

[1] Leeper (1991), Sims (1994, 1997), Woodford (1995, 1996, 2001), and Cochrane (1998, 2001) developed the FTPL.

is that this does not matter. The argument goes that since mature economies are characterized by low inflation with seigniorage constituting only a small part of overall government revenues, fiscal policy does not impact monetary policy. Budget deficits and public debt have no effect on price stability because of Ricardian equivalence (Barro, 1974) and central bank independence. The problem with this is that all too often expectations of fiscal policy are precisely the opposite—that it will be non-Ricardian. In such circumstances, the application on the monetary side of rules such as a Taylor rule could have dramatic consequences for inflation. We already noticed in the case of Russia in 1998 how an exchange rate peg could lead to a massive financial crisis since the peg served not only as a counterinflationary anchor but also, on the fiscal side, as the lure—along with rising interest rates—for funding ballooning budget deficits. Loyo (1999) takes the example of Brazil where attempts at controlling the inflation rate at the beginning of the 1980s resulted in large increases in nominal interest rates on Treasury bills. This created a vicious circle where those interest rate increases led to an explosion of public debt and the inflation rate. This was a case of the "tight money paradox" or "inflation without money," whereby "given the primary budget deficits, tighter money leads to faster growth of outside wealth, and to more rather than less inflation" (Loyo, 1999: 2). We saw as well that the effects of high levels of outstanding debt on monetary policy were neglected in the early literature. The standard explanation for hyperinflation as resulting from large primary deficits financed by seigniorage tended to ignore the importance of a large overhanging stock of public debt—or, put another way, the calamitous effects of a sharp rise in the cost of debt service when monetary policy is tightened to counter inflation while underlying fiscal problems are left unaddressed.

The main question as put by Woodford (2001) is why inflation did not spiral in the United States in the 1980s as happened in Brazil. The answer is that Volker tight monetary policy was accompanied by Ricardian fiscal expectations. Measures were taken to adjust annual budgets to rein in public debt. The conclusion is that monetary authorities cannot be indifferent to fiscal expectations. As William Silber (2012: 2) wrote in his biography *Volcker: The Triumph of Persistence*,

> Volcker's linkage of responsible monetary policy with fiscal virtue carries a message for today, as the United States emerges from the greatest financial crisis since the Great Depression.

For mature economies, this reality applied to the aftermath of the bursting of the credit bubble in 2007–8 when private-sector retrenchment (balance sheet repair) had stifled other sources of demand. The policy mix thrown up by this crunch was a combination of both monetary and fiscal stimulus.

Faced with almost zero interest rates, traditional interest rate instruments proved to be ineffective, so the Fed and the BOE followed in the footsteps of Japan by engaging in debt monetization (i.e., creating money in order to buy debt). The conscious goal was to avoid at all costs a repeat of the sharp deflation, money supply contraction, and output fall of the 1930s. No central banker seemed to be better qualified for the job than the U.S. Fed Chairman Ben Bernanke, who described himself in the preface of his book *Essays on the Great Depression* as a "Great Depression buff." Faced with the collapse of asset prices and financial markets, Bernanke was keen to avoid repeating the mistake of tightening monetary policy at the wrong time. He drew on the historical evidence that the correct priority was to flood the economy with liquidity. Conventional monetary instruments such as the discount window and open market operations were supplemented (or supplanted) by a plethora of extraordinary facilities to provide reserves, guarantees, and short-term credits to banks.

On the fiscal side, meanwhile, the crisis generated huge budget deficits and public debt through a combination of discretionary fiscal stimulus, lower revenues on the back of deep recession, and socializing the losses of the banks. Fiscal constraints in mature economies therefore built up very sharply. If the size of budget deficits is such that the stock of debt has reached the point where explicit taxation and expenditure cuts have reached the limit beyond which the government is unwilling or unable to go without risking its hold on power, inflation will be just around the corner. To stave off the threat of national insolvency, the governments of many fiscally troubled industrialized countries launched austerity programs. Their success would be conditioned by the level of public confidence and tolerance for hardship in the form of higher taxes and decreased spending. Raising taxes risks undermining growth. Lupton and Hensley (2010: 26) found, while warning that the relationship is not perfect, that on average over the previous two decades, a 10 percentage point increase in the government revenue share of GDP was associated with a 0.7 percentage point lower rate of potential growth and a 1.2 percentage point higher level of structural employment.

Escape from this fiscal predicament would be assured by a return to solid economic growth. Should this happen, the public finances would improve without the need for a retrenchment so painful as to undermine the government's credibility. In the absence of growth, bond markets would doubt whether debt sustainability could be restored and would start dumping government debt—causing interest rates to jump.

This brings us back to the monetary stimulus, which, of course, is designed to fuel demand and growth. This stimulus was delivered through the above-mentioned unconventional monetary policy instruments under the general label of "quantitative easing" initiated in response to the financial crash in 2008 and pursued in successive phases (launched in November 2010 and September 2012). To succeed, this approach needed to stimulate domestic demand (by injecting funds into U.S. banks to finance domestic loans and refinance mortgages) without in the meantime undermining confidence in the future value of money or sustainability of the public finances and debt.

On the first count of growth, the previous experience of Japan had not been encouraging. After the Bank of Japan started QE in 2001, injecting trillions of yen into bank reserves, these funds (also known as "high-powered money") sat there and failed to encourage firms and consumers to invest and spend. The aim of unconventional monetary stimulus like QE is to raise inflationary expectations, thereby inducing people to borrow and spend to drive up demand. But the U.S. public was trying to reduce borrowing given its high level of indebtedness; and table 4.1 suggests that lower interest rates had little effect on these deleveraging intentions.

To a much greater extent than it stimulated aggregate domestic demand, QE stimulated demand either for international assets (such as commodities or emerging market bonds) or safe domestic havens such as excess reserves and government securities.

That last point on demand for U.S. government debt takes us back to the fiscal link with this monetary stimulus. Partly due to the direct purchases of U.S. Treasuries by the Fed under QE, this monetary stimulus helped to prevent damaging fears building up about the fiscal position despite the dramatic underlying deterioration in the U.S. public finances. For QE to work a certain "Keynesian myopia" is necessary—defined by Benjamin and Kochin (1984: 596), as economic agents failing "to perceive the future tax liabilities implied by current deficit finance." Put another way, QE's desired effect on aggregate demand hinges on the public not expecting near-term tax increases and hence reining in consumption spending. The requirement is to persuade the public that future primary surpluses will be smaller than the real value of outstanding debt (even if people do not think consciously in such terms). One of the internal critics of QE among voting members of the FOMC was Thomas Hoenig (2010: 10), president of the Federal Reserve Bank of Kansas City, who, while recognizing the usefulness of the first phase of QE at the height of the crisis, objected to its continued use ("QE2") in a period of recovery as the central bank risks becoming the government's agent financing fiscal programs.

TABLE 4.1

Growth of domestic nonfinancial debt, percentage changes;
quarterly data are seasonally adjusted annual rates.[a]

Date	Total	Households	Business	State and local governments	Federal
2000	5.0	9.1	9.3	1.4	−8.0
2001	6.3	9.6	5.7	8.8	−0.2
2002	7.3	10.6	3.0	11.1	7.6
2003	8.0	11.8	2.2	8.3	10.9
2004	9.3	11.1	6.6	11.9	9.0
2005	9.2	11.1	8.9	5.5	7.0
2006	8.5	9.8	10.8	3.7	3.9
2007	8.4	6.6	13.6	5.4	4.9
2008	5.9	−0.1	6.1	0.7	24.2
2009	3.1	−1.7	−2.3	3.9	22.7
2010	4.1	−2.2	0.8	2.2	20.2
2011	3.6	−1.5	4.5	−1.9	11.4
2010Q1	3.7	−2.8	0.1	2.4	20.6
2010Q2	3.7	−2.2	−2.0	−0.5	22.5
2010Q3	4.0	−2.2	2.7	2.1	16.0
2010Q4	4.6	−1.5	2.3	4.8	16.4
2011Q1	2.4	−1.6	4.1	−3.3	7.9
2011Q2	2.4	−3.0	5.0	−3.5	8.6
2011Q3	4.5	−1.1	3.8	0.0	14.1
2011Q4	4.9	−0.2	4.9	−1.0	13.1
2012Q1	4.7	−0.4	5.2	−1.8	12.4

Source: Federal Reserve Statistics Release, Z.1, http://www.federalreserve.gov/releases/z1/current/accessible/summary.htm.

a. Changes shown are on an end-of-period basis.

But Hoenig's main concern was focused on the risks inherent in the project of stimulating inflation expectations by just enough but not too much. He warned that given the size of the Fed balance sheet and government indebtedness, inflation expectations might become unanchored with the inflation rate ending up at a much higher level than the Fed's ideal of around 2 percent. This would "soon be followed by a rise in long-term treasury rates, thereby negating one of the textbook benefits of the policy" (Hoenig, 2010: 7).

Here we see various routes toward the unhappy destination of lost public confidence in the authorities' ability to control inflation; but all these routes pass sooner or later through the territory of the public finances. Either inflationary expectations generated by monetary stimulus cause government bond yields to rise, in turn making public debt look unsustainable, or else the effect of QE in disguising the underlying weakness of the public finances proves short-lived, and when the reality of the fiscal emergency becomes impossible to ignore, the response that generates the least political resistance is to inflate the debt away. In other words, the fiscal limit to monetary policy would have been reached and the time for "remembering inflation" on a big scale would be nigh.

From Unpleasant Monetarist Arithmetic to Unpleasant Fiscal Arithmetic

We saw earlier in Barro's model how government uses public debt (deficits) to smooth tax rates over time. Thus, public debt finances transitory spending and taxes finance permanent spending. Christiano and Fitzgerald (2000: 25) observed that "Barro's (1979) policy of absorbing fiscal shocks by raising taxes in the future can be represented as non-Ricardian fiscal policy."

The same authors noted that the risks attached to such non-Ricardian policies provide the rationale for the IMF and Maastricht Treaty on European Monetary Union to recommend an upper bound in public debt (Christiano and Fitzgerald 2000: 7, 25). As soon as public debt reaches a predefined threshold, fiscal policy is called upon to bring it down, as for instance in the 1980s and 1990s in the United States, and therefore there is no effect on the price level arising from periodic fluctuations in the fiscal balance. If instead governments choose to exceed the public debt upper bound thereby forcing the price level to increase in response to fiscal shocks, the Ricardian equivalence is breached (Woodford, 1996).

Both non-Ricardian and Ricardian policies have been observed at different periods. When highly indebted governments adjust their fiscal policy accordingly, there will be no effect on the price level. In other cases such as in the 1960s and 1970s in mature economies fiscal constraints seem to have been ignored (Sargent, 1987: 112). As a result, it is perhaps reasonable to suppose that the non-Ricardian assumption held for that period (Christiano and Fitzgerald, 2000: 6).

The FTPL is much tougher than the analysis of Sargent and Wallace (SW) reviewed in chapter 2 since it contends that regardless of whether the central bank is independent, fiscal constraints such as an increase in the public debt or a decline in the primary budget surplus have implications for price stability. In SW the intertemporal budget constraint is indeed a constraint on fiscal policy forcing the government to adjust its taxes net of spending; in other words shocks to the real primary surplus are financed by opposite movements later on, and only if the central bank is weak will these shocks have implications on the price level. In SW all government debt is assumed to be indexed to inflation meaning that the government does not benefit from the loss in the real value of debt when prices increase. In the FTPL the intertemporal budget is not a constraint but an equilibrium condition with money creation adjusting passively to maintain equilibrium. Even if the central bank is tough, price stability will not be restored (Christiano and Fitzgerald, 2000). Inflation reduces the real value of outstanding government bonds and other liabilities specified in nominal terms, giving the government the benefit of a reduction in the real value of debt. Given the existence of nominal government debt, unexpected inflation as a result of fiscal shocks may reduce the real value of outstanding government liabilities (Woodford, 1995).

In contrast to SW, in which debt is fixed in real terms, the FTPL focuses on nominal rather than real debt. This means that money creation does not need to actually occur for inflation to take place; instead, the mere expectation of future fiscal problems is enough for economic agents to dump domestic debt. Contrary to the standard Ricardian equivalence (Barro, 1974), in the FTPL scheme of things, economic agents dump debt today suspecting that in the future the debt will be monetized and that future primary surpluses will not be raised, that is, taxes will not be increased nor will expenditures be decreased. The market price of nominal debt obligations fluctuates in line with the ratio of nominal debt to the present value of real primary surpluses,

$$\frac{B}{P} = d$$

where d = present value of future surpluses with B being the outstanding nominal public debt and P the price level.

And the present value of future primary surpluses in turn hinges on expectations. This has led Cochrane (2011: 6) to liken nominal debt to equity, in the sense that its price reflects changing expectations of future cash flows.

When fiscal policy has Ricardian properties, any change in the level of the outstanding public debt entails an exactly equivalent adjustment in the present value of future government surpluses regardless of the path that price and interest rates may follow. Changes in the government budget balance and hence the level of the public debt therefore have no effect upon aggregate demand.

Yet—and as we have seen—it is far from inevitable that fiscal policy will be Ricardian. If fiscal policy is not Ricardian, and shocks occur that change the expected present value of current and future government budget balances, there will no longer be any expectation of stable prices or output. This is because under a non-Ricardian regime, fiscal shocks do change households' intertemporal budget constraints at what would otherwise have been equilibrium prices and interest rates; hence markets fail to clear at those prices.

In the presence of nominal rigidities and despite the assumption of rational expectations,

> the unexpected increase in the primary deficit, not offset by any expected reduction in future primary deficits, stimulates aggregate demand, temporarily increasing both inflation and output. (Woodford, 1996: 17)

The reason is that

> [a]n increase in the present value of the government deficit increases the present value of total consumption that the representative household can afford, if prices and interest rates do not change, and thus induces an increase in the aggregate demand for goods (at those given prices). (Woodford, 1996: 17)

Contrary to the Ricardian household, non-Ricardian households do not expect to have to repay this budget deficit in the future by increased taxes. Consequently, they feel richer due to a reduction in the present value of their tax liability and therefore increase their consumption until the price level and/or interest rates adjust so as to preserve equality between the value of outstanding government liabilities and the present value of future primary surpluses (counting seigniorage income) (Woodford, 2001).

When long-term debt is present, the nominal value of the debt depends on nominal bond prices, which in turn depend on expected future price levels (Cochrane, 1998). Suppose that there is bad news about future surpluses; if there is no long-term debt, the nominal value of government debt is fixed, so the price level must rise to reequilibrate. However if long-term bonds are outstanding, their relative price and therefore the outstanding nominal debt might fall instead. Lower bond prices correspond to expectations of higher future price levels, so when these prices fall in response to bad news about future surpluses, this results in future rather than current inflation. A government may decide that it will not repay its debt and will roll over the debt forever but the willingness of private lenders to hold the current debt stock will depend on the present discounted value of future government surpluses equaling the market value of the debt stock. Most government debt issuance comes together with an implicit or explicit promise to increase future surpluses. The government smooths the effects of a negative surplus shock by issuing long-term debt and by promising to raise future surpluses. It follows that fiscally driven inflation will be predicted by higher long-term interest rates (Cochrane, 2011).

No Country Is Immune

For most of the present-day cohort of decision makers whose professional memory does not extend much further back than the 1980s, debt defaults and high inflation (which is just another form of debt default) have been associated with emerging and other exotic markets rather than developed countries like the United States or members of the Eurozone. That assumption was jolted during the aftermath of the 2007–8 financial crisis, which produced a serious prospect of national insolvency in Portugal, Ireland, Greece, and Spain (and this list reflecting the situation at the time of writing has clear potential to become much longer). These developments bear out the force of the message of the historical overview of financial crises by Reinhart and Rogoff (2009)—that no country is immune. In the aftermath of the financial crisis, a central question for global finance and the world economy is, of course, what event could trigger a buyer's strike in the government debt market of the United States itself.

The answer offered by Ferguson and Kotlikoff (2003: 27) is, a piece of financial news. They illustrate their argument by the example of what happened in the Weimar Republic after the announcement that the definitive reparations liability amounted to 132 billion reichsmarks, making clear to investors the unrealistic scale of the fiscal adjustment that would be required to settle this liability. A similar dawning realization could quite abruptly shift inflationary expectations and long-term interest rates in the United States. And when financial markets turn suddenly, the consequences can be dramatic.

Governments cannot issue indefinitely new debt since there will always be the question of who will absorb this new debt and at what price. Cochrane (2011: 4) argues,

Difficulties in rolling over short term debt in the face of higher interest rates are one of the first signs of a fiscal inflation driven by expected future deficits, and a central mechanism by which future deficits induce current inflation.

The literature in the 1980s investigating the impact of large budget deficits on interest rates in the United States is extensive, running from Evans (1985, 1987), Mascaro and Meltzer (1983), and Makin (1983) who found no relation between the two to Cebula, Bates, and Roth (1988), Hoelscher (1986), Tanzi (1985), and others who found a relation. One of the reasons for the negative results of the 1980s literature is that in the mid-1970s increases in inflation were larger than increases in nominal long-term interest rates, which, as a result, were negative in real terms. Given that high inflation and the financial regulations that prevented inflation are fully reflected in nominal long-term interest rates, it is not surprising that no relation was detected.

Baldacci and Kumar (2010) investigated the impact of fiscal deficits and public debt on long-term interest rates in the period 1980–2008 for thirty-one mature and emerging economies. They report a broad finding that an expansion in the fiscal deficit by 1 percent of GDP will raise long-term interest rates by 30 to 60 basis points and that an increase in the debt-to-GDP ratio of 1 percentage point is reflected in an interest rate increase of 2 to 7 basis points. Their conclusion is that raising fiscal deficits and public debt levels will put upward pressure on sovereign bond yields over the medium term. This empirical evidence is highly supportive of the reasoning underlying the FTPL.

Is the United States at Risk?

At the time of writing, debates were still raging between prominent public commentators about whether inflation or deflation should be reckoned the main economic danger to the United States. Studies taking a longer view of what could disturb the low inflation in the period immediately following the financial shock of 2007–8 (in 2010 the trend annual rate of headline CPI inflation in the United States was about 2 percent) highlighted the ominous dynamic of the U.S. debt-to-GDP ratio. Here lies the key source of serious inflationary risks over the medium and long term.

As mentioned in the discussion in chapter 2 on the dynamic or intertemporal fiscal constraint, what matters when assessing debt sustainability is the gap between the interest rate paid on debt and the nominal growth of GDP. The Office of Budget and Management (OBM) in its *2009 Financial*

Report of the United States Government highlights the historical path of the U.S. government debt-to-GDP ratio.[2] From being very low (often close to zero) before WWI, the ratio reached 110 percent of GDP at the end of World War II, decreasing to below 60 percent in 1953, and reaching 35 percent of GDP in 1966. Hall and Sargent (2010: 13) note that from 1946 to 1974, about 20 percent of the decline in the debt-GDP ratio came from using inflation to deliver negative returns to bond holders and that the remaining 80 percent was shared about equally between growth in GDP and running primary surpluses. Under the Fed chairmanship of Paul Volcker (1979–87) inflation was brought under control and positive returns larger than real GDP growth were paid to bond holders, resulting in a rising debt-to-GDP ratio. Under President Clinton (1993–2000) primary budget surpluses drove the reduction in the debt-to-GDP ratio with positive real interest rates paid to bondholders roughly matching the rate of growth in real GDP. During the presidency of George W. Bush (2001–9), primary fiscal surpluses turned into deficits, increasing the debt-to-GDP ratio. By 2010, that ratio had risen to about 62 percent due to tax cuts, the financing of wars after 2001, and the rising costs of health care, social security, and net interest on the federal debt (figure 4.1).

But despite this surge in the amount of outstanding public debt, net debt service stayed relatively low thanks to low interest rates on Treasury securities interest rates (figure 4.2) with three-month Treasury bill yields falling from an average of 4.4 percent in 2007 to 0.1 percent in 2010, while the yields on ten-year Treasury notes contracted in the same period from 4.6 percent to 3.2 percent.

Thanks to these low interest rates (which were, of course, a direct consequence of the financial crash of 2007–8 and the "flight to safety" in the U.S. government debt market), net debt service payments as a percentage of GDP fell from 1.7 percent in 2007 to 1.4 percent in 2010. A range of weighty institutional modelers in the CBO (2010a), OMB (2009), and IMF (2010c) concluded that without a fiscal adjustment this benign environment would soon change for the worse. The OMB (2009: 25) predicted that net debt service payments would rise to 3 percent of GDP in 2015, 10 percent in 2040, and 35 percent in 2080 (figure 4.3).

In summary, the United States emerged from the crisis of 2008 set on a path of increasing government borrowing and burden of debt service.

---

[2] The report is available at http://www.gao.gov/financial/fy2009financialreport.html. The entire report can be downloaded, as can individual chapters. The "Management's Discussion and Analysis" chapter presents the essence of the report.

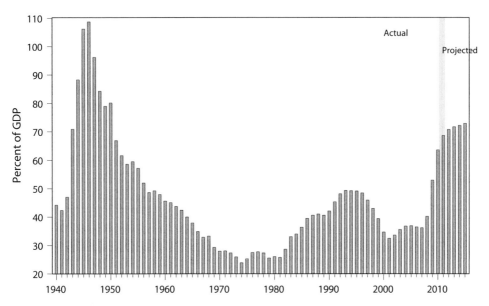

Figure 4.1. Net federal debt at the end of the year in percentage of GDP (1940–2015).
Source: Office of Management and Budget.

Taking into account the effect of population aging, social security, and health expenditures, the CBO (2011) warned that if most of the tax cuts enacted in 2001 and 2003 were to be continued (and a decision to that effect was taken by the U.S. Congress in December 2010) revenues would be 20.7 percent of GDP in 2020, expenditures 23 percent, and debt about 76.2 percent, while by 2035 the debt-to-GDP ratio would have jumped to 185 percent (table 4.2).

One useful measure to assess how much revenues and spending will have to adjust in order to ensure a sustainable debt path is the fiscal gap. This measurement establishes the immediate change in spending or revenues that would be necessary to make the projected debt-to-GDP ratio the same at the end of a given period as at the beginning of the period. The fiscal gap quantifies the projected long-term shortfall of revenues relative to expenditures in present value terms. That same CBO *Financial Report* for 2009 concluded that to avoid an unsustainable acceleration of the debt-to-GDP ratio over the following twenty-five years, the government would need to take immediate action to close the gap between expenditures and revenues

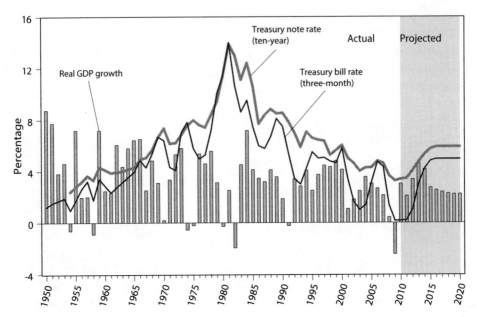

Figure 4.2. Gap between three-month and ten-year treasury bills and real GDP growth (1950–2020).

Sources: Congressional Budget Office and Federal Reserve.

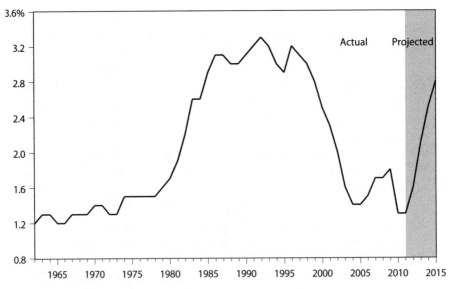

Figure 4.3. Net interest outlays in percentage of GDP (1962–2015).

Source: Office of Management and Budget.

TABLE 4.2
Projected spending and revenues under CBO's long-term budget scenarios.[a]

	2010	2020	2035
Total spending	23.8	23.9	35.2
Primary spending	22.4	20.6	26.4
Interest spending	1.4	3.3	8.7
Revenues	14.9	20.5	19.3
Deficit (−) or surplus			
Primary	−7.5	−0.1	−7.2
Total	−8.9	−3.2	−15.8
Debt held by the public[b]	62.1	76.2	185.0

Sources: Congressional Budget Office (2010b: 7, table 1.2) and Congressional Budget Office (2011: 15, table 1.4).

a. Rounding explains why percentages do not add up.

b. At the end of the year.

by 4.8 percent of GDP (equivalent to about $700 billion in FY2010) either through increasing revenues by broadly 25 percent relative to the amount projected for 2020 and later years or by decreasing primary spending by about 20 percent (CBO, 2010b:15). The report warned that any delay would make the fiscal adjustment more painful.

Such warnings were not, of course, confined to government agencies. Laurence Kotlikoff declared the "US is bankrupt and we don't even know it" in an interview with *Bloomberg* (August 10, 2010). Kotlikoff here refers to an issue that he has raised in a series of books and articles (for instance in Ferguson and Kotlikoff, 2003; Kotlikoff, 2010)—namely, the imbalance between a growing elderly population starting to collect Medicare benefits and the decreasing number of workers able to pay for these benefits. This analysis is based on generational accounting (Auerbach, Gokhale, and Kotlikoff, 1991), which calculates, assuming no debt default or other change in policy, the amount of net taxes current and future generations will have to pay. When this prospect is combined with the existing large fiscal imbalance, the conclusion must be the U.S. public debt will rise unsustainably over the medium and long run.

Despite these alarming long-term debt forecasts, the investing public apparently expected the authorities to succeed in restoring fiscal sustainability, otherwise demand for U.S. government paper would have collapsed. The assumptions at work here are worth examining. What matters is not how large or small the debt-to-GDP ratio is but how government liabilities compare to the resources available to service them. The resources in question are various—ranging from political will to public tolerance for higher taxes and including perhaps most important the vulnerability of an economy's growth dynamic to the damaging effects of increased taxes such as distorted incentives, tax evasion, and a brain and wealth drain. In short, financial markets might view a 100 percent debt-to-GDP ratio as sustainable in one country and not in another. Fiscal sustainability is essential for sustained economic growth, but the measures required to restore fiscal sustainability—higher taxes and lower public spending—risk being self-defeating by undermining growth and causing, in turn, a further deterioration in the public finances.

If a country is already at the top of the Laffer curve where higher taxes fail to raise more revenues and manage only to impede growth, fiscal inflation cannot be far away (Cochrane, 2011). Judging how close a country is to reaching that point of diminishing returns from higher taxes depends on how efficient the tax system is, and on historical public tolerance for taxation. Russia for instance has a uniform tax rate on individuals' income of 13 percent, reflecting low tolerance of government interference, and the consequential reality that any higher rate of personal income tax would result in tax evasion rather than increased revenues. Table 4.3 highlights that the U.S. net debt/GDP ratio is quite small compared to Japan and European countries experiencing over 100 percent, but the concern is that the United States generates considerably less revenue than some of the European countries. As a result—and as also shown in this table—the relatively modest U.S. debt-to-GDP ratio of 64 percent in 2010 translated into a debt to revenue ratio of 430 percent—the highest reading in this group of advanced countries.

This underlines the importance of the efficiency of countries' tax systems. Trabandt and Uhlig (2009) compared the limits of firms' and households' tolerance of higher taxes in the United States and fourteen EU member states. Basing their assessment on actual tax rates from 1995 to 2007, and assuming fixed productivity growth and no labor mobility between the United States and the EU, they found that the United States could increase tax revenues by 30 percent by raising labor taxes and 6 percent by raising taxes on income and capital, while the corresponding scope for raising these tax rates in the EU-14 would be 8 percent and 1 percent, respectively. As regards the EU, considerable variations are observed between countries. For instance, the United Kingdom could raise labor taxes by 17 percent while France by only 5 percent, Italy by 4 percent, and Belgium by 3 percent. As for capital

TABLE 4.3

Debt ratios estimates (2010), in percentage.

Country	Net debt/GDP[a]	Revenue/GDP	Debt/revenue
Belgium	91.4	48.2	189.5
France	74.5	48.3	154.2
Germany	58.7	42.1	139.5
Greece	109.5	39.5	277.0
Ireland	55.2	35.4	156.1
Italy	99.0	46.0	215.0
Japan	120.7	30.1	400.7
Netherlands	45.8	44.1	103.9
Portugal	78.9	40.4	195.3
Spain	54.1	36.3	148.8
Switzerland	37.8	35.3	106.9
United Kingdom	68.8	36.5	188.7
United States (federal)	63.6	14.8[b]	429.7

Source: Calculated with estimates from the International Monetary Fund, World Economic Outlook Database, October 2010; data for the United States are from the OMB.

a. Net debt is calculated as gross debt minus financial assets corresponding to debt instruments. These financial assets are monetary gold and special drawing rights, currency and deposits, debt securities, loans, insurance, pension, standardized guarantee schemes, and other accounts receivable.

b. CBO (2010b: 12): "Federal revenues have fluctuated between 15 percent and 21 percent of GDP over the past 40 years, averaging about 18 percent."

taxes in the EU-14 only 1 additional percent could be raised on average, with zero scope for increasing these taxes in France, Italy, and Belgium.

Interestingly and logically—given for instance the persistence of high unemployment in France since the 1970s—the model found that for the United States 32 percent of a labor tax cut and 51 percent of a capital tax cut are self-financing, while in the EU-14 the equivalent figures are 54 percent and 79 percent, respectively, rising in the case of France to 62 percent and 88 percent. Trabandt and Uhlig (2009: 27) conclude

> that there rarely is a free lunch due to tax cuts. However a substantial fraction of the lunch will be paid for by the efficiency gains in the economy due to tax cuts.

Eurostat (2010) reports that in general the EU is a high tax area due to the size of the public sector. In 2008 the overall tax ratio that is taxes and social security contributions in EU-27 amounted to 39.3 percent of

GDP, this compared to 26.9 percent in the United States and 28.3 percent in Japan. The level of taxation however varies widely, with taxes above 40 percent in the Nordic countries (Denmark, Sweden, and Finland) and in Belgium, Austria, France, and Hungary.

As the figures quoted above suggest, this applies in particular to countries in the Eurozone, where the tax structure could be considerably improved by implementing taxes with lower distortions, adopting lower rates of taxation on both individuals' income and firms' profits, and simplifying the entire system by reducing the quantity of different tax rates with the effect of both facilitating collection of taxes and reducing tax evasion. Tax evasion can give some measure of how inefficient a tax structure is. Lupton and Hensley (2010: 28) reported that the proportion of legal market-based economic activities deliberately concealed from the government amounts to between 20 percent and 30 percent of reported GDP in Greece, Italy, Spain, and Portugal. These estimates exclude all illegal and non-market-based activity, put at 17 percent in Germany and around 10 percent in Japan and the United States.

In short, both the United States and EU countries have considerable potential for efficient fiscal adjustment provided that each chooses the adjustment path most suitable for its own conditions (tax rises in the case of the United States and, in the EU, spending cuts partially offset by efficiency-boosting tax cuts). This leaves the question of whether the political will exists to make such adjustments. Markets price the risk of that will proving to be lacking. In the case of the United States, that risk assessment by investors is complicated by the various attractions of the U.S. government debt market besides the creditworthiness of the issuer.

On this question of who will finance the U.S. budget deficit in the medium term, the position at the end of 2010 was that outstanding public debt was 53 percent owned by domestic entities and 47 percent by foreign entities (mainly from China, Japan, and the United Kingdom) (see table 4.4).

As of the end of March 2010 among central banks that report their currency holdings, the dollar's weighting had fallen to a record low of 61.5 percent, with the world's smaller central banks diversifying their international reserves into an increasingly wide basket of currencies (figures 4.4 and 4.5). China and other large surplus countries are most likely to cushion the U.S. fiscal adjustment given the scale of their reserve asset requirements—that is, their dependence on the depth and the valuation of the U.S. Treasury market. This is reflected in the IMF baseline projections of demand for U.S. government debt, which see China continuing to buy Treasuries at a rate

TABLE 4.4

Holders of public debt at the end of fiscal years
2005 and 2010 in percentage of total.[a]

	2005	2010
Domestic holders	56.7	52.8
Individuals	10.9	12.0
Federal Reserve	16.0	9.0
Pension and retirement funds	6.8	8.6
Mutual funds	5.2	6.7
State and local governments	9.8	5.6
Other	8.0	10.8
Foreign holders[b]	43.3	47.2
China	6.7	9.8
Japan	14.7	9.6
United Kingdom	2.1	5.1
Oil exporters[c]	1.4	2.6
Brazil	0.6	1.8
Other	17.9	18.4

Sources: CBO (2010a: 13, table 1-3), based on Board of Governors of the Federal Reserve System, *Flow of Funds Accounts of the United States; Flows and Outstandings* (December 9, 2010) (for domestic holders and total foreign holders); Treasury International Capital Survey (November 16, 2010) (for individual foreign countries).

a. Percentages do not add up due to rounding.

b. Data for foreign countries include holdings by individuals, businesses, and government entities. Data for individual foreign countries were estimated by the Federal Reserve on the basis of its survey holdings.

c. Includes Algeria, Bahrain, Ecuador, Gabon, Indonesia, Iran, Iraq, Kuwait, Libya, Nigeria, Oman, Qatar, Saudi Arabia, United Arab Emirates, and Venezuela.

of 36 percent of its official reserve accumulation (which was roughly the average ratio for the period 2000–2007).

Such projections of stable Chinese demand for U.S. Treasuries were reflected in the actual market pricing. Yet experience in emerging markets suggests that the loss of confidence in governments' ability to service their debts tends to come abruptly. No indicators exist to predict when confidence in a government's debt is going to be undermined; there is no guarantee of a soft warning, let alone a soft landing. Any piece of news can make interest rates on government debt jump sharply, leading to a decline in value of the outstanding government debt generating huge losses for

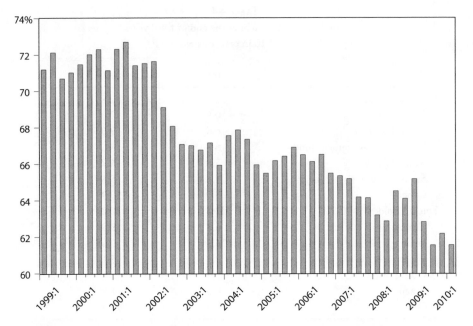

Figure 4.4. Claims in U.S. dollars as a percentage of identified total foreign exchange holdings (1999:Q1–2010:Q1).

Sources: Calculated from the IMF Statistics Department COFER Database and International Financial Statistics.

all bondholders. At that point, if the costs of a sharp fiscal adjustment are perceived to be too high both economically and politically, the affected government is left to choose between default or the monetization of its deficit, with strong inflationary consequences.

We saw in chapter 2 that Friedman's (1969) "Optimum Quantity of Money" and Phelps (1973) viewed monetary policy in an optimal taxation framework. The optimum rate of inflation is determined in the light of minimizing the distortions from the overall tax system given the range of fiscal instruments available to governments needing to raise revenue.

In this context of designing an optimal monetary policy tied to fiscal policy, one fiscal instrument at the disposal of governments is the inflation tax—or, more precisely, surprise or unexpected inflation; and this option may seem particularly attractive in conditions of a fiscal shock combined with practical difficulties in implementing the necessary increases in *explicit* taxes. Unanticipated inflation would reduce the real value of debt and an unexpected decline in the price of long-term debt further reduces the real

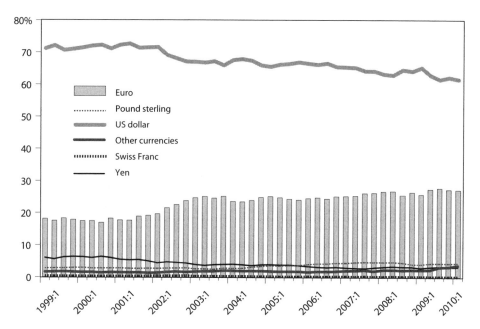

Figure 4.5. Claims in U.S. dollars compared to claims in euro, yen, Swiss franc, pound sterling, and other currencies as a percentage of identified total foreign exchange holdings (1999:Q1–2010:Q1).

Sources: Calculated from the IMF Statistics Department COFER Database and International Financial Statistics.

value of debt with longer maturities. But a rise in the inflation rate not only augments revenues from the inflation tax but also weakens money demand as the opportunity costs of holding money increases, and, as a result, the inflation tax base is decreased. In other words the relation between the inflation rate and the inflation tax is not one-to-one. The practical outcome is likely to be an extremely volatile inflation rate. It follows that routine use of the inflation tax can never be an optimal policy, and that price stability will retain its primacy among monetary policy goals (Canzoneri, Cumby, and Diba, 2011: 983).

Applying Inflation Targeting to Fiscal Sustainability

In February 2010, Olivier Blanchard, Giovanni Dell'Ariccia, and Paolo Mauro published a paper titled "Rethinking Macroeconomic Policy." One of their most controversial proposals was to alleviate the risk of deflation by increasing the inflation target from the level of around 2 percent typical of most developed country inflation-targeting regimes to 4 percent. Their proposal was heavily criticized, notably by Willem Buiter (2010: 3):

> What makes it in our view a very bad idea are the political economy dimensions of raising the inflation target. It would be the first step on the slippery slope of "inflation creep."

This objection appears to overlook the potentially greater dangers involved in maintaining a stated target, which is bound to be systematically missed since it is so obviously incompatible with the fiscal policy and general economic situation in the period following the financial crisis of 2007–8. As one of the protagonists of this book—Mervyn King—wrote in an article titled "What Has Inflation Targeting Achieved?" and published well before this crisis (2005b: 11),

> I think that monetary stability, or macroeconomic stability more generally, is a bit like healthy living, you need to find a way of setting policy that can be sustained.

IT aims to anchor inflation expectations; so for the whole policy to succeed, the anchor has to be realistic. The key condition for a realistic—hence stable—anchor is the theme of this chapter—namely, the proper coordination of monetary and fiscal policies; and this discussion also exemplifies the overarching theme of this whole book—that credibility is indispensable. For if the authorities explain transparently why they have to raise the inflation target, this will enhance credibility. The alternative would be hasty actions to bring back inflation into an unrealistic target band. While this might enhance the central bank's own reputation for determination, the tactical gain could equally be overwhelmed by wider negative consequences such as a political backlash against the IT regime.

This approach of adapting IT rules to shocks found support in economists' thinking before the onset of financial crisis in 2007 (and therefore unrelated to that crisis). In particular, Sims (2005: 297–98) recommends that IT could be improved by treating fiscal policy—once it proved to be a constraint on the inflation target—just like any other shock:

> Fiscal policy ought to be treated as a potential source of shock. Ideally, when fiscal policy that undermines central bank control of inflation is a real possibility, this should be accounted for, discussed in inflation reports and reflected in central bank projections.

This argument boils down to a critique of a formulaic approach to central bank independence—that is, the assumption that the conduct of monetary policy will always be a purely technocratic affair, in contrast to the politically charged environment of fiscal policymaking. The IT regime introduced in the United Kingdom in 1997 implicitly acknowledges the force of this argument by providing that the inflation target that the technocratic MPC is mandated to pursue will be determined, and possibly varied from time to time, by Parliament—that is, a political decision.

Failure to be flexible in this way could jeopardize the credibility built since the 1970s. In the United Kingdom, for example, the target rate of 2 percent was continually exceeded by more than a whole percentage point for four consecutive years from 2006—and, at the time of writing (2011), this overshoot was heading for two whole percentage points. The key point about such overshoots is that whatever their immediate causes, and regardless of the validity of arguments about the transience of inflation drivers (such as, in this U.K. case history, one-off tax hikes and currency devaluations), the credibility of the central bank will be called into question. The consequent risk of the loss of BOE independence and a rule-based monetary policy could have major negative consequences.

This discussion of credibility should be viewed in the perspective of the differences between the mandates of the world's main monetary authorities. As already noted, the United Kingdom's MPC is given the single task of pursuing an inflation target set by Parliament. This contrasts with the plurality of goals contained in the mandate of the FOMC as defined in the Federal Reserve Act: "to promote effectively the goals of maximum employment, stable prices, and moderate long-term interest rates." It might be supposed that the Fed's task of simultaneously pursuing several objectives means that its overall credibility is less bound up with inflation targeting. Yet, the BOE's more narrowly defined price stability mandate turns out, on inspection, to be similarly linked to broader goals of growth and employment:

> Low inflation is not an end in itself. It is however an important factor in helping to encourage long-term stability in the economy. Price stability is a precondition for achieving a wider economic goal of sustainable growth and employment. High inflation can be damaging to the functioning of the economy. Low inflation can help to foster sustainable long-term economic growth. (Monetary Policy of the Bank of England)[3]

---

[3] See http://www.bankofengland.co.uk/monetarypolicy/index.htm#.

The conclusion must be that regardless of formal mandates, credibility does hinge first and foremost on hitting inflation targets. Both the MPC and the FOMC rationalized in precisely this spirit their persistent attachment to zero-interest policies in the wake of the 2008 financial crash by highlighting that the risk of deflation was equal to or greater than the risk of inflation. But beneath this rationalization lurked concerns about our central focus here—namely, the fiscal position and its implications for monetary authorities' inflation targeting efforts.

Thomas Hoenig, who as we have seen was a prominent internal critic of the Fed in this period, highlighted the general risk of zero interest rates (the unintended consequences of financial market distortion, mispricing of risk, and subsidizing borrowers at the expense of savers), but stressed above all that uncertainties about the U.S. fiscal situation were the biggest brake on economic growth. That last observation highlights a key point for the purposes of this discussion: rock-bottom nominal interest rates were designed not only to stimulate growth but also to reduce budget deficit funding burdens until such time as revived growth improved the fiscal position. The risk of this policy mix undermining the credibility of monetary authorities' control of inflation was dismissed by central bankers with reference to continued investor demand for low-yielding government bonds. That argument was disingenuous since demand was supported not by low inflation expectations (which, on the contrary, could be discerned in the rising price of gold and widening yield spread of indexed bonds over ordinary government paper), but rather by QE (in the case of the Fed and the BOE) and concessional repurchase operations in the case of the ECB.

In reality, then, the price stability mandate was overridden by growth and fiscal policy considerations. Central bankers feared that if monetary policy were tightened, not only would the slow recovery be stopped in its tracks but also governments' ability to afford the resulting increase in the cost of funding their huge budget deficits might start to be questioned. This reality appeared in particular stark form in the Eurozone crisis borne of fundamental economic divergence between Germany and the periphery. As the astute *Financial Times* commentator Wolfgang Munchau remarked in a January 2011 column titled "Time to Get Real on Europe's Inflation Target," the higher interest rates required to resist inflationary pressure in Germany would aggravate the sovereign debt crises in the periphery. But forgetting about the inflation target altogether would spell loss of credibility, and the resulting uncertainty would in turn undermine prospects for revived economic growth.

This circle can be squared by increasing the inflation target. IT aims at anchoring inflation expectations in a transparent rule-based framework. Given the fiscal problems present in most mature economies, raising the inflation target from 2 percent to 4 percent would accommodate fiscal constraints while allowing monetary authorities to preserve credibility by explaining clearly the constraints they face and how they aim to reach their goals.

In a fiscal perspective, there are two reasons for advocating an increased inflation target. The first reason has its source in the literature reviewed earlier emphasizing that controlling inflation finds its limit in fiscal policy. The second reason is to use "controlled" inflation in the form of IT to reduce the debt burden. To return to the case history of the Eurozone, given the drastic fiscal adjustment required in the peripheral members—both in terms of reduced public spending and increasing the burden of explicit taxation—the 2 percent inflation target does not create enough seigniorage to make fiscal policy sustainable. The case for varying the relative contributions to budget revenue of seigniorage and explicit taxes was made by Cukierman, Edwards, and Tabellini (1989: 25), who argued that

> the equilibrium efficiency of the tax system and hence seigniorage also depend on political stability and polarization. The evidence supports this implication: more unstable countries rely relatively more on seigniorage to finance the government budget than stable and homogeneous societies.

Now turning these results upside down suggests that to limit the level of political instability created by an exceedingly tight budget constraint, inflation targeting with a raised target could come to the rescue by providing for a limited period of time some of the additional revenue needed for these European countries to get out of the crisis without defaulting or incurring exorbitant political costs. The key cost is a blocked collective decision-making process—a problem that the lubricant of increased seigniorage could help resolve.

To clarify the reasoning behind this set of arguments, let us recall equation (5), which simply shows the various options at the disposal of a government in financing its expenditures in the form of direct and indirect taxation, domestic and foreign debt, seigniorage, and inflation tax.

$$d + rb_{-1} + Er^* b^*_{-1} = \Delta b + E \Delta b^* + \Delta mb + \frac{\pi}{1 + \pi} mb_{-1} \qquad (5)$$

Equation (5) for the purpose of this section can be rewritten as equation (7). To avoid any confusion with b, let us call mb the monetary base m and also to aggregate domestic bonds and foreign bonds:

$$d + (r - n)b_{-1} - \frac{\pi}{1 + \pi}m_{-1} = \Delta b + \Delta m \qquad (7)$$

Equation (7) is the same as equation (6), only highlighting that the left-hand side shows the government deficit net of inflation tax revenues while the right-hand side shows how the budget deficit is financed by issuing either interest-bearing bonds or money.

The Limit of CBI and Inflation Targeting

Leeper (1991) analyzed monetary and fiscal policy interactions and distinguished between "active" and "passive" policies. The monetary authority sets the nominal interest rate in order to control the inflation rate around the target inflation. The fiscal authority chooses a level of direct taxes that depends on the quantity of real government debt held by the public. Policies are either "active" or "passive" when one policy dominates the other. Leeper (1991: 137) illustrates his dichotomy quoting SW's (1981: 2) unpleasant monetarist arithmetic, which arises because "fiscal policy dominates monetary policy" and "the monetary authority faces the constraints imposed by the demand for government bonds."

Four permutations of Leeper's dichotomy can be logically derived:

1. Monetary policy is active—that is, actively seeking to control the inflation rate, while fiscal policy is passive—with settings designed simply to meet the conditions necessary to stabilize government debt from whatever starting point that debt happens to be at.
2. Both fiscal and monetary policy are passive: the fiscal authorities are unable to stabilize government debt for economic or political reasons, leaving the monetary authorities no choice but to allow passively the money supply to expand to prevent an explosive government debt path.
3. Fiscal policy is active in seeking to stabilize the borrowing requirement, but monetary policy must "passively" contribute to that fiscal adjustment.
4. Finally, both monetary and fiscal policies are active, with budget constraints ignored.

This analysis leads to the conclusion that a necessary condition for monetary policy independence in the presence of public debt is that fiscal policy is passive—that is, its primary objective is public debt stabilization. Monetary policy is able to keep the inflation rate close to target provided that fiscal policy shoulders the burden of controlling public debt. Woodford

(1996, 2001) suggests that a Taylor rule for monetary policy should be accompanied by targets for the size of government budget deficits. In the opposite case, it is monetary policy that must take the burden of bringing public debt back to a sustainable level.

Piergallini and Rodano (2009) extend Leeper's results. They show that when government debt increases above a certain level, it becomes unfeasible for the fiscal authority to respond passively to public debt dynamics by generating more income tax revenues. Passive fiscal policy means that the authorities stabilize public debt by increasing tax rates, which in turn decreases output, money demand, and hence inflation tax at the targeted inflation rate. The effect is that at the given targeted inflation rate the fiscal authorities have to increase tax further to prevent an explosive debt path until they reach the limit where an increase in taxes stops generating more revenues. At this threshold, the choice is for the monetary authorities either to abandon IT and to adjust passively to fiscal constraints by letting the inflation rate jump to whatever level would ensure the stability of real public debt; or alternatively to increase the inflation target.

Trouble lies in store when monetary authorities continue to pursue actively an unchanged inflation target while fiscal policy is not stabilizing the debt. For as the monetary authorities peg inflation to the target through the nominal interest rate, interest debt payments will increase and inflation tax decrease, leading to an explosive debt path just as Loyo (1999) mentioned in the case of Brazil.

The other solution is the one adopted by the United Kingdom in the aftermath of the 2008 crisis. This solution (corresponding to Leeper's third option in the above list) entails where fiscal policy is active. While the BOE paid lip service to the official 2 percent inflation target, in practice that target was set aside. As noted by Leeper (1991: 138),

> Without the additional constraint imposed by one authority behaving actively, there are many money growth processes—indexed by the initial money stock—that are consistent with the equilibrium conditions. This reproduces Sargent and Wallace (1975) price level indeterminacy result, which shows up algebraically as a system with no unstable roots.

As already noted, the risk here is to unanchor inflation expectations. In such conditions (in the United Kingdom by 2010, inflation expectations were broadly set around 4 percent rather than the official 2 percent target—see figure 4.6), it would make more sense to target consciously and openly a moderately higher level of inflation.

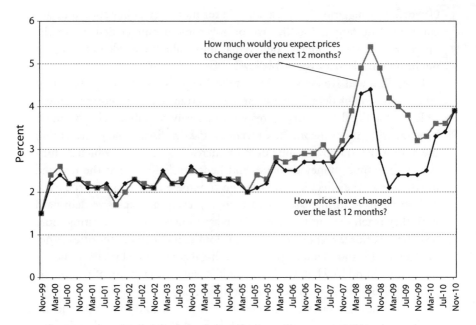

Figure 4.6. U.K. inflation expectations.
Sources: Bank of England/NOP Inflation Attitudes Survey.
Notes: GfK NOP interviewed a quota sample of 2,057 people aged sixteen and over, in 175 randomly selected output areas throughout the United Kingdom between November 11 and November 16, 2010. The raw data were weighted to match the demographic profile of the United Kingdom as a whole. The methodology is explained in http://www.bankofengland.co.uk/statistics/nop/nopias.pdf.

Well-anchored inflationary expectations can withstand the impact of an inflationary shock, in other words the shock is absorbed. Conversely, and to quote Mervyn King again (2005b: 13),

if you let inflation expectations drift too far away from the target, you can end up in quite serious difficulty with a costly process to bring them back again.

Piergallini and Rodano's (2009) conclusion is that for any given target inflation there exists a threshold level of public debt beyond which the inflation target should be raised as the dynamics of public debt can be controlled only by means of higher inflation tax revenues. If the central bank intends to continue controlling inflation by IT, it must fix a sufficiently higher target inflation rate. Both household participation and Laffer effects explain why there is a threshold level of public debt beyond which monetary policy independence is undermined. The central bank can maintain inflation control around the steady state by applying IT, provided it targets a higher inflation rate. Otherwise inflation must endogenously rise in line with the fiscal theory of the price level.

Public Debt Erosion

This idea of raising the inflation target—as a way of preserving a monetary policy framework oriented toward long-term price stability in the face of a fiscal shock—can contribute to the older and more general debate about the pros and cons of using inflation to alleviate debt burdens. Many commentators believe that given the huge budget constraints faced by governments, inflation will be the widely preferred expedient to ease those constraints. But the consequent risks would be reduced by incorporating this strategy into a transparent IT regime rather than through the back door.

Two papers, one by Hall and Sargent (2010) and the other by Aizenman and Marion (2009), address the issue of the extent to which inflation could reduce the debt-to-GDP ratio. Both studies compare the post–World War II situation with the aftermath of the 2007–8 crisis. The first (already noted earlier in this chapter) concludes that growth—together with primary budget surpluses—was four times more important than inflation (acting through negative real returns on government bonds) in reducing the postwar government debt. The study by Aizenman and Marion calculates for the period 1946 to 2009 the impact of various inflation scenarios (1 percent, 3 percent, and 5 percent) on the percentage decline of the debt-to-GDP ratio. The assumptions in this exercise are that all debt is denominated in domestic currency (true for the United States), none is indexed (in fact about 5 percent is), and the maturity is invariant to inflation (this last assumption has a strong empirical foundation). Aizenman and Marion (2009: 9) found that if inflation had been 3 percent higher in FY2009 and stayed at that higher level over the average life of the debt (3.9 years in 2009, compared to 9.4 years in 1947), the effective debt-to-GDP ratio would be about 12 percent lower. With a 5 percent higher inflation, the debt-to-GDP ratio would be about 20 percent lower—at 43.4 percent instead of 53.8 percent.

Finally, these authors apply an optimizing model (weighing the costs and benefits of using inflation to erode public debt) to the post-2008 situation. They note the similarities with the post-WWII period where the debt-to-GDP ratio was large and inflation low. They also note the differences: first, foreigners hold a large (47 percent) share of the public debt—allowing the partial export of the costs of inflation but at the risk of increased tensions with international creditors making the financing of public debt more costly and difficult; second, the average maturity is about 3.9 years instead of 9 years (and, in the period 2008–10, the proportion of debt maturing in less than a year jumped from about 30 percent to over 40 percent).

In this perspective, conditions in the period after WWII were particularly favorable: as a result of a combination of the long average maturity of domestic public debt and low inflation (but still higher than expected). Aizenman and Marion find that inflation reduced the 1946 debt-to-GDP ratio by almost 40 percent within a decade. The shorter average debt maturities seen in the present day reduce the potential for inflation to erode the public debt burden, since the market will simply require a higher yield when short-dated paper is refinanced. (In the extreme cases of zero maturity or fully indexed debt, the government would have no scope to reduce its debt burden through inflation). Taking all these factors into account the Aizenman and Marion (2009: 17) "model predicts that a moderate inflation of 6 percent could reduce the debt/GDP ratio by 20 percent within 4 years."

Despite the variations in their conclusions due to differences in the data used and analytical methods, all these authors are careful to stress the riskiness of using inflation to address debt problems. The risks derive in good part from the above-mentioned problem of shorter "duration," but this in turn can lead to other dangers. The basic problem comes from the "Fisher effect" whereby nominal interest rates on new debt issues adjust to the expected rate of inflation. Government attempts to restrain increases in interest rates could undermine confidence (especially on the part of foreign debt holders). The threat to confidence would arise if, for example, central banks continued to purchase government paper ("quantitative easing") even against the background of rising inflation; and the dangers would clearly be greater still if governments resorted to more drastic measures such as altering indexation contracts (a more explicit form of default than the inflationary effects of monetary deficit financing).

More generally, the effect of rising inflation expectations can accelerate increases in nominal yields to the extent of raising the real cost of debt service and the overall deficit-to-GDP ratio (this effect will be all the more marked when the existing stock of domestic public debt is high as in the case with the United States and other rich countries coming out of the

2007–8 crisis). That would be the very opposite of the desired effect of eroding the real value of public debt—which, as we have seen, depends primarily on an unexpected increase in inflation reducing the real value of previously issued debt obligations. A final risk arising from rising inflation expectations is a perception of a decline in the government's capability to raise revenue through the inflation tax or to borrow abroad; and this, in turn, may reduce foreign investors' willingness to buy that government's new debt issues.

In short, the potential benefits of higher inflation in reducing the debt and tax burden of future generations and clearing balance sheet liabilities must be weighed against the material risk of inflation expectations becoming "unanchored." Raising the inflation target could materially reduce if not eliminate this risk. The best way to guard against a "moderate" inflation getting out of control would be to deploy the same instruments and principles developed in the wake of the 1970s inflation—that is, relying on a clear and credible rule. The benefits of this approach would be all the greater in countries with a reasonable track record of inflation targeting, since the track record built up in previous years would preanchor inflationary expectations around the new (raised) target for a defined period, and ease the task of returning thereafter to the normal (lower) target without creating a recession. In short, inflation targeting could be used as a flexible framework, facilitating the resolution of a major economic shock in a way that limits the tax burden on future generations and the risks of much higher inflation in the future.

Pursuing this goal—of eliminating a substantial portion of government debt by resetting the inflation target to a higher level, say 4 percent, for a defined period—would need to be done in a coordinated fashion by the world's major central banks to limit damaging volatility in exchange rates. And the costs and limitations even of this optimal approach should still be kept in mind.

The most obvious limitation is, as already noted, the trend toward shorter average maturities of government debt, especially in the United States. In addition, the scale of the U.S. government's index-linked liabilities (social security and Medicare benefits) is such that, as Cochrane (2011: 20) has remarked,

> even an infinite price level—a default of all outstanding US debt, cutting future interest payments to zero—is not enough to pay for the CBO's projections of social security and Medicare deficits.

As for the costs, the losers from any such controlled increase in inflation would be fixed asset holders: but here again, the losses incurred as a result of a modest level of inflation would be offset by the benefits of restoring the financial system to health and relieving crippling indebtedness. The more general social costs of inflation are the subject of the next chapter.

Who Is Voting for Low Inflation and Why?

> Economic analysis of the costs of inflation—the mirror
> image of the benefits of price stability—is inevitably
> disappointing to the many . . . who know that inflation
> is a deep societal problem. The question is whether
> what the many know is merely difficult to prove,
> or rather is substantially exaggerated.
> —Fischer (1984a: 33)

WE SAW IN previous chapters that to control persistent high inflation it is necessary to carry out a sweeping and lasting regime change (Sargent, 1993). Reducing deficits and controlling the money supply, when carried out radically and quickly, can be immediately beneficial politically as well as economically (Shleifer and Treisman, 2000). Often however governments have carried out "cosmetic" reforms that succeed in reducing inflation while failing to address the root cause—namely, the fiscal deficit. This results in nothing better than a temporary inflation reduction followed by relapse (Sargent, Williams, and Zha, 2009), leading Bruno (1993: 263) to ask,

> Why does a country's past experience, or the experience of other countries in crisis, not convince policy makers of the futility of successive attempts at short term solutions?

One of the answers he considers in the case of democratic systems is the short-term approach to boosting voters' incomes that may stem from governments being elected for terms lasting no more than a few years. Alesina and Drazen (1991) emphasize that there may be a general consensus for radical reforms but that the bottleneck comes when the question turns to the group who is going to have to pay higher taxes or incur the expenditures cuts necessary for achieving the necessary fiscal adjustment. Despite repeated efforts by governing authorities to initiate anti-inflationary policies, long-lasting stabilization can prove elusive if the reforms undertaken are half-baked. Reducing inflation is one thing, keeping it down is the real challenge.

This was the experience of some Latin American countries in the 1970s and 1980s, Russia in the 1990s (Granville, 2001), and Argentina in the 2000s (Kehoe, 2003). One typical mistake was to choose the exchange rate as the nominal anchor. As we saw in chapter 3, this was especially notable in Russia, which adopted a de facto ruble peg in 1995. That example of an exchange rate peg causing the derailment of reforms was far from untypical; and the conclusion we noted was that money-based stabilization programs work better than those based on exchange rate management. The exchange rate peg allows the inflation rate to be reduced quickly, but its effect is temporary as governments often use lower inflation as a reason to delay the necessary fiscal tightening leading eventually to the collapse of the exchange rate peg and inflation striking back with a vengeance. But monetary based stabilizations are no panacea, and likewise can work only in conjunction with fiscal tightening (as demonstrated by the Sargent and Wallace model).

Bruno, Di Tella, Dornbusch, and Fischer (1988) relate the failures and successes of stabilization programs in the 1980s, showing how the lack of fiscal consolidation resulted in failures in Argentina with the Austral Plan (1985–87) and in Brazil with the Cruzado Plan (1986–87), while radical plans of the kind seen in Israel and in Bolivia succeeded. Israel's program launched in July 1985 not only stopped high inflation but also did not produce a recession; after six consecutive years in which the annual inflation rate remained above 100 percent (peaking at 400 percent in 1984), drastic cuts in the budget deficit resulted after just three months in the inflation rate falling to an annualized rate of less than 20 percent. In Bolivia in February 1985 the monthly rate of inflation reached 182 percent, convincing the government and the population that inflation had to be stopped. The Supreme Decree 21060 issued on August 29, 1985, contained the main elements of the money-based stabilization program including fiscal correction, a unification of exchange rates, a flexible exchange rate, and a return to full convertibility (Morales, 1988).

The question is why it took so long and so many failed attempts for countries to learn about budget and foreign exchange constraints. Part of the answer appears to lay in large income inequalities—or rather the effects of attempts to correct such inequalities by means of various experiments rooted in a range of development economics theories. One such was the dependency theory, which was most dominant in Latin America as its most illustrious instigator and proponent was the Argentinean Raul Prebisch who ran the United Nations Economic Commission for Latin America (ECLA) in the 1950s. The world was divided into core and periphery, the core being the industrialized countries and the periphery the developing countries. Since the main function of the periphery was to provide natural resources to the core, one of the natural policy prescriptions was for the periphery to develop its own industries in order to become competitive and to overcome the core over time. To this end, the "infant" industries had to be protected from outside competition by imposing tariffs and to be "nourished" by subsidies. However, the so-called import substitution industrialization (ISI) came at a high cost: it failed to create competitive industries and to generate economic growth, while leading to deficit finance and high inflation.

Unstable governments frequently resort to deficit financing and price controls—policies with a populist appeal that can enable politicians to gain support in the short term. Such policies then lead to frequent macroeconomic crises, which, in the long run, can especially hurt the urban poor who were the usual audience for such appeals and the supposed beneficiary of the associated policies. This is the point at which democracy can be undermined by a threat that it has itself generated. For Sachs (1989), populism is motivated by governments' concern to correct sharply unequal income distributions. In *The Macroeconomics of Populism in Latin America* Dornbusch and Edwards (1991) illustrate this phenomenon with case studies on Argentina, Brazil, Chile, Mexico, Peru, and Nicaragua in the 1970s and '80s, and show how concerns about income inequality on the part of populist governments in these countries resulted in the overuse of deficit financing causing financial crises and ending by ironically hurting the very same people—the lowest income groups—that such policies were trying to help. At that time a deep confusion seems to have reigned, stemming in part from stabilization programs being seen as costly for social welfare and in part because of "economic populism," understood by Dornbusch and Edwards (1991: 9) to mean

> an approach to *economics* that emphasizes growth and income redistribution and de-emphasizes the risks of inflation and deficit finance, external constraints, and the reaction of economic agents to aggressive nonmarket policies.

The effects of protracted high levels of inflation are easily born by the well-off, and governments too can survive the effects of expansionary policy up to the point of crisis. Nevertheless, in the medium and especially the long run high inflation can have severe political and social costs for governments, so blinkered shortsightedness seems insufficient as a sole explanation of the tendency for stabilizations to be delayed and avoided in democracies. Most additional explanations have to do with the perception that stabilization must cause higher income inequality—a perception that helps influential lobbies oppose and forestall counterinflationary programs. Such lobbies may weaken the normal functioning of democratic accountability while fiscal accounts are meanwhile stretched to fulfill the promises of populist politicians. Persistent high inflation may result in institutional adjustments and expectations that impede the kinds of fiscal and monetary reform required to attain a low inflation rate (Sturzenegger and Tommasi, 1998). There are difficulties in both the formation and implementation of stabilization policy in countries where market institutions are weak or highly distorted and political structures inhibit regime shifts (Alesina, 1989). A typical obstacle is the federalist fiscal arrangements found in many countries whereby the budget is distributed at different levels of government—central, state/regional, municipal—and all these government bodies may have different budget constraints and constituencies making it difficult to reform.

Populist leaders of all political affiliations wishing to project an image of caring government motivated by concern for income redistribution and poverty alleviation have embarked on massive spending programs quickly financed by money creation. The effect on inflation has usually been rapid and countered by imposing price controls that, in turn, result in shortages. The end point of this road is social unrest, sometimes involving violent social conflict. At this point, the IMF—cast in the role of "bad guy"—has typically been called upon to promote the radical reforms that were needed in the first place. Such reforms usually comprised liberalizing prices and eliminating subsidies to remove shortages and to restore fiscal balance. In the 1980s and even after the 1997–98 financial crises, however, the tough remedy prescribed by the IMF was far from being supported by the majority of the population; and more than one IMF adjustment program collapsed amid riots and violence. Dornbusch and Edwards (1991: 8) write,

> More impressive perhaps, is the fact, so clearly illustrated throughout this volume, that in the end, foreign exchange constraints and extreme inflation forced, in every country, a program of violent real wages cuts that ended, in many instances, in massive political instability, coups and violence.

Such experiences have deterred governments from implementing policies to reduce inflation such as removing price controls and subsidies. Adverse social reaction to such policies tends to be particularly feared in countries where the government sector covered a large share of the economy. More often than not, the economic consequences of stabilization policies have not been well understood by policymakers themselves or at least not well explained to the population. Cardoso and Helwege (1995: 176) highlighted the example of free university tuition in Brazil, which mainly benefited the middle class and therefore eliminating the subsidy was not regressive.

The motivation to stabilize was further weakened by the reality that evidence for inflation being bad for the poor and economic growth either theoretically or empirically was not established. On the contrary, expansionary policies and inflation were often thought to be better for the poor than tighter monetary and fiscal policies policy on the grounds that real incomes adjusted to inflation and no real damage was inflicted on the economy. This view has always enjoyed considerable support and received its most compelling expression in the writings of Paul Krugman (1999).

Particularly strong criticism was leveled against the stabilization policies attempted in early post-Soviet Russia. Many such critics suggested that it was a "fetish" to keep inflation down and that belt tightening was likely to hurt the most vulnerable sections of the Russian population. My work with Judith Shapiro and Oksana Dynnikova in 1996 showed, on the contrary, that when inflation had been higher, the extent of poverty was more severe. Unlike the rich, the poor did not have access to income-bearing, indexed, or otherwise protected assets. The condemnation of Russia's successive stabilization packages became a commonplace of academic and expert commentary on Russia's tumultuous first decade after the collapse of Soviet central planning in 1991. The principal causes of the poverty seen in that decade were to be found in the circumstances of that collapse rather than the attempts by the Yeltsin administration (which came into power following the collapse) to combat the resulting inflation. General defenses of the benefits of the stabilization packages (Åslund, 1995, 1997; Granville, 1995, 2001; Shleifer and Treisman, 2000) did not succeed in dispelling that confusion or the related commonplace association of those hesitant counterinflationary efforts with "shock therapy"—a misnomer for the partial liberalization of prices in 1992 that brought into the open the preexisting high inflation rate that had been camouflaged up to that point by price controls. The perception was that the so-called shock therapy pushed the bulk of the population into poverty (see among others Murrell, 1995; Stiglitz, 2000).

A review of the literature reveals a turnaround in economists' understanding between the postwar period up to the 1970s, when most such analysis appeared to show that inflation had no adverse impact either on poverty or growth, and the period after 1980, when studies using superior data sets and econometric tools suggested that inflation could aggravate poverty and, at levels above 3 percent per year, impair growth performance. The difficulty is that at least for mature economies where inflation rates were relatively low, the causal influence of inflation on growth and/or poverty is likely to be small, and small effects are hard to detect empirically. The difficulty is compounded by endogeneity issues, given that high inflation, low growth, and high poverty are also joint effects of some other causes. Consequently, existing research is inconclusive about the extent to which inflation impairs growth and aggravates poverty.

At the same time, total agnosticism on the consequences of inflation would be misplaced. As Persson, Persson, and Svensson (1998: 45) put it,

> One result seems clear, though: inflation does not improve long term growth. At best it is neutral, at worst it can cause a sizeable deterioration, particularly at high inflation rates. The exact costs of high inflation depend on details in the institutional framework, especially the tax system, and can hence vary from country to country.

And if theoretical and empirical studies have struggled to demonstrate definitive answers to the question of whether inflation adversely affects economic growth and poverty, a growing trend of anti-inflation preferences expressed by voters, and in turn reflected in policymakers' choices, suggests that the "real-life" answer to this question has become established. At the level of policymaking, the preceding chapters have told the story of how from the 1980s onward new economic thinking shaped counterinflationary programs into coordinated frameworks linking both fiscal and monetary policy. Many central banks were meanwhile mandated to pursue price stability on the assumption that inflation hurts the public and the economy. These developments emanated not only from the academic ivory tower, but also from the street.

Sturzenegger (1992: 24) remarked that by the 1990s, stabilization programs became popular—to the extent of enjoying electoral successes as with the Real Plan in Brazil in 1994. He added that this is not

> puzzling, when we consider the strong regressivity of the inflation tax in these economies, where a long history of inflation has led to an expansion of financial institutions and pervasive dollarization of the economy. (Sturzenegger, 1992: 24)

Still this raises the important question of who votes for low inflation—that is, influencing governments to take measure to enforce price stability—and why.

The public in general dislikes unemployment, inflation, and low growth. The good reasons for this are summed up by Mankiw (2001b: 4):

If a nation enjoys low and stable inflation, low and stable unemployment, and high and stable growth, the fundamentals are in place to permit prosperity for most of its citizens.

Some interesting insights were thrown up in a survey titled "Why Do People Dislike Inflation?" carried out in 1995 by Shiller (1996). A total of 677 people comprising economists and noneconomists, young and old, from three countries, the United States, Germany, and Brazil, were asked what they thought about inflation. Germany was selected for its historical record of low inflation and inflation aversion linked to its high inflation experience of the 1920s (Ferguson and Granville, 2000) and Brazil because of its history of very high inflation. Shiller first notes, using a computer search of news stories, that the word "inflation" was mentioned more often than unemployment—and even more than the word "sex," with 45 percent and 34 percent more mentions, respectively. Asked to choose between high inflation and high unemployment, most respondents chose high unemployment on the grounds that "inflation erodes their standard of living" (Shiller, 1996: 5). In particular, pensioners and those dependent on social security transfers were focused on uncertainty about the timing and extent of the negative impact of inflation on their incomes.

Shiller (1996: 25) refined his survey by distinguishing between economists and noneconomists in the United States: presented with the statement that over the long term "my own income will not rise as much as such costs will," only 5 percent of the economists in the sample agreed, in contrast to 66 percent of the noneconomists. Economists know that over the long run any nominal variable series will move in line with the aggregate price level, while members of the general public interpret any temporary decrease of their real income as caused by inflation and any temporary increase as a reward for their productivity or other merits. Both the public and the economists were supportive of stabilization policy in the belief that preventing inflation will promote a higher average real income, in other words that economic growth is affected by inflation. Other concerns about the effects of inflation explored by Schiller were on the psychological, moral, and political planes. There is a sense that inflation is deceptive by giving the impression that people are making more money while their actual spending power is declining and that some people use inflation to trick others. In both the United States and Germany but not in Brazil, Shiller found that there was a sense that high inflation increases the risk of a political breakdown, weakening social cohesion and national unity. National prestige is also mentioned; the national currency is seen as a symbol, and therefore the depreciation of the currency is equated with a loss of international prestige especially among people born before 1940 in the United States and Germany.

Shiller highlights the lack of communication between economists and noneconomists as revealed by the survey—since the public's notions about inflation are fundamentally different from those of the economists (moreover, the public thinks that if inflation is dominant as a topic in the news, this is due to economists). German respondents believe more strongly than U.S. respondents that their government has to be committed to low inflation. But the most striking result is that differences between the young and the old are more important than international differences; the differences of attitudes toward inflation among Germans and Americans are bigger between those born in 1950 and after and those born before 1940 than the differences between the two countries overall. Shiller (1996: 63) concluded with this warning:

> The people in our sample born before 1940 are now at least 56 years old; those of them in public life are probably at the peak of their influence or of declining influence. Their ability to prevent a resurgence of inflation must be waning. People who must evaluate the long-term outlook for inflation (such as those investing in long term bonds) should bear this in mind, before concluding (as many seem to have concluded) that we are entering a new regime of steady low inflation in coming decades.

Another survey—conducted by Scheve (2004)—also found that people are concerned with the effects of inflation on their living standards. In this exercise, forty-four surveys in twenty mature economies were examined in selected years from 1976 to 1997. To measure the demand for low inflation each survey used a question of the form,

> What do you think the (NATIONAL) Government should give greater priority to, curbing Inflation or reducing Unemployment?

Responses were controlled for the current economic context (i.e., the expectation that demand for low inflation should increase with rising inflation). Variations in demand for low inflation among different sections of society and between respondents from different countries are explained, respectively, by the effects of inflation and unemployment on income distribution and by differences in institutions and economic structure impacting on the aggregate costs of inflation and unemployment.

Scheve concluded that aversion to inflation is strongly correlated to nominal asset ownership. How badly people are affected by inflation depend on the amount and nature of assets they hold. Individuals who own nominal assets and receive fixed incomes not fully indexed such as pensions and state transfers are more inflation averse than people whose incomes are indexed. When the rate of unemployment is high, people seem to be less worried about inflation. Individuals on low incomes are more likely to face unemployment and therefore may be more concerned about unemployment than inflation. This sensitivity toward unemployment will be accentuated if the individual is currently unemployed.

Countries differ in their level of inflation aversion. Variations across countries seem to be explained by the historical experience of price instability, the size and structure of the financial market, as well as the country's dependence on trade and capital flows. The demand for low inflation will also depend on the extent of fiscal pressures facing the country in question: the public may be less averse to inflation than to explicit tax increases.

As regards the impact of historical macroeconomic performance and more or less vivid national memories of inflation, Germany is often singled out as being particularly inflation averse due to the country's experience of hyperinflation in the 1920s. In Ferguson and Granville (2000), we apply Sargent and Wallace's "unpleasant monetarist arithmetic" to that episode (viewed in the comparative perspective of the high inflation that accompanied the collapse of Soviet central planning in Russia), as did Sargent and Velde (1995) in their explanation of the macroeconomic features of the French Revolution. We showed how high inflation can carry a high social cost, with potentially destabilizing political consequences. Scheve confirmed that on average Germans are more inflation averse than respondents in the United Kingdom—and also France.

The survey by William Easterly and Stanley Fischer (2001) was undertaken between February and May 1995: polling data for 31,869 households in thirty-eight countries (nineteen industrialized and nineteen transition and developing) were used, and allowing for country effects, the poor were found more likely than the rich to mention inflation as a top national concern. Those same authors also compared countries' propensity to mention inflation as a top national problem with the actual inflation rate in the decade preceding the 1995 survey (1985–94). They found that in general there is a significant positive relationship (i.e., respondents were more pro–price stability when asked in the 1980s and 1990s than in the 1970s, reflecting the high and volatile inflation experience of the 1970s), but also some outliers reflecting the historical experience of these countries. For example, inflation was consistently cited as a top problem by respondents from China and Hungary—perhaps reflecting both countries' experiences with WWII hyperinflation. In this same study, using pooled cross-country data, the authors confirmed that the poor are right to dislike inflation, since their results indicate that the poor suffer more from inflation than the rich—with inflation found to be negatively correlated with the change in the poor's share of national income, the percentage decline in poverty, and the percentage change in the real minimum wage.

Meltzer (2005: 147) wrote about the United States that

> by the 1980s, the public and policymakers had learned that inflation was costly. Voters elected a President committed to reducing it, and the Federal Reserve had a Chairman who changed procedures and, most importantly, remained resolute in the commitment to reduce inflation.

This lesson was transferred from the United States to other parts of the world. Kaufman and Stallings (1991: 31) noted that the United States through its involvement in the IMF, the World Bank, and other international organizations was able to influence other countries such as in Latin America to tighten fiscal and monetary policies and downsize the public sector. This especially applied to Argentina, Chile, Brazil, Bolivia, and Uruguay, all of which had high inflation rates in the 1960s and '70s. In the 1980s this lesson was reinforced by the demonstration effect provided by the economic successes of Chile, which relied on tight fiscal policy, trade liberalization, and privatization, and the successful stabilization programs in Bolivia and Israel. This was why by the 1990s demand for low inflation had gained momentum in Latin America and other emerging economies. Sturzenegger (1992) attributes this newfound popularity of stabilization policies to the long history of high regressive inflation leading the population to support radical reforms. Cardoso and Helwege (1995: 166) mentioned that in October 1988 a poll in Peru revealed that 75 percent of respondents supported an IMF agreement suggesting that they ranked reducing inflation as a top priority. Another factor that may have contributed was the collapse of the Soviet Union in 1991, which left the United States as the arbiter of international economic intervention and the home of what appeared to be the sole successful economic model.

This growing public demand for inflation to be controlled leads us back to the findings of empirical analyses conducted since the middle of the twentieth century about whether inflation aggravates poverty and impairs economic growth. Can we at this stage say for sure that the costs of inflation surpass its benefits? Does inflation have an adverse impact on economic growth and living standards, and is there a level at which it can be said for sure that inflation is damaging for welfare? For example, how strong is the rationale for targeting one or another level of annual inflation, be it 2 percent, 5 percent, or even a 10 percent inflation target?

The Complex Link between Inflation and Growth

We saw in chapter 1 that the classical school of economics held that money was neutral over the long run—that is, changes in the level of the money supply affect nominal variables such as the general level of prices but not real variables such as unemployment or output. In this perspective, the link between inflation and growth is not straightforward. The theoretical literature highlights that the effects of inflation on real output in the long run depend on how money is introduced into the various models and on the specifications of those models. As we will see, in most such theoretical studies, the conclusions stem from the relative weight given to cash balances, capital accumulation, or consumption. Assessments of the welfare costs of inflation also vary depending not only on "shoe leather" costs—that is, the cost involved in minimizing cash balances in an inflationary context (Bailey, 1956) when money is primarily considered as cash (i.e., as a means of exchange), but also on whether an evaluation of these costs is made in addition from the perspective of money as a store of value. Put another way, the costs and benefits associated with inflation need to be considered in relation to money both as a flow (affecting trade) and as a stock (affecting liquidity). Turning from such conceptual questions to empirical studies, here too researchers have had difficulty establishing a clear impact of inflation on economic growth in the long run. Still a consensus seems to emerge in favor of inflation being nonneutral and its long-run effects on growth being negative.

To start by looking more closely at the more theoretical analysis, and from the perspective of the function of money as being a medium of exchange, economists working on this track have considered money either as a consumer good yielding a flow of services contributing to utility and/or a producer good contributing to output. Either way, money's welfare effects are direct. The opportunity cost of holding money, the nominal interest rate, should equate to the social opportunity cost of creating additional money, which is zero.

To measure the welfare cost of a permanent increase in the rate of inflation is to evaluate the losses that occur at each instant of time. The traditional measure of this loss is the value of the liquidity services that society foregoes because of inflation. Both Bailey (1956) and Friedman (1969) measured this loss in terms of the extent to which people reduce their cash balances due to anticipated inflation. The nominal interest rate broadly equals inflation, and the real interest rate is the "price of money"—that is, the opportunity cost of holding cash in order to perform exchanges instead of holding alternative assets. For Friedman (1969) because hardly any cost is involved in the production of money, money should be freely available to economic agents.

By creating and spending money, which can cause prices to rise, a government increases the opportunity cost of holding cash balances and as such discourages the public from holding the "optimum quantity of money" (Friedman, 1969). Friedman demonstrated that this concept of the optimum quantity of money is valid regardless of the structure of the economy, while other economists suggested what this optimum amount of money should be in order to maximize welfare (the "Full Liquidity Rule" or "Chicago Rule"; Niehans, 1978: 93). This leads to the recommendation that the rate of money growth rate be set to yield a zero marginal opportunity cost of money, that is, the nominal interest rate is zero. The service provided by money is economic exchange; inflation obstructs the smooth delivery of this service by increasing the cost of holding real balances, thereby creating an incentive for economic agents to use other means of exchange such as a reserve and parallel currency, or credit and barter, which may be more costly or less efficient. For example in the 1990s the early transition process from command to market economies in the former Soviet bloc unleashed high inflation, which was previously repressed by price controls, and people used DM and U.S. dollar cash to save and hold their wealth.

We saw in chapter 2 that the Friedman rule was modified by Phelps (1973) to take into account the fact that government finances would have to compensate for the "lost" seigniorage.

The literature distinguishes between the inflation tax and the way that inflation undermines the role of money as a medium of exchange by acting as a tax on cash balances (Kohn, 1984). Assuming that no interest is paid on currency but that interest is paid on bank deposits, a tax on cash balances will reduce the amount of cash held and increase "shoe leather" costs but will have no effect on the level of economic activity. The shoe leather cost metaphor refers to the number of trips that people make to the bank to withdraw cash, a trip they make to match the cash and the purchase in an attempt to minimize the amount of purchasing power lost in case of inflation, but in the process their shoes get worn (Bailey, 1956: 100–102). The cost referred to here is that of the public using scarce resources to minimize the expense of holding cash balances—resources that could be used in more productive ways. The metaphor is equally applicable to a situation (prevalent in many developed economies at the time of writing) in which the price of most purchases is settled not by cash, which has to be physically withdrawn from banks, but by electronic transfers from bank account balances on which, unlike cash, interest is paid—but the interest rate is below the inflation rate. So these deposit account balances are also taxed as a result of inflation, resulting in other manifestations of suboptimal use of "shoe leather."

Turning from theoretical assessments of the welfare impact of inflation from the perspective of the function of money as a means of exchange to those assessments hinging on money as a store of value, the criterion for optimal social welfare is maximum consumption per head. In this perspective, economists have treated money as one among various alternative assets which an economic agent can choose from when building an optimally diversified asset portfolio. For example, Tobin (1965) contended that inflation would make money less attractive as an asset compared to capital. This effect of higher inflation in increasing the capital stock would offset the negative effect of higher inflation in inducing people to save more (consume less), with the overall result that aggregate demand and economic growth would be maintained.

This so-called *Tobin effect* was challenged in 1967 by Sidrauski, who argued that increases in the rate of inflation render consumption more appealing than real cash holdings, decreasing savings and reducing capital accumulation.

Despite their differences, both Tobin and Sidrauski arrived at the same practical conclusion—in line with classical economics—that the level of the money supply has no permanent real effects. Sidrauski went even further by contending that money was "superneutral," meaning that the long-run real output growth path is independent of the growth rate of money supply and inflation. Various papers have challenged the superneutrality result, but these critiques of the Sidrauski model have not established for sure whether an increase in the rate of money growth leads to a higher or lower capital stock and output. For example Stockman (1981) established a negative relation (on the grounds that investment transactions become more costly as a result of inflation, reducing capital accumulation), while Fischer (1979) elaborated the Tobin effect by developing a model incorporating inflationary expectations.

The notions that growth is not threatened, and might even be supported, by monetary expansion, and that inflation is a "necessary evil" prevailed in the postwar period until the last two decades of the past century. This theoretical perspective on inflation as innocuous for growth was supported by the early empirical research on the subject conducted in the 1950s and the 1960s. Bruno and Easterly (1998) draw attention to various papers published in *IMF Staff Papers* before the inflation shock of the 1970s (Wai, 1959; Dorrance, 1963, 1966; Bhatia, 1960) as evidence that even the double-digit inflation rates seen in various Latin American countries (Pazos, 1972; Galbis, 1979) were at that time reckoned to have no effect on economic growth.

By the 1980s, the empirical research effort had become more intense as a consequence of the high and persistent inflation experienced in the late 1970s and early 1980s. Despite the increasing sophistication of data analysis in empirical studies, the results were still uncertain. Many surveys of long-run relationships between money and output (e.g., Geweke, 1986, for the United States) found no negative or positive correlation between inflation and the long-run growth rate of real output. Bullard and Keating (1995), exploring postwar data for fifty-eight countries, found that only in countries where the rate of money growth was already high did a permanent increase in money growth rate translate into a negative correlation between inflation and the long-run growth rate of real output (i.e., higher inflation caused lower output).

Kormendi and Meguire (1985) explore the effects of inflation on economic growth using data from the IMF's International Financial Statistics covering the period from 1950 to 1977. They did not find any Tobin effect; on the contrary they found evidence of a negative effect of inflation on economic growth—the effect seeming to operate through the investment channel—that is, the proportion of aggregate income devoted to capital formation. Kormendi and Meguire's results confirm the earlier finding of Alan Stockman (1981) of a negative long-run relationship between output and inflation:

> As long as capital cannot be costlessly obtained by barter, however, higher inflation reduced the steady state capital stock. (Stockman, 1981: 393)

In Kormendi and Meguire's paper too, and contrary to the Tobin effect, inflation was found to act as a tax on investments. Karras (1993) challenged the conclusions of Kormendi and Meguire, arguing that the form of the growth equation that they had used could not establish a causal relationship between inflation and growth. Other technical criticisms of the treatment of data in such empirical studies have highlighted the problems of "error autocorrelation" (Levine and Renelt, 1991) and basing analysis on differences in variables while ignoring the actual level of those variables (Ericsson, Irons, and Tryon, 2000). Applying his conclusions on analytical techniques to a good-size data set (annual data from thirty-two countries for the period 1958–87), Karras did not find evidence of either negative or positive effects of inflation on real economic growth and concluded that "long-run money neutrality probably prevails" (Karras, 1993: 673). But the growing sophistication of modeling techniques did not put an end to contradictory conclusions. For example, growth regressions run on a panel of twelve Latin American countries using six-year moving average data for the period 1950–85 found that high inflation negatively affected growth mainly by impairing total factor productivity (De Gregorio, 1991a).

Despite all these rather ambiguous results, progress was made in two directions: first that the Tobin effect did not hold and second that the irrelevance of money supply growth and inflation to long-term real output ceases to hold once due account is taken of uncertainty. Danthine, Donaldson, and Smith (1987: 495) generalized Sidrauski's production growth model, and testing for "superneutrality" in an equilibrium with uncertainty they found that money was not superneutral. They found that, on the one hand, an increase in inflation will lead to increased mean values of consumption, output, and capital stock; but, contrary to Tobin, their optimizing macroeconomic model revealed these positive effects to be quantitatively insignificant in real terms, while the negative effects were proportionately greater. They concluded, "[H]igher inflation must be unambiguously identified with lower welfare."

The foundation for such conclusions resulted from two lines of thought that started to emerge in the 1980s. The first concentrates on the uncertainty that inflation entails, while the second hinges on the intuition that the effects of inflation on real activity may be nonlinear—that is, an increase of the inflation rate through a certain threshold could have a disproportionately large impact.

Uncertainty

For some authors, the costs of inflation stem from the average rate of inflation being excessively high; while others, such as Arthur Okun (1971) in "Mirage of Steady Inflation" and Milton Friedman in his 1977 Nobel lecture, emphasize how inflation uncertainty regardless of the absolute level of inflation impairs real economic activity. From these varied perspectives on the adverse effects of inflation emerges the overall thesis that businesses and households will rein in their economic activity when inflation is high and unpredictable.

This insight gave rise to the problem of establishing what is the threshold—as regards both the absolute level of inflation and the volatility (unpredictability) of the inflation rate—above which real economic growth will be harmed. First, Harry Johnson (1969: 281) in his essay "Is Inflation the Inevitable Price of Rapid Development or Retarding Factor in Economic Growth?" observes that

> inflation, defined broadly in the factual sense of an upward trend of prices, includes the possibilities of both mild and rapid, and steady and erratic, upward price movements; and each of these distinctions is connected with important differences in the economic consequences of inflation.

The connection between inflation and uncertainty needed to be not only established but also explored in more depth. Ball and Cecchetti (1990) filled this gap by distinguishing between short- and long-term uncertainty and countries' different experiences of inflation depending on whether price level shocks are temporary or permanent. Their sample covered forty countries from 1960:2 to 1989:1 with quarterly data seasonally adjusted for the CPI and either the GNP or the GDP deflator drawn from the IMF's International Financial Statistics and data series published by the OECD. These countries' inflation rates during that period ranged from average quarterly inflation of 2 percent in Europe and the United States to 10 percent and above in Israel and Latin American countries. The authors reached the conclusion that higher levels of inflation are associated with more persistent variability of the inflation rate, causing long-term uncertainty—and strengthening the case for governments to adopt a low inflation policy. They also showed that inflation increases both variability, the variance of changes in inflation, and uncertainty, the variance of unanticipated changes. This finding, because it was based on a long-term time horizon, contradicted the conclusion of Engle (1983), who found no relation between high inflation and uncertainty, arguing that although the variability of inflation is indeed high when its level is high, even high levels of variability can be predicted. Ball and Cecchetti (1990) also found not only that high inflation has a strong effect on uncertainty, but also that the same goes for moderate levels of inflation. This finding emerged from focusing on the twenty-eight countries in their sample with an average quarterly inflation rate below 3 percent and coming up with results that were essentially similar to the findings for the high inflation countries.

The relationship between inflation and uncertainty consists in both consumers and producers becoming less confident about the future level of prices, in turn making it difficult to plan for the future and thereby undermining investment and growth. Imperfect information introduces inefficiency in resource allocation, and economic agents confuse aggregate and relative price movements (Lucas, 1972, 1973).

Even expected inflation introduces uncertainty about relative prices inducing misallocation of labor and capital. Not all firms will raise their prices by the same level or at the same time leading to a temporary demand imbalance, which will have costs and result in output variability. The uncertainty generated by inflation leads to expectations of macroeconomic and financial instability and intensifies the distortionary effect of taxes on income that is derived from capital—in turn, discouraging capital accumulation (Feldstein, 1997, 1999a).

Inflation retards growth not only by discouraging productivity-boosting investment but also by leading the public to prioritize current consumption over saving and investment. The costs for the public of anticipated inflation include the devaluation of savings of real money holdings, in turn adversely affecting real money demand. High inflation disrupts economic exchange by rushing people into consuming to avoid the inflation tax instead of allowing them to take the time to search for the best bargain, shifting resources toward less productive uses and leading to resource misallocation and welfare loss for both buyers and sellers. Firms must change product prices at the rhythm of the price increase, generating so-called menu costs (the term comes from restaurants having to print new menus as prices change).

Casella and Feinstein (1990) develop a theoretical framework encompassing these inefficiencies and welfare loss that they illustrate with this historical quotation referring to the hyperinflation episode in the Weimar Republic:

> Almost daily at the ten o'clock break I used to see the teachers trooping down into the [school's] playground where their friends and relatives were waiting, into whose hands they thrust the money that they'd just received so that it could be spent before the prices went up. (Dorothy Haenkel in Guttman and Meehan, 1980: 80, quoted in Casella and Feinstein, 1990: 2)

Tommasi (1999) extends the Casella and Feinstein model of economic exchange under hyperinflation by considering heterogeneous firms and highlighting the real effects on output. Because high inflation induces traders to rush to get rid of their cash, the search process of identifying the best match is altered. Given a limited amount of resources, in an environment of high inflation resources tend to be channeled to less efficient firms, reducing the incentives for cost reduction, and thereby adversely affecting social welfare. As efficient and inefficient firms became indistinguishable, economic growth suffers.

Inflation redistributes wealth between creditors and debtors because contracts are not continuously renegotiated. Unanticipated inflation or delayed indexation benefit nominal debtors with real capital gains at the expense of nominal creditors who suffer real capital losses. It erodes the value of saving and the purchasing power of pensioners, welfare recipients, workers, and other holders of fixed nominal incomes not fully indexed to inflation. This wealth redistribution of inflation may be large "of the order of 1 percent of GNP per 1 percent unanticipated increase in the price level" (Fischer and Modigliani, 1978: 827).

Savers and borrowers may demand a risk premium in response to the uncertainty created by inflation. This same uncertainty also deters people from entering into long-term contracts, in turn impairing long-term investment since investors will have confidence only in the real value of returns that can be extracted in the short run (Briault, 1995: 34). Inflation redistributes wealth between those who can hedge against its costs and those who cannot, creating winners and losers. Those who are rich enough can avoid the inflation tax by investing some of their wealth into financial assets, leading in turn to imbalances in the financial sector (English, 1996). These imbalances will generate dysfunctions in the economy, adversely affecting economic growth (Mishkin, 1999). Moreover some people may suffer from the money illusion, confusing the numerical value of money with its purchasing power leading them to make poor financial choices (Mishkin, 2007b).

Nonlinear Effects

In another study with a similar scope to the ones already mentioned (in this case, covering 120 countries between 1960 to 1990), Robert Barro (1995) found a relatively small negative effect of inflation on real output growth (an increase in average inflation by 10 percentage points per year reduces the real per capita GDP growth rate by 0.2–0.3 percentage points per year and a decrease in the ratio of investment to GDP by 0.4–0.6 percentage points). Perhaps his most interesting finding was that this relationship holds good only when average inflation rates are above 15 percent.

This highlights an important aspect of the question of the impact of inflation on growth—whether this impact depends on the level of inflation.

Many studies have demonstrated that the macroeconomic effects of inflation are indeed nonlinear. Four levels of inflation emerge from economists' attempts at categorization: low, moderate, high, and very high (or hyperinflation); but there is no "agreed convention" (Fischer, Sahay, and Vegh, 2002: 12). The range of values defining these magnitudes tends to be rough and open to disputes about whether high is really that high or moderate is really that moderate. In other words, these levels are not set in stone but vary not only from author to author, but also in the light of successive empirical studies and according to whether the countries under consideration are qualified as mature, emerging, or poor. Such variation of definitions in economic studies published over a period of several decades has blurred conclusions on whether and at what level inflation is bad for growth.

The definition of moderate inflation is particularly difficult, but generally means "an annual percentage rate that can be counted on the fingers of one or at most two hands" (Johnson, 1969: 281). This poses a problem, however, given the widely accepted notion that high inflation is anything above 40 percent a year for two years or more (Bruno and Easterly, 1998). Fischer, Sahay, and Vegh (2002: 12) answer this conundrum by categorizing inflation by ranges so "moderate to high" is defined in the 25 to 50 percent range.

High and hyperinflation are easier to identify, as well as the damaging effects of such inflation being clearer. No one would argue, for example, with the classification of Zimbabwe's inflation in the 2000s—that reached the level of approximately 24,000 percent in 2008—as very high. Fischer, Sahay, and Vegh (2002: 9) define very high inflation as inflations in excess of 100 percent per annum. Hyperinflations, which are relatively rare, have been identified and defined by Philip Cagan in 1956 as increases in the general price index reaching a monthly rate of 50 percent.

Given the lack of precision of these definitions, Heymann and Leijonhufvud (1995) offer more precise criteria where low, moderate, and hyperinflation are differentiated by whether people refer to the inflation rate in annual, monthly, or weekly terms. Low and moderate inflation is quoted by the year, high by the month, and anything below monthly is a clear indicator that inflation has reached some very high level.

Testing for nonlinear effects of inflation, Stanley Fischer (1993) regressed growth, capital accumulation, and productivity on inflation, with breaks at inflation rate levels of 15 and 40 percent. Contrary to his initial intuition, he found that the negative association between inflation and growth is actually stronger at moderate levels. This result endorses the economic wisdom of eliminating double-digit inflation while at the same time raising the question of whether inflation targets should be set at less than 7 percent if there is no appreciable loss of economic efficiency attached to inflation rates below that level. Bruno and Easterly (1998) identified a magnified negative effect kicking in only at much higher levels above 40 percent.

But Fischer was not going to be the only one to find that inflation hurts growth at much lower levels than first assumed. This result was further supported by Michael Sarel, who in a study published in 1996 pooling information from eighty-seven countries for the years 1970 to 1990 discovered a structural break in the relationship between rates of economic growth and inflation. The break is estimated to occur at an annual inflation rate of 8 percent. Between zero and 8 percent Sarel found that the inflation rate either has no effect or has even a slight positive effect on economic growth. Above 8 percent per annum, the estimated negative effect of inflation on growth rates is significant, robust, and extremely powerful. Sarel speculated that this may also explain why earlier studies did not notice any negative correlation between inflation and growth, since before the 1970s it was relatively rare to experience inflation rates above this threshold of 8 percent.

The results of later tests further narrowed the critical range of the inflation rate. Ghosh and Phillips (1998), covering 145 countries in the period 1960–96 (3,603 annual observations), found a robust negative relationship between inflation and growth at inflation rates above 3 percent a year, while at annual levels below 3 percent per year the relation was positive. Interestingly, their results point to inflation being more damaging to growth when increasing from 10 to 20 percent than from 40 to 50 percent. Khan and Senhadji (2001), using data from the *World Economic Outlook* (WEO) with an unbalanced panel of 140 countries from 1960 to 1998, support the findings of Ghosh and Phillips (1998). They found the threshold to be lower for developed countries than for developing with estimates ranging respectively from 1–3 percent annually and 11–12 percent. They are careful to add that while their results on the relation between inflation and growth are robust, the channels through which the relation takes place are not specified. The effect is most likely to take place through productivity since their regression analysis already controls for investment and employment.

Such studies do present some unresolved difficulties. There is a potential problem of endogeneity as inflation is not an exogenous variable in the growth inflation regression. In addition, the low threshold of 3 percent above which inflation is suggested to damage growth in developed countries is problematic since data on very low inflation over a sufficiently long time span remain quite sparse. As Andersen and Gruen (1995: 39) note,

[T]he lowest annual inflation rate in the OECD over the 30 years, 1960–89, was achieved by Germany with a 4 per cent average. Over the shorter period, 1960–73, the lowest average annual inflation rate was in the United States, again with 4 per cent, while over the period 1974–89, Japan had the lowest inflation with an annual average of 3 percent.

The overall tendency of all these developments in empirical research on the relationship between inflation and growth is well captured in a study by Andres and Hernando (1999) estimating the long-run effects of inflation on growth over the period 1960 to 1992 for the OECD countries. Their sample of countries therefore is characterized on average by relatively low and moderate levels of inflation. They found evidence of a robust negative relationship between inflation and output in the long run. Their main finding is that current inflation has never been found to be positively correlated with higher income per capita over the long run, confirming that the only certain result is that in the long term there is no Tobin effect.

The Link between Inflation and Poverty

To establish a relation between poverty and inflation is not easy as numerous trade-offs need to be accounted for. We saw earlier that monetary theory reveals inflation to be a tax of the most regressive kind mainly because the rich can always minimize the use of the inflated domestic currency. Sturzenegger (1992: 1) describes the process as follows:

Real money demand depends negatively on expected inflation, the alternative cost of holding money. In addition, financial adaptation is an unavoidable process in the presence of seigniorage financing. Financial adaptation is reflected in the shifts of the whole money demand curve, with less money being demanded at each rate of inflation. Financial adaptation may take several forms, shifts into foreign assets or shifts into interest-bearing domestic assets, goods, investments or real estate.

In other words the rich can easily escape the inflation tax while the poor cannot. In decreasing their demand for the inflated domestic currency, the rich narrow the inflation tax base, and this has a redistributional effect from poor to rich. The relatively worse impact of inflation on poorer people is aggravated by the reality that they cannot avoid using the inflated domestic currency:

[T]he poor have a consumption pattern that is biased towards goods that are always purchased with domestic currency. Financial adaptation is equivalent to a change in the tax structure that increases the tax on these commodities, therefore, with financial adaptation, the poor pay a higher inflation tax on their purchases and are made worse off. (Sturzenegger, 1992: 2)

This discussion begs an initial question of defining and quantifying the group labeled "poor." The literature on poverty is extensive and too large to be surveyed in any detail here. It may be sufficient to mention the work of Nora Lustig (2011), who explains the complexities of defining the concept of poverty and its measurement. In brief, the term "poverty" can refer either to absolute poverty meaning the lack of basic necessities or relative poverty referring to the differences in wealth between people. Poverty either absolute or relative is defined by a threshold, the poverty line—with that part of the population whose earnings or consumption fall below that line being classified as poor. Relative poverty lines are constructed by choosing a level of income or consumption relative to a country's average income or consumption, most typically less than 60 percent of median household income.

The Evidence

Decades of detailed empirical studies produced ambiguous results. Easterly and Fischer (2001: 161) noted that most studies such as Powers (1995) and Blank and Blinder (1986) dealing with the United States using annual data on poverty rates and inflation did not support a strong relationship between inflation and poverty, with the exception of Cutler and Katz (1991: 7) who found that increases in inflation reduced the poverty rate in the period 1959–89. One reason for such inconclusive results may be that the benefits to the poor of bringing down inflation are clearest when inflation is reduced from high levels, while in the United States that "base" has never been particularly high.

Romer and Romer (1998) produced findings about the short- and long-run effects of expansionary monetary policy on poverty, which at first glance appear contradictory. In the first part of the paper the authors investigated the effects of monetary policy on the absolute well-being of the poor in the short run in the postwar United States. They reached the conclusion that while expansionary monetary policy may reduce poverty in the short run, this can only ever be a temporary effect, the cyclical effects of monetary policy being inherently temporary. In the second part of the paper using a cross-country dynamic analysis they asked how the poor fare "in countries where monetary policy has kept inflation low and demand stable relative to countries where policy has produced high inflation and unstable demand" (Romer and Romer 1998: 21). Addressing this question, they considered two samples: the first composed of sixty-six countries while the other sample comprised the nineteen industrialized countries that made up the OECD in 1973. Their overall conclusion was that sustained high rates of inflation increase poverty levels in the long run:

> [T]he cross-country relationship between monetary policy and poverty suggests that monetary policy that aims at low inflation and stable aggregate demand is the most likely to result in improved conditions for the poor in the long run. (Romer and Romer, 1998: 38)

This may suggest that the evidence for the inflation-poverty link emerges as stronger in studies dealing with poorer countries and higher rates of inflation.

In Cardoso's study of the effects of inflation on poverty in Latin America from 1970 to 1990, the inflation tax has a minor impact on the poor below the poverty line because they hold little cash in the first place. The poor have no savings, and the frequency with which they are paid accelerates as inflation accelerates—that is, from monthly to weekly to daily. As inflation accelerates, workers tend to buy all they can on the day they get paid. In Brazil, the rate of inflation increased from 20 percent in 1970 to 100 percent in 1980 on an annual basis. Cardoso calculated that while some income groups lost as much as 2 percent of their income, the penalty levied by inflation on the very poor was no more than 0.3 percent of their income. When the Brazilian inflation rate increased to 2,700 percent in 1990, the very poor lost no more than 1.5 percent of their income to inflation. However, since middle-class savings were wiped out, the effect was to increase the number of the poor and therefore poverty. In other words it does not affect those who are already poor but creates more poor. Cardoso also found that real wages are affected by inflation. Nominal wages do not keep up with high increasing inflation with a consequent reduction in real income. Using a panel of seven Latin American countries (Argentina, Columbia, Costa Rica, Chile, Mexico, Peru, and Uruguay) between 1977 and 1989, she found an elasticity of average real wages to inflation of −0.14. In other words, the poor are vulnerable to inflation through this effect of reduced real wages.

In "Who Would Vote for Inflation in Brazil?" Kane and Morisett (1993) noted that official income distribution figures based on household survey data underestimate inequality in Brazil as they ignore capital income. This is even more the case in an inflationary environment where income from capital becomes a more important channel through which income distribution is altered. In other words, real wages and cash holdings are not enough to assess the impact of inflation on income distribution. Adjusting for financial assets magnifies the observed increase in inequality in Brazil in the 1980s. Taking into account indexed assets to which some economic agents switch when inflation rises, in a framework including money, demand deposits, and bonds as well as real wages, the authors show that income distribution in Brazil worsened as a result of inflation during the period 1980–89 with the lowest quintile losing about 19 percent, divided between 16 percent due to real wage erosion and 3 percent to the inflation tax. The middle class was found to be the main loser (of about 30 percent of their income), while the top quintile managed to insulate themselves from inflation by taking advantage of high real interest rates on demand deposits without losing on the labor income side. In short, the poor are affected because their real wages are eroded, the middle class because they do not have the same range of assets at their disposal to hedge against inflation.

Brazil After the Real Plan

The experience of the Brazilian coalition whose leaders implemented the Real Plan (1994), a coalition with ample representation of the lower-income people who were paying most of the inflation tax, illustrates how inflation is liable to affect the poor. Inflation being regressive there is a higher inflation aversion among the poor. In contrast to the two preceding plans to reduce Brazil's high inflation, the Real Plan tackled the budget deficit and was considered a success by bringing inflation under control from the outset (figure 5.1):

> Our model says that the 1994 stabilization is different from the earlier cosmetic reforms; this time the stabilization was accompanied by a persistent reduction in the mean and volatility of seigniorage.... Thus, Brazil provides an interesting example of some futile cosmetic reforms ultimately being followed by a successful sustained fiscal reform. (Sargent, Williams, and Zha, 2009, 238)

The preceding Cruzado Plan (1986) and Collor Plan (1990) froze retail prices, the exchange rate, and most private wages and blocked bank accounts (creating an immediate panic among investors).

The lessons of those failed anti-inflation efforts in Brazil are instructive—not only for the impact of inflation on poverty but also as an illustration of the importance of harnessing fiscal policy to any stabilization effort,

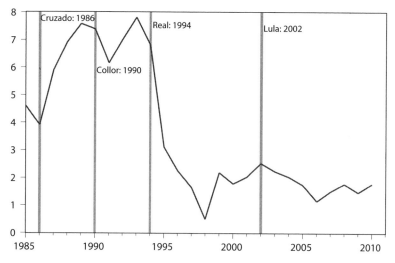

Figure 5.1. Brazil—Annual inflation (in logs), December to December (CPI), 1985–2010.
Source: Central Bank of Brazil.

as discussed in the previous chapter. Launched in February 1986, the Cruzado Plan replaced the cruzeiro by the cruzado as the unit of the national currency, with three fewer zeros. After twenty-one years of military rule, the new republic was declared. Da Fonseca (1998: 624) mentions that the main difference with the military regime was that the political base of the government broadened to include several parties and all public-sector workers each claiming a share of the government budget. The budget deficit increased rapidly, putting upward pressure on the inflation rate. After the debt crisis of 1982, international financial markets were closed to Brazil, putting pressure on domestic sources for financing the fiscal deficit.

At that time Brazilian policymakers were convinced that economic growth was essential for alleviating poverty and income inequality and that the causes of high inflation, contrary to IMF recommendations, were not to be found in lax fiscal and monetary policies but lay instead in the inertial effect of the indexation of wages and prices. The remedy was therefore simple, as explained by Cardoso and Helwege (1995: 191–94), that is, freezing prices, exchange rates, and wages. Such actions, it was reckoned, would create a break with the past.

The inflation rate was reduced quickly. This "success" meant that the authorities saw little need of going through the painful process of reducing the budget deficit; in fact it was argued that budget deficits and inflation were not related. While inflation was repressed, shortages developed. But "zero inflation" allowed the authorities just like in the Soviet Union to deny the existence of repressed inflation and to claim success at least until the November 1986 election. Both the Cruzado and the Collor Plans managed to reduce temporarily the inflation rate while failing to tackle the budget deficit, with the result that inflation quickly picked up again. Sargent, Williams, and Zha (2009, 238) sum up as follows:

> Thus, our model interprets the recurrent inflations and stabilizations before 1994 in the manner of Marcet and Nicolini (2003), namely as recurrent escapes followed by cosmetic reforms ... inflation is reset but not beliefs, reflecting the incomplete credibility that the public attaches to the reform.

The Real Plan was different and its effects surprising. While the immediate objective of the Real Plan was not the reduction of poverty, its success was especially felt by the poor. Averbug (2002: 932) gives the following description:

> The tranquility of knowing that a "cup of coffee with milk and a piece of bread with butter" (typical Brazilian breakfast) would cost next week the same as today, changed people's perspectives and a wave of optimism took over the country. Furthermore, the Plan increased the purchasing power of the poor and contributed to a natural (though still modest) process of flattening the income distribution.

Various reports from the World Bank (2007) confirm that since the inflation stabilization the situation of the Brazilian poor has improved. Using the World Bank definitions of extreme poverty (living on less than $1.25 in terms of purchasing power parity per day) and moderate poverty (less than $2 a day), table 5.1 shows that between 1993 and 2009 the percentage of the population below the respective two poverty lines declined from 13 to 3.8 and from 24.7 to 9.9, respectively. The success of the reduction in poverty is attributed to both the inflation rate stabilization and social policy reforms. Ravallion (2011) explains how the Real Plan by finally tackling inflation through a fairly orthodox stabilization program and reforming social spending of the federal government managed to reduce poverty and this while relatively little economic growth was generated. Ferreira, Leite, and Ravallion (2010) find that the effects of macroeconomic stabilization

TABLE 5.1
Brazil, poverty head count for 1981–2009 using $1.25 PPP per day
and $2 PPP per day, percentage of population.

	At $1.25 a day (PPP) (% of population)	at $2 a day (PPP) (% of population)
1981	17.1	31.1
1982	17.5	31.3
1983	20.9	36.0
1984	20.6	36.1
1985	17.5	31.5
1986	12.3	24.8
1987	16.7	29.4
1988	17.7	30.5
1989	14.6	26.8
1990	15.5	27.8
1991	—	—
1992	13.3	24.4
1993	13.0	24.7
1994	—	—
1995	10.5	21.9
1996	11.4	22.6
1997	12.0	23.3
1998	11.0	22.6
1999	11.2	23.0
2000	—	—
2001	11.0	22.3
2002	9.8	21.3
2003	10.4	21.7
2004	11.7	20.9
2005	7.8	18.3
2006	—	—
2007	—	—
2008	4.3	10.4
2009	3.8	9.9

Source: World Bank, Development Research Group. Data are based on primary household survey data obtained from government statistical agencies and World Bank country departments. For more information and methodology, see PovcalNet (http://iresearch.worldbank.org/PovcalNet /jsp/index.jsp).

Note: Data for 1991, 1994, 2000, 2006, and 2007 are not available because the household survey was not conducted that year. The international poverty lines of $1.25 at PPP in terms of household consumption in 2005 and $2 at 2005 PPP per day correspond to about $38.00 and $60.84 per month, respectively. The $1.25 poverty line corresponds to the average poverty line found in the poorest 15 countries in a data set on national poverty lines across 75 developing countries, while $2 is the median poverty line for all developing countries (Ravallion, 2011: 95).

and social spending on poverty were far greater than the effects of changes of economic growth. What is especially striking in Ravallion's (2011) comparison with India and China is that Brazil achieved a higher success against poverty than India while having a relatively low real growth rate of about 1 percent per year in the reform period. He found that for all three countries, controlling inflation is of primary importance in the fight against poverty.

Those findings confirm results by Ferreira and Litchfield (1998) and Ferreira, Leite, and Litchfield (2006), which identified accelerating inflation as one of the reasons for increased inequality and poverty in Brazil during the 1980s. Income inequality as measured by the Gini coefficient for the distribution of household income per capita rose from 0.574 in 1981 to 0.625 in 1989; the Real Plan and its aftermath saw the Gini coefficient decreasing to 0.591 in 1995 to 0.539 in 2009 (figure 5.2).

High inequality in the 1980s slowed down progress toward poverty reduction. The poor were found to have more difficulty in protecting themselves against the inflation tax and to lose more from the effects of lagged

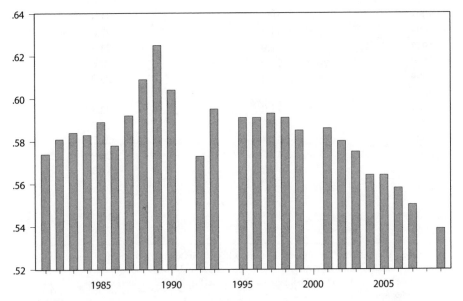

Figure 5.2. Brazil—Gini coefficient, 1981–2009.
    Sources: The data from 1981 to 2004 are from Ferreira, Leite, and Litchfield (2006: 6, table 1); the data from 2005 to 2009 are from the World Development Indicators, World Bank.

indexation than the well-off. Ferreira and Litchfield's (1998) overall conclusion is that the main lesson of the 1980s is that any attempt at alleviating poverty and income inequality through improving education opportunities and other structural factors can be effective only in a benign macroeconomic environment of low inflation, which, as this Brazilian experience demonstrates, depends in turn on prudent fiscal policy.

Monetary and Financial Stability
Conflict or Complementarity

> I'm baffled. I find it hard to believe.... What I'm puzzled
> about is whether, and if so how, they suddenly learned
> how to regulate the economy. Does Alan Greenspan
> have an insight into movements in the economy and
> the shocks that other people don't have?
> —Milton Friedman (2001: 105), quoted in Mankiw
> (2001b: 1)

JACKSON HOLE IS a place in Wyoming where the Federal Reserve hosts an annual retreat at which central bankers, economists, and various observers discuss topical issues facing monetary and broader economic policymakers. The Jackson Hole gathering in 2005 was the last to be held during the long Fed chairmanship of Alan Greenspan. Joining the chorus of praise for Greenspan on that occasion, the governor of the Bank of England, Mervyn King (2005a:5), said that one of the main lessons to be drawn from Greenspan's tenure at the Fed was that "economics is not a set of doctrines but a way of thinking." It was this very "Greenspan" way of conducting monetary policy that would be called into question by the financial crisis that began in 2007.

Even on that celebratory occasion—that is, well before the gravity of the coming financial crash became apparent—one skeptical voice could be heard. The killjoy was the then IMF chief economist Raguram Rajan, who gave a prophetic talk titled "Has Financial Development Made the World Riskier?" This well-founded foreboding of financial instability stemmed from analysis of the combination of the explosive growth of credit and its securitization in financial markets with those markets' increasing complexity and opacity—a development to which regulators proved unequal. The degree of culpability of financial market regulators as regards the credit bubble that so calamitously burst in 2007–8 is the subject of fierce controversy that is unlikely to be resolved any time soon. The more relevant question for us is the role of *monetary* policymakers. For in addition to the easily identifiable causes of financial instability—in particular the effects of misguided regulation (manifest in the appearance of ever more complex traded derivative instruments)—the conditions for that instability emerged at a time of, as we have seen in the preceding chapters, remarkable monetary *stability*.

This has led to speculation that the successful pursuit of low and stable inflation contributed to the dramatic financial destabilization experienced in the years following 2007. This hypothesis deserves to be examined since, if it were supported by evidence, the conclusion would be that welfare gains from monetary stability can be offset by the damage to welfare dealt by related financial instability. This chapter also investigates the broader relation between monetary and financial stability, looking at possible chains of cause and effect running in both directions between them—from the possibility that an unexpected tightening of monetary policy increases the mean probability of financial system distress (as posited by De Graeve, Kick, and Koetter, 2007: 3), to the general risk of monetary stability being undermined by financial instability.

In contrast to the straightforward definition and measurement of monetary stability as price stability, the concept of financial stability is vaguer and its opposite "financial instability" is easier to grasp. For Mishkin (1999: 6) financial instability occurs

> when shocks to the financial system interfere with information flows so that the financial system can no longer do its job of channelling funds to those with productive investment opportunities.

Others such as De Graeve, Kick, and Koetter (2007: 3) focus on distress in one or more major banks. Whatever definitional issues remain unresolved by professional economists, there is little difficulty identifying the period beginning in August 2007 with the emergence of credit problems in the subprime segment of the U.S. mortgage market as one of financial system instability.

The relationship between monetary stability and broader financial stability hinges on the combined responsibilities of most central banks for the value of the currency and the functioning of credit markets (through direct supervision of the banking system and/or the mandate to prevent and contain financial crises as lenders of last resort [LLR]). Central banks therefore focus on both monetary and financial stability. Financial sector policies (whether conducted by central banks on their own or in conjunction with other specialized financial regulators) affect financial stability at both the microeconomic and macroeconomic levels. At the microeconomic level, regulation helps to reduce the risk of failure of an individual financial institution, while at the macroeconomic level it aims at protecting the entire financial system.

The idea that monetary stability encourages financial instability is controversial. We saw in the previous chapter that inflation is often the root cause of financial instability by distorting information flows between lenders and borrowers, leading to asset bubbles and over investment. Therefore if anything monetary stability should promote financial stability in the long run and not the other way around. Most empirical evidence tends to support this view. But while monetary stability is a necessary condition for financial stability, it is not a sufficient one. In other words, financial instability can still occur even with the inflation rate under control.

As regards the opposite chain of cause and effect—namely, monetary stability being jeopardized by financial instability—the nature of the threat is more straightforward. A conflict can arise between inflation targeting and LLR activities. LLR activity undermines the credibility of inflation targeting, because in the event of a financial crisis, the typical response of central banks is to flood the banking system with liquidity. The question to consider therefore is the kind of regulatory reforms needed to support the credibility of inflation targeting.

Does Monetary Stability Undermine Financial Stability?

As already mentioned, although this question is counterintuitive, the stakes for general welfare are high enough to justify a careful review of the evidence on whether the success of counterinflationary monetary policy strategies arising from the economic principles discussed in earlier chapters has ended up destabilizing the financial sector—in particular, by creating the conditions for credit bubbles, the fallout from which might in turn lead to the return of inflation through the "back door." The idea is that success in controlling inflation on the back of central bank credibility (which is further enhanced by that same success) can both cause and conceal imbalances that ultimately lead to higher asset price volatility with serious macroeconomic consequences. This possibility has been labeled the "paradox of credibility" (Borio, 2006: 3408):

> [T]he establishment of a regime yielding low and stable inflation, underpinned by central bank credibility, may have made it *less likely* that signs of unsustainable economic expansion show up first in rising inflation and

more likely that they emerge first as excessive increases in credit and asset prices ("the paradox of credibility").

Various authors express doubt about any such "credibility paradox" and the purported need to reconsider the monetary framework on the grounds that the achievement of low inflation gives rise to a "new environment" (Borio and Lowe, 2002; Borio, English, and Filardo, 2003). Issing (2003) advanced the logical objection that given the lack of evidence that inflation benefits financial stability there is no reason to suppose that monetary stability encourages financial instability. Taylor (2010: 8) argued that as long as the monetary authorities follow closely the monetary framework derived since the 1970s from empirical models refined over time and stick to the "rule," there is no need for a new monetary paradigm.[1]

For Taylor it was the deviation from the principles enshrined in his own "Taylor rule" that led to the 2007 financial crisis, not the other way around. During the first five years of Greenspan's tenure as chairman of the Federal Reserve—1987 to 1992—the federal funds rate was set in a way designed to fulfill the Fed's dual mandate of price stability and employment and in doing so conformed broadly to the Taylor rule. The reverse was true at the end of his tenure. Between October 2002 and April 2005, the years leading to the financial crisis, the federal funds rate was negative in real terms. Other academic economists and economic commentators such as Tirole (2010: 15) have defended the same view that one of the reasons for the 2007 crisis was that monetary policy was too loose after the dot-com bust (figure 6.1). Taylor (2009a) demonstrates that this deviation from the rule—what he called "monetary excesses"—was a deliberate decision by the U.S. monetary authorities motivated by "a fear of deflation." That fear was misplaced. As pointed out by Rajan (2010: 106), unlike Japan the United States did not "experience a debt crisis, only a meltdown of the overvalued tech stocks," and the CPI during this period never went into deflationary territory. But the low interest rate policy bears a part of the responsibility for the boom and bust of the housing market, and therefore of the general financial crisis, by encouraging all population segments to buy houses regardless of the sustainability of mortgage credit for the many low-income households that now gained access to such credit for the first time. House prices started to rise, leading to the vicious circle where low-income people were able to borrow ever larger sums secured on the collateral value of their

---

[1] Some of these models are listed by Taylor (2010: 6, figure 1).

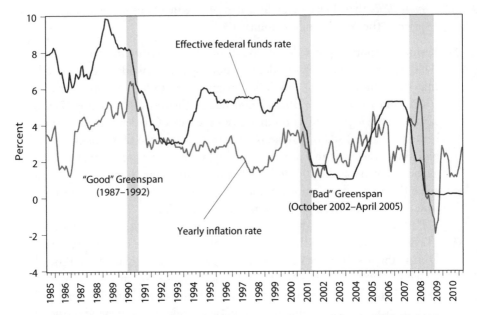

Figure 6.1. Effective federal funds and CPI percentage change, July 1985–March 2011.

Sources: U.S. Department of Labor, Bureau of Labor Statistics and Board of Governors of the Federal Reserve System.

Notes: Shaded areas indicate recessions. Consumer price index is for all urban consumers, all items, seasonally adjusted, monthly percentage change from a year ago. Effective funds rate is the average of daily figures.

homes. The bubble expanded with skyrocketing asset and house prices, only to burst once the Fed started to increase interest rates.

Mankiw (2001b) reinforces Taylor's view by showing that soon after Greenspan took charge of the Fed, the federal funds rate was increased drastically to fight inflation (figure 6.1), with the resulting stabilization success showing up in the 1990s in the form of a lower standard deviation of inflation rates (see table 6.1).

Each inflation rate increase was immediately answered by a greater increase in the federal funds rate. Mankiw (2001b: 39) notes that a 1 percentage point increase was met by a 1.39 percentage point increase in the federal funds rate, with the result that inflation was kept under control. Still, for Mankiw the positive 1990s performance not only for inflation but also for employment and growth owed more to good luck than good monetary policy, as this was a period free of supply shocks in key markets such as energy and food.

TABLE 6.1
The U.S. inflation experience, decade by decade.

	1950s	1960s	1970s	1980s	1990s	2000s
Average inflation	2.07	2.33	7.09	5.57	3.0	2.57
Standard deviation of inflation	2.46	1.46	2.71	3.53	1.13	1.42
Maximum inflation	9.6	5.9	13.3	14.6	6.4	5.5
Date of maximum inflation	Apr	Dec	Dec	Mar	Oct	Jul
	1951	1969	1979	1980	1990	2008

Sources: Mankiw (2001b: 7, table 1), updated with U.S. Department of Labor, Bureau of Labor Statistics and author's calculations.

Note: Decades refer to the first month of the decade to the last month. Consumer price index for all urban consumers, all items, seasonally adjusted, monthly percentage change from a year ago.

This conclusion seems to be supported by the experience of the 2000s when after the bursting of the dot-com bubble monetary policy was loosened. The Fed justified its action on the grounds that an expanded money supply was necessary to stimulate aggregate demand and therefore growth and employment. To the extent that in the 2000s the Greenspan Fed never seemed to recover its 1990s "magic" touch, this may be attributed in part to the possibility suggested by Mankiw (2001b: 53) that during the 1990s the Fed had conducted "covert inflation targeting" at a rate of about 3 percent, whereas in the 2000s the "rule" seems to have been abandoned. What is sure is that with hindsight Greenspan's legacy is limited not only as no explicit "rule" was ever announced but also because many observers now blame Greenspan for having preferred a discretionary approach to a more rule-based monetary policy.

Turning from the United States to Europe, a study that I coauthored with Sushanta Mallick (2009) investigated the impact of price stability (or inflation targeting) on financial stability on the twelve Eurozone countries between 1994:Q1 and 2008:Q2. For the purposes of this study, monetary stability is defined in terms of changes in the CPI and the ECB's policy rate, while financial stability is defined in terms of changes in equity market prices—together with interest rate spreads, the nominal effective exchange rate, house price inflation, and the loan-to-deposit ratio of the banking system. Examples of recent authors who have found that monetary policy affects these financial variables in the short run are Kuttner (2001) and Rudebusch (1995) who have focused on the term structure of interest rates, Bernanke and Kuttner (2005) on share prices in the United States, and Honda and Kuroki (2006) on both term structure and share prices in Japan.

In our study, we found that the interest rate instrument used for inflation targeting promotes financial stability. In the specific case of the ECB policy rate on which this study focused, moves in the policy rate stabilized share prices in the sense that a 1 percent easing in the policy rate produced a rise of around 2 percent in share prices in the medium term, and vice versa. There is clear evidence of a long-run procyclical relationship between monetary stability and financial stability—that is, sustained periods of low inflation have a steadily positive impact on share prices (seen as a proxy for financial stability).

The fourteen-year period from which data were taken for this study of twelve countries using the euro ended on the eve of the global financial crash of 2008, which led to a severe sovereign debt and banking crisis in the Eurozone. Those difficulties resulted from the flawed design of the European Monetary Union rather than the ECB's successful pursuit of monetary stability: in other words, and as we have already noted, monetary policies aimed at price stability are a necessary but not a sufficient condition for financial stability.

Should Central Banks Mandated to Achieve Low Inflation Take Account of Asset Prices?

The criticism that effective counterinflationary policies cause growing financial instability brings us to the debate about the correct monetary policy response to asset price shocks. For if runaway asset prices are not stabilized, a trade-off between monetary stability and financial stability might materialize after all. Once interest rates are reduced in response to the bursting of an asset price bubble, the resulting increase in liquidity may encourage further high risk taking in financial markets, causing new bubbles to form and then burst—a cycle that could ultimately undermine inflation targets or the general pursuit of price stability. As we noted in the response of the Greenspan Fed to the dot-com bust, the decision to reduce interest rates to head off the risk of recession now appears to be one of the causes of the financial crisis that began a few years later, in 2007.

In the wake of that crisis, the central bank response to asset price movements such as housing and stock prices took center stage. The question therefore is whether asset prices should be integrated into the monetary policy framework based on a credible inflation targeting regime and, if so, how this might best be achieved.

The central banks' prevailing view described by Issing (2011: 5) as the "Jackson Hole Consensus" is that asset prices should not be targeted by central banks. Most central bankers including of course Greenspan and Bernanke share the view that asset price stabilization is their job only if there is an inflation risk. The argument here is the money authorities' poor credentials for determining the "right" price for any asset—at least relative to private market participants who have better incentives in this area. On this view, monetary policy, with its set of traditional instruments, is badly armed to cope effectively with asset price bubbles. Controlling an asset bubble with the interest rate is seen as risky and costly in terms of output. Moreover as we saw in previous chapters a monetary policy regime that can control inflation while avoiding large reductions in output and welfare may depend on having sufficient credibility to anchor expectations. Any such "anchoring" credibility would be undermined if the regime added one or more additional targets—related to asset prices—to its existing target, since the frequently high volatility of asset prices—from stock markets to housing markets—is incompatible with maintaining the credibility of a single explicit target.

This does not mean that information about asset prices should be ignored by monetary policymakers. Arguments are building for information on financial markets to be better represented in the various macroeconomic models used by central banks to achieve their inflation-targeting mandates, as set out in a paper by the IMF (2010a). This approach should help central banks spot when changes in asset prices are such as to signify excess risk taking in asset markets. At this point, and on this view, central banks should put pressure on banking system and financial market regulators to rein in excessive risk taking by financial institutions.

One lesson for monetary authorities from the events of the early twenty-first century is that because of the difficulty they have in preempting asset price bubbles, their role in dealing with prospective asset price bubble threats should be secondary to that of financial system regulators. At the same time, they should be ready to react as quickly as possible to a bubble bursting by running simulations at the macro and micro levels, preparing them for such an eventuality (Goodhart, 2006). Changes in asset prices affect spending, which in turn has important effects on inflation and output (in an upward direction during the period when an asset bubble is forming and spending is buoyant, and in a downward direction after the bubble has burst). The avoidance of such shocks to price stability caused by the formation and bursting of asset price bubbles should better be dealt by regulatory instruments than the interest rate (an argument made by Blinder, 2010, and others). This brings us to the debate on the role of central banks in relation to the financial system.

Conflict between Inflation Targeting
and Lender of Last Resort Activities

In 1978, John Kareken and Neil Wallace (1978: 436) wrote,

> The historical record would seem to suggest that making bank liabilities safe and, say, keeping the price-level constant are conflicting objectives.[2]

The contradiction or tension facing central banks is that while they lack the means to prevent an asset price bubble, their LLR function obliges them to provide the economy with liquidity in time of a financial crisis. At the end of the 1990s, financial commentators labeled the U.S. version of this "asymmetry" the "Greenspan put" after Greenspan remarked before the Committee on Banking and Financial Services at the U.S. House of Representatives on July 22, 1999, that

> it is the job of economic policymakers to mitigate the fallout when it [the bursting of an asset price bubble] occurs and, hopefully, ease the transition to the next expansion.

Those remarks were repeated at the Jackson Hole conference in 2002. Issing (2011: 5) has set out powerfully the dangers of this asymmetry:

> However, restricting the role of the central bank to be totally passive in the period of the build-up of a bubble and practically pre-announcing the bank's function as a "savior" once a bubble bursts represents an asymmetric approach, one that might create moral hazard and over time contribute to, if not trigger, a sequence of ever larger bubbles and following collapses.

For Rajan (2010: 113) the "Greenspan put"

> told traders and bankers that if they gambled, the Fed would not limit their gains, but if their bets turned sour, the Fed would limit the consequences. All they had to ensure was that they bet on the same thing, for if they bet alone, they would not pose a systemic threat.

Rajan observed that telling financial institutions that the Fed will stand ready to flood the market with liquidity in case of trouble was like telling them

> Don't bother storing cash or marketable assets for a rainy day; we will be there to help you.

---

[2] Kareken and Wallace (1978: 414) define lender of last resort as "in effect, the insurer of bank liabilities."

Tirole (2010: 27) found the *mot juste* to capture central banks' predicament at the onset of the crisis: they were "stuck." By pouring liquidity into the financial system, the Fed and other central banks' aim was to limit the extent of the recession by making sure that the majority of financial institutions could continue to function. The Fed succeeded, but, as highlighted by Bordo (2008) and other observers, this has implications. Since avoiding economic disaster entails bailing out major banks ("too big to fail"), the seeds are thereby sown for a future financial crisis of even bigger proportions. Here we can certainly see instability in the financial system posing a threat to long-term monetary stability.

This reality was well captured in the conclusion of the Squam Lake Report (French et al., 2010: 1) on "fixing" the financial system:

> Though the crisis led to a severe downturn, a repeat of the Great Depression has so far been averted. The interventions by government around the world have left us, however, with enormous sovereign debts that threaten decades of slow growth, higher taxes and the dangers of sovereign default or inflation.

The question therefore is to see if there is a way out—that is, do central banks always have to be "stuck"? As with most big questions, the answer begins with further questions: what is the origin of this problem, and is there an alternative to bailing out financial institutions for fear of a total economic collapse? This whole topic presents a tough challenge for economists. Their response has focused on two fundamental issues. The first one is how to prevent financial crises from reaching the intensity experienced after 2007 (assuming, of course, that crises cannot be eliminated altogether since by definition risk is part of the financial trade). The second fundamental issue concerns the role of central banks: do they have to perform the lender of last resort function, and, if they do, how can it be performed at least cost to the taxpayer? Put another way, what regulations and reforms can remove the moral hazard now seen in the financial system whereby the gains of risky activities are enjoyed by the banks while the losses are picked up by the taxpayer? This is an old debate revisited every time a financial crisis takes place. The difference now is that the sheer scale of the crisis that began in 2007 has called into question the very role of the financial system together with the LLR role of central banks.

Proposed reforms occupy a wide spectrum—touching upon issues that have preoccupied economists for centuries—from laissez-faire (which, in this context, means allowing unrestricted financial intermediation) to strictly limiting banks to their traditional function of connecting lenders to borrowers. In the rest of this chapter, I review the principles underlying the opposite ends of that spectrum: at one end, the laissez-faire real bills doctrine and, at the other end, the strict regulation associated with narrow banking and its variant, what Lawrence Kotlikoff calls "limited purpose banking" (LPB), where banks would not be allowed to "gamble" with public money.

The Real Bills Doctrine versus Narrow Banking: Efficiency versus Stability

In his 2010 Phillips Lecture at the London School of Economics, Thomas Sargent revisited a debate that has occupied economic thinkers since at least the seventeenth century. The debate is between, on the one hand, advocates of strictly regulating "banks' portfolios ... to foster a stable price level and stable monetary (narrow) aggregates" (Sargent, 2011: 199) and, on the other hand, proponents of free banking, which, as interpreted by Sargent (2011: 198), can comprise "recommending that a central bank stand ready to purchase sound evidences of commercial indebtedness at an interest rate set with an eye to promoting prosperity." This debate has come to be labeled as "narrow banking versus the real bills doctrine."

Sargent's starting point is that "the real bills doctrine is alive ... and provides justification or consolation for the massive holdings of private securities on central bank balance sheets" (Sargent, 2011: 198). The Fed for instance reacted to the 2007–8 financial crisis by providing liquidity not only through its discount window and open market operations but also through other measures such as the Troubled Asset Relief Program (TARP), the Term Auction Facility (TAF), the Term Securities Lending Facility (TSLF), and the Primary Dealer Credit Facility (PDCF). In doing so the Fed bought all kind of "assets" such as long-term debts and mortgages.

The origin of this debate is to be found in the nature of the banking system. While a full account of the development of modern banking is well beyond the scope of this study, a digression is nevertheless required here into the history of the fractional reserve banking system and its corollary, the LLR.

Fractional reserve banking as practiced in most countries allows banks to hold in reserve only a small portion of the deposits that they lend out to their borrowing customers. The principle is to borrow short to lend long (a practice known as "maturity transformation"). Douglas Diamond and Philip Dybvig (1983) recognized that maturity transformation weakened the financial industry as bank runs are not easily predictable and conclude that deposit insurance should provide some protection against panics. John Kareken and Neil Wallace (1978: 414) take the opposite view:

We, however, are not so sure that a fractional-reserve banking industry is inherently unstable, . . . on certain assumptions, as we show in this paper, the liabilities of banks, although uninsured, are nevertheless safe, even when banks are not bound by a 100% reserve requirement. It is only required that creditors, actual and would-be, know what portfolios banks hold and that bankruptcy would be costly. Then, there is no risk of bankruptcy. Bank liabilities are safe—free, that is, of default risk. And deposit insurance is, in a word, unnecessary.

Since deposit insurance systems enjoy public funding in most advanced countries, this also leads to the moral hazard of the losses facing a failed bank's creditors (depositors) being taken on by the taxpayers. In short,

[I]n the real world, we're in a situation where we have to worry about [bank] runs and we also have to worry about moral hazard. (Sargent, 2010: 32)

Historically the fractional reserve banking system has developed out of commodity money. The story has been well told by Ferguson (2008: 41–52). Bank notes originated as receipts given by goldsmiths and others for the deposit of gold and silver coins for safe keeping. Depositors soon find it convenient to settle their larger debts by endorsing over these receipts to their creditors rather than having to go to the trouble of drawing out the gold and silver coins. To assist this development the goldsmiths began to issue receipts in the form of promises to pay the bearer on demand in multiples of round sums, such as five pounds sterling. Notes started to circulate instead of metal.

Goldsmiths noticed that gold and silver depositors rarely came to claim their specie at the same time. They started to invest a proportion of the deposited gold and silver, bringing them additional revenue but meaning as well that promissory notes—the receipt for the gold and silver deposited—were issued in excess of the metal in their possession. Goldsmiths thus found themselves in a new role of intermediating between savers and investors—that is, a banking function. These notes guaranteed to the depositors that upon receipt the depositor will be paid and that the note could be redeemed at any time. This promise to pay became known as a bank note, bearing the inscription "payable to bearer on demand."

While such a system is safe most of the time, danger stems from the implicit assumption that depositors will not want to redeem their bank notes at the same time. For if they did, a bank run would occur, which, in the absence of a lender of last resort, would result in the bankruptcy of the institution concerned. The key questions arising here are these: What portion of reserves should a bank hold as a safety cushion—should it be 100 percent or none at all or somewhere in between? Should this amount be fixed by law or at the discretion of each bank?

Financial Institutions: Middlemen or Money Manufacturers

In the seventeenth and eighteenth centuries various views were held about the nature and role of bank notes. The works of three thinkers are especially relevant to an understanding of the real bills doctrine versus narrow banking debate: John Law (1671–1729), Richard Cantillon (1680/90?–1734), and Adam Smith (1723–90). At the heart of this debate lies the question of whether financial institutions are mere intermediaries or the manufacturers of money, and whether money and credit should be separated.

The origins of the real bills doctrine are to be found in the work of John Law. Law, whom Schumpeter ([1954] 1997: 295) reckoned among the greatest monetary theorists of all time, published in 1704 *Essay on a Land Bank* and, in 1705, *Money and Trade Considered with a Proposal for Supplying the Nation with Money*. Law's idea was to create a land bank that would "issue legal tender paper money up to a certain proportion of the value of land and receive as deposits for *placement* money that would otherwise lie idle, so that money would never be either too cheap or too dear" (Schumpeter, [1954] 1997: 295).

Law's pioneering rationale for paper money was founded on a premise that, so self-evident today, requires imaginative effort to understand as the innovative notion that it was in early modern Europe—namely, that the first duty of government was the material well-being of the country it ruled over. His most radical argument was not so much that expanding the supply of paper money would support growing trade and prosperity but that, specifically, paper money was preferable to precious metals as a means of exchange. For him, money is not wealth. Wealth depends upon trade and trade depends on the money of account. Money has no value other than facilitating economic activity; it is a simple promise to pay a debt issued by the sovereign. Metallic money is undesirable because its quantity depends on the extent of discovery and production of the relevant metals and its value depends on the whims of the sovereign, who may decide at any point in time to debase or devalue it. Law called debasement or devaluation "an unjust tax" (Schumpeter, [1954] 1997: 321). Taking his inspiration from the Bank of England (set up in 1694), Law was strongly in favor of a central bank, but contrary to the Bank of England his bank would issue large amounts of legal tender paper money. He was perhaps the first economic thinker to intuit the conceptual basis of what would later become a banking system based on credit. Law's thinking evolved beyond his *Essay on a Land Bank* to conceive of a banking system that would no longer rely on a real asset (whether metals or land) underpinning the creation of a growing amount of liabilities (and specifically, promissory notes in the form of paper money); instead, the issuance of bank notes would be guaranteed by loans rooted in real trading activities.

Law's historical reputation results from his winning the confidence of the Duke of Orleans, who became Regent of France after the death of Louis XIV in 1715.[3] The regent was confronted with a gigantic royal debt bequeathed, in the memorable words of the contemporary courtier and memoirist, the Duke of Saint-Simon, by "a profuse and corrupt monarch [i.e., Louis XIV], whose profuseness and corruption were imitated by almost every functionary, from the highest to the lowest grade, [and which] had brought France to the verge of ruin" (Mackay, [1848] 1852: 1.10).

As things stood, France was unable to service its debt:

> The national debt amounted to 3000 millions of livres, the revenue of 145 millions, and the expenses of government to 142 millions per annum; leaving only three millions to pay the interest upon 3000 millions. (Mackay, [1848] 1852: 1.10)

Saint-Simon's advice was to default on the national debt and to declare the state bankrupt, a proposal rejected by the regent, who instead launched a campaign to raise revenue through the corrupt existing tax system. The result was a failure: the campaign produced a mere 80 million livres for debt repayment, with another 100 million being embezzled by courtiers (Mackay, [1848] 1852: 1.15). This gave Law his opportunity to initiate an alternative approach consisting of issuing paper money and establishing a central banking system. Law proposed a bank that, inspired by the recent pioneering central banking institutions of Great Britain and Holland, would issue notes secured on tax revenues, which it would manage, and on land holdings (Mackay, [1848] 1852: 1.17). The Bank (named Banque Générale Privée) was duly established in 1716 and was licensed to issue notes redeemable at face value in gold and silver.

> [Law] made all his notes payable at sight, and in the coin current at the time they were issued. This last was a master-stroke of policy, and immediately rendered his notes more valuable than the precious metals. The

---

[3] See Mackay ([1848] 1852) and Murphy (1997) for a full account of Law's life and theory.

latter were constantly liable to depreciation by the unwise tampering of the government. . . . He publicly declared at the same time that a banker deserved death if he made issues without having sufficient security to answer all demands. The consequence was, that his notes advanced rapidly in public estimation, and were received at one percent more than specie. (Mackay, [1848] 1852: 1.20)

The resulting improvement in general confidence boosted trade and tax revenues. But this success sowed the seeds of the undoing of Law's project. Now thoroughly persuaded of the merits of paper money, in 1718 the regent brought the bank—for which Law had initially envisaged governance arrangements at arm's length from the crown—under the crown's direct tutelage and renamed it Banque Royale de France. Until then the issue of notes was carefully managed, but now the notes, which were legal tender and the mandatory means of tax payments, were printed in "thousand of millions" brought about by the regent. The country was flooded with paper money, "which based upon no solid foundation, was sure to fall, sooner or later" (Mackay, [1848] 1852: 1.23).

At first sight, Law would appear in the flush of his initial success to have forgotten his principle that paper money should be adequately collateralized. But the reality was more nuanced. Law strove to associate the Royal Bank with real trading and economic activity to absorb the burgeoning liabilities (in other words, preempting adverse effects of the paper money issue). The bank accordingly obtained monopoly rights in the tobacco trade and the refining of precious metals; but the most important initiative by far notionally embraced the national commerce more generally—in the sense of the prospective new colonial trade. So it was that the Banque Royale was, in effect, merged with the Compagnie de la Louisiane ou d'Occident, known as the Mississippi Company. The rationale was to centralize in one institution all financial proceeds of trade and taxation, and to direct the resulting profits to repaying the debt. In that connection, and in a striking display of financial innovation, Law engineered a debt-for-equity swap of crown debt into the company's shares, and the prospective profitability of the company attracted speculative investment in its stock from all over Europe (and resulted ironically in the British, no longer in their accustomed position of financial leadership, imitating Law in the form of the South Sea Company, into which state debt was similarly off-loaded). Law's experiment unfortunately failed because all the Mississippi Company could show for its activities was losses. Schumpeter ([1954] 1997: 295) notes that "if these ventures had been successful, Law's grandiose attempt to control and to reform the economic life of a great nation from the financial angle ... would have looked very different to his contemporaries and to historians." Unfortunately this failure overshadowed the merits of Law's theory and tainted "the evolution of what eventually became the classic theory of banking."

Richard Cantillon was a major economic theorist and financier described by Schumpeter ([1954] 1997: 217n4) as "a Paris banker of Irish extraction."[4] Like Keynes, he combined brilliance of economic thinking with a taste for financial speculation—in Cantillon's case including a successful foreign exchange bet against Law's Mississippi System. The failure of Law's experiment most probably had a strong influence on the thinking of Cantillon. Contrary to Law's viewing money as a promise to pay, Cantillon, in his *Essai sur la Nature du Commerce en Général* (Essay on the General Nature of Trade), written in 1730, does not regard paper money as money but as a surrogate used to "accelerate the circulation of money" (Cantillon, 1964: 30, quoted in Bordo, 1983: 237). The value of money depends on the quantity of land and labor necessary to produce it. The cost of production of precious metals determined the "intrinsic" value of money (*valeur intrinsèque*), but the demand and supply of metals affect its commercial value (market prices) around this intrinsic value of money (relative prices). In other words "Cantillon clearly distinguished between relative prices and money prices," as pointed by Michael Bordo (1983: 240) in his essay, "Some Aspects of the Monetary Economics of Richard Cantillon."

The influence of the variation in the quantity of money on the economy and on market prices depends first on the velocity of circulation and second on the level of economic activity. Banks do not create money, they act purely as intermediaries. Banks increase the velocity of money by issuing bank notes in excess of the gold deposited with them, but bank notes are not part of the money supply. Banks act as intermediaries by lending the part of the deposit not needed by the depositor using bank notes, which are a more convenient means of payment than metals and circulate more quickly.

An increase in the quantity of money will lead to a relatively either high or low rise in market prices depending on the level of economic activity. Cantillon saw that a change in the quantity of money led to a change in market prices but that the rise in market prices was not strictly proportional to the rise in the quantity of money because the velocity of circulation may vary.

One of the big differences between Law and Cantillon concerns the role of the banks. For Law the banks that are useful are those that create

---

[4] See Murphy (1986) for a full account of Cantillon's life and contributions.

money, while for Cantillon the principal function of banks is to make money circulate.

Adam Smith, who is generally credited with the formulation of the real bills doctrine, was inspired both by Law and Cantillon. For Smith just as for Law, money is merely a means of exchange, a "voucher to purchase" with no "intrinsic" value. Its value is derived instead from its purchasing power:

> Money is neither a material to work upon, nor a tool to work with; and though the wages of the workman are commonly paid to him in money, his real revenue, like that of other men, consists not in money, but in the money's worth; not in the metal pieces, but in what can be got for them. (Smith, [1776] 1986: 392)

Smith distinguishes between fixed and circulating capital and classifies money as being part of the latter, excluding it from the country's national income:

> The great wheel of circulation is altogether different from the goods which are circulated by means of it. The revenue of the society consists altogether in those goods, and not in the wheel which circulates them. In comparing either the gross or the net revenue of any society, we must always, from their whole annual circulation of money and goods, deduct the whole value of money, of which not a single farthing can ever make any part of either. (Smith, [1776] 1986: 385)

Since it is much cheaper to produce paper money than metallic money, replacing gold and silver with paper will increase the national income (Smith, [1776] 1986: 388). This substitution is operated thanks to the banking system. Bank notes are issued when bankers discount a bill of exchange whereby they advance to the merchant their own promissory notes not gold and silver (Smith [1776] 1986: 395). Smith noticed that banks can issue notes in excess of the value of their cash holdings. The issuance of notes therefore can lead to an increase in the quantity of money in circulation. But for Smith there exists a fixed ratio between the annual production of a country and the quantity of money in circulation. If the quantity of money in circulation increases while "that annual produce cannot be immediately augmented by these operations of banking ... that sum being over and above what can be employed in the circulation of the country must overflow" (Smith, [1776] 1986: 390). And since this overflow of money cannot be used at home, it will be exchanged for foreign goods. But since bank notes will not be accepted in payments abroad, only gold and silver will be used (domestic business being carried out by paper, international trade by gold and silver). Thus, in the event of excessive quantities of paper money being issued,

> Many people would immediately perceive that they had more of this paper than was necessary for transacting their business at home, and as they could not send it abroad, they would immediately demand payment of it from the banks.... There would immediately, therefore, be a run upon the banks to the whole extent of this superfluous paper, and if they showed any difficulty or backwardness in payment, to a much greater extent; the alarm which this would occasion, necessarily increasing the run. (Smith, [1776] 1986: 398)

Therefore on the one hand, Smith established,

> The whole paper money of every kind which can easily circulate in any country never can exceed the value of the gold and silver, of which it supplies the place, or which (the commerce being supposed the same) would circulate there, if there was no paper money. (Smith, [1776] 1986: 397)

On the other hand banks are beneficial to economic growth by creating new means of payment conditional on their quantity being strictly limited. For a bank to not overissue paper money and therefore being free of risk, it should first restrict itself to "advance to a merchant or undertaker of any kind ... that part of it [capital] which he would otherwise be obliged to keep by him unemployed, and in ready money for answering occasional demands" (Smith, [1776] 1986: 401–2).

Thanks to the respect of this rule, a bank should be able to limit the risks of overissuance of paper money (i.e., loans to borrowing customers in the form of promissory notes issued by the lending bank) leading to bank runs and bankruptcy. To guarantee that a bank carries out a careful lending policy, the liabilities issued should be backed by safe assets or "real bills." Those "real bills" are interpreted by Sargent (2011: 199) as "safe short-term evidences of private indebtedness":

> [A] bank discounts to a merchant a real bill of exchange drawn by a real creditor upon a real debtor, and which, as soon at it becomes due, is really paid by the debtor. (Smith, [1776] 1986: 402)

Smith's monetary thinking in effect synthesized the main ideas of his predecessors Law and Cantillon. His analysis had a profound influence on the controversies about monetary and banking policies that took place well into the nineteenth century and laid the foundations for modern monetary and banking theory. He influenced both the "currency" and the "banking" schools of thought—the currency school with his doctrine, which we have already noted, of paper money as mere vouchers whose face value should not exceed the precious metal collateral value, and the banking school with the real bills doctrine: there cannot be an excess money supply as long as a bank discounts only real bills and because the reflux mechanism, that is, the paper issued by a bank, will be returned in repayment of the loans:

> The payment of the bill, when it becomes due, replaces to the bank the value of what it had advanced, together with the interest. The coffers of the bank, so far as its dealings are confined to such customers, resemble a water pound, from which, though a stream is continually running out, yet another is continually running in, fully equal to that which runs out; so that, without any further care or attention the pound keeps always equally, or very near equally full. Little or no expense can ever be necessary for replenishing the coffers of such a bank. (Smith, [1776] 1986: 402)

Overissue of banknotes is further discouraged by a free competitive banking system. Assuming that

> banks are restrained from issuing any circulating bank notes, or notes payable to the bearer, for less than a certain sum, and if they are subjected to the obligation of an immediate and unconditional payment of such bank notes as soon as presented, their trade may, with safety to the public, be rendered in all other respects perfectly free. (Smith, [1776] 1986: 429)

Free competition of banks

> obliges all of them to be more circumspect in their conduct, and, by not extending their currency beyond its due proportion to their cash, to guard themselves against those malicious runs. . . . By dividing the whole circulation into a greater number of parts, the failure of any one company, an accident which, in the course of things, must sometimes happen, becomes of less consequence to the public. This free competition, too, obliges all bankers to be more liberal in their dealings with their customers, lest their rivals should carry them away. (Smith, [1776] 1986: 429)

Sargent (2011: 199) explains,

> The real bills doctrine emphasizes the efficiency gains associated with financial competition. It prescribes disarming legal barriers that separate money and credit markets. Legal barriers to competition can be either torn down directly to allow unrestricted financial intermediation, or circumvented, by having a central bank issue notes that it uses to purchase

enough private loans to eradicate the rate of return wedges that the legal barriers were designed to sustain.

Regulation or Laissez-Faire: A Tension Forged in the Development of Modern Banking

In the 1790s William Pitt's extensive use of the "line of credit" to finance war with France (1793–1815) meant that an alarming number of bills were being presented to the Bank of England for redemption into gold. As provider of the government's financial needs, the Bank of England had to comply, but the result was the severe depletion of its gold reserves. The Bank of England kept asking Pitt to limit his demands and warning him of the danger of going bankrupt in the face of the gold stock going seriously low. At last, on February 26, 1797, the Bank Restriction Act came into force, suspending convertibility of its notes, saving "the Bank from a state of chronic insolvency which would have demoralized public as well as private credit" (Silberling, 1924b: 398). As things turned out, the suspension lasted until 1821.[5]

Although the act, which applied only to the Bank of England, did not make the bank's notes official legal tender, they became just that in practice as a reflection of the trust that the public had in the Bank of England (Silberling, 1924b: 399). Thanks to war finance and the Bank Restriction Act, every part of the financial British system, that is, Treasury, Bank of England, London private banks, and country banks at the time of the Napoleonic Wars, prospered; by 1800 the financial system was well developed with its network of banks both in London and in the country issuing notes and providing credit to the commercial and industrial activities of England. Put another way, the expedients of war finance proved coincidentally apt for providing financial underpinning for the broader economic developments of the period—that is, the surge in output and productivity stemming from the technological advances that were to become known as the Industrial Revolution.

In the years that followed the Bank Restriction Act, it was observed that the pound depreciated in terms of gold, that prices were rising, and that the price of bullion was high. This led to a debate (known as the Bullionist Controversy) on the causes of the pound's depreciation. On opposite sides of this controversy were the so-called bullionists and the anti-bullionists, who respectively blamed and exonerated the Bank of England.

---

[5] See Hawtrey (1918) for a full account of the circumstances imposing the Bank Restriction Act.

The anti-bullionist cause was founded on the real bills doctrine. There was no need to restore convertibility since bank notes were issued in exchange for merchants' bills of exchange. As long as these bills of exchange were "real," resting on the "needs of trade," banks would not issue bank notes in excess of what commerce demanded.

The most serious spokesman of the bullionists was Henry Thornton (1760–1815), who is described by Silberling (1924b: 407) as "an eminent and highly respected London banker," who as well as being a banker was a member of Parliament and a philanthropist, and whose *Enquiry into the Nature and Effects of the Paper Credit of Great Britain* (1802) is much praised by Schumpeter ([1954] 1997: 689): "the book reads as if he himself had not been aware of [its] novelty.... He was one of those men who see things clearly and who express with unassuming simplicity what they see." Thornton's criticism of the Bank of England was moderated by his respectful acknowledgment that both the government and the Bank of England had exerted as much caution as permitted in time of war:

> Government spent lavishly. But it also did its best, by the introduction of an income tax and in other ways, to keep the inflationary advances from the Bank down to a minimum, and its finance never ceased to remain competent and responsible. (Schumpeter, [1954] 1997: 691)

Thornton was supported by the famous economist David Ricardo (1772–1823), who advocated the return to convertibility into gold in order to prevent banks issuing notes in excess of gold, which would lead to an excess of money and therefore to inflation. For Ricardo the depreciation of the paper currency, the high price of bullion, and the increase in commodity prices were due to the Bank of England's discretionary overissuance of notes. The bullionists therefore concluded that to restore a stable pound sterling, the gold standard was a necessary discipline.

Access to the actual data would have allowed Ricardo to exercise better judgment; instead he could only guess "the size of the Bank of England's note issue, and to the volume of its discounts ... from occasional figures published in response to official enquiries" (Sayers, 1953: 35). Moreover Niebyl (1940: 763) notes that "Thornton and his fellow bullionists ... do not seem to be interested in the fact that the volume of production at that time was increasing considerably." Niebyl attributes this lack of interest to the fact that most of them were "London merchants, and as such primarily interested in foreign *trade* relations rather than domestic, and that their commercial activity was intimately bound up with the price of silver." They also ignored the role of the country banks in "providing an expanding productive society with the necessary capital for such an expansion" (Niebyl, 1940: 763). The importance of the country banks in financing expanding industry was combined with speculative credit expansion that contributed more to inflation than (as the bullionists argued) the paper issue of the Bank of England (Silberling, 1924b: 438–39). To give an example, "the banking house of Messrs. Daintry and Ryle of Macclesfield, with its bank at Manchester, incurred heavy losses because of advances that they had made for a scheme to run steam carriages on ordinary turn-pikes" (Niebyl, 1940: 770).

The bullionists' influence was reflected in the conclusions of the Report on the High Price of Gold Bullion of the Select Committee of the House of Commons set up in February 1810.[6] This "Bullion Report" recommended a return to the gold standard, convertibility of the note issue, and control of the supply of paper money.

The views of the Bullion Report prevailed in the form of Peel's Resumption Act of 1819, which prescribed a progressive return to convertibility during the following four years (with guaranteed convertibility in coins starting on May 1, 1821). But despite the apparent defeat of the anti-bullionists and the proponents of the real bills doctrine, the debate was revived in the face of the reality that expanding economic activity required financing. In this new cycle of controversy, the equivalent of the bullionists and anti-bullionists became known as the currency and banking schools, referred to above in our brief look at the influence of the monetary thinking of Adam Smith.

By the 1820s, the Bank of England had various roles to perform: a statutory duty to maintain the convertibility of banknotes into gold, a political duty to attend to the government's financial needs, a commercial duty to pay dividends to its shareholders, and a lender of last resort role whereby the bank was the ultimate source of cash and credit for the banking system. It was thus the guardian both of the currency and of the credit structure (Schumpeter [1954] 1997: 686n12). The tensions engendered by this combination of functions led to the controversy described by Eltis (2001: 6), quoting Lord Overstone, as follows:

> The leading political economists who contributed to the debate were divided between those who focused on the role of the Bank as "manager of the currency" and those who emphasized its role as "head of the

---

[6] See Silberling (1924a) for a full account of the Bullion Report. The literature on the bullionist controversy is large and not reviewed here.

banking operations of the country." The labels currency school and banking school were a natural consequence.

The controversy boiled down to whether money and credit should be integrated or separated. The system ushered in by the 1821 Resumption Act was predicated on a preference for separation. In its support for this system, the currency school (among its members were Lord Overstone, Samuel Jones Lloyd, and Robert Torrens) argued that bank notes should be regarded as though they were the gold specie they represented so that the quantity at issue should fluctuate in accordance with the balance of payments. In other words the existing mixed currency (gold and notes) should be made to operate as a purely metallic currency. As a result, gold flows would automatically be matched by a change in the money supply, and therefore the automatic functioning of the system will be preserved and with it the classical principle of international trade equilibrium. The trouble was that domestic credit was not integrated into this system. The currency school did not think to regulate deposits, which, albeit from a low base (hence the lack of attention to them), contributed to money supply growth and further credit growth. It was therefore impossible for the system to work toward equilibrium, as credit expansion counteracted the mechanism established by the 1821 act. Awareness of this problem led to a first reform in 1833 which gave the Bank of England discretionary power to set the rate of discount as an instrument of credit control.

> An Act passed in 1833 exempted the Bank of England, in so far as its discounts of short-term paper were concerned, from the legal maximum interest rate of 5 percent under the usury laws, and thus gave it the power to use the discount rate as an instrument of credit control. (Viner, 1937: V.2)

Against the currency school stood the banking school (prominent adherents included Thomas Tooke, John Fullarton, and John Stuart Mill). They were afraid that the currency school principles would lead to excessive rigidity in the issuance of bank notes. "Like many modern theorists, Tooke insisted that it was national income based effective demand and not the money supply which determined prices" (Eltis, 2001: 11). The banking school's ideas were close to the real bills doctrine. They did not see an increase of the money supply (composed of notes and deposits) through the discounting of "real" bills as inflationary. Its members were concerned by the "straitjacket" imposed by the currency school. In other words, the rigidity imposed by such a system would not offer the necessary flexibility necessary to cope with shocks such as droughts and bad harvests or, conversely, abundance. The quantity of bank notes should be demand determined; banks should be able to accommodate changes in the demand for currency associated with changes in real activity. Any overissue of bank notes could happen only for a short time since the notes exceeding money demand would be returned to the issuer for loan repayment.

Such concerns of the banking school were borne out by the sequence of booms and busts experienced by the British economy during this period. The busts—in 1825, 1837, and 1839—stemmed from the deflationary effects of convertibility, which became increasingly difficult to maintain as gold reserves were repeatedly prone to depletion. Each crisis cycle sparked new controversies about the role of the Bank of England and the note-issuing banks. The reason why gold reserves were under constant pressure was that the Bank of England compensated for the shortage of gold by issuing more bank notes. Eltis (2001: 8) notes,

> In other words the Hume/Ricardo mechanism by which a loss of gold will depress domestic demand, reduce prices and boost exports bringing gold back was not at work. There could not be any improvements in the terms of trade since the loss of gold was compensated by the Bank issuing currency notes leaving the mixed monetary base intact (gold plus currency notes). The Bank of England was following what became to be known as the "Palmer rule."

This Palmer rule, which took its name from John Horsley Palmer, who was governor of the Bank of England from 1830 to 1832, was a pragmatic arrangement designed to accommodate the conflicting pressures on the bank described above: This rule

> called upon the Bank to back one-third of its short term liabilities of currency notes plus short term deposits with gold and silver bullion, and the remaining two-thirds with interest-yielding earning assets. The Bank had no rule which specifically linked its currency issues to its gold reserve, and as the gold ran out in 1825, in 1837 and in 1839, it merely sold investments to sustain the two thirds ratio, while it actually expanded its note issue. (Eltis, 2001: 8)

The controversy culminated when the Bank of England's charter came up for renewal in 1844. The Bank Charter Act of 1844 (known as the Peel Act) reorganized the Bank of England. It was thought that the best way to rein in issuance of bank notes by the Bank of England was to separate money and credit. To achieve this separation, the bank's operations were divided by creating an Issue Department and a Banking Department. The

Issue Department was designed to be in charge of issuing and controlling the money supply, defined strictly as bank notes and coins, while the Banking Department was left with the banking business. In other words the control of the currency was to be independent from banking. Gold reserves were to be held by the Issue Department, and bank notes were to be issued in strict accordance with those reserves, but always in excess by

> £14 million, which was close to the lowest level to which it had fallen between 1821 and 1844. The note issues of the country banks would be gradually phased out and two-thirds would then be absorbed into the permitted fiduciary issue of the Bank of England. The extent of the Bank's note issue would be continually held at its bullion reserve (at least three quarters in gold) plus £14 million plus whatever it absorbed from the country banks. Hence Britain's monetary base of notes plus bullion would precisely track the Bank's gold and silver reserve upwards and downwards. (Eltis, 2001: 9)

The gold in the Issue Department was made unavailable for external payments, except as the Banking Department had a disposable reserve of notes that it could exchange for Issue Department gold. The Issue Department of the Bank of England could increase its issue of notes only on the condition that it obtained more gold through international trade, that is, an increase of exports or in case of crises. Schumpeter ([1954] 1997: 694) notes that the Bank Charter Act "enforced what may be described as a '100 percent reserve plan' for bank notes."

As such, this act represented a victory for the adherents of the currency school, just as the 1821 Resumption Act had done for their bullionist predecessors. However, the authors of the act, in their haste to make sure that the Issue Department had no discretion as regards sterling being as good as gold, overlooked the Banking Department and in doing so left it free to act for the Bank of England as the "lender of last resort" (Triffin, 1946–47: 55). The bank moved to bring the operations of the subordinates or commercial banks under its control, and as such became the bank of the banks. And, once again—that is, similar to the previous cycle that started with the 1821 Resumption Act—as the volume of transactions expanded, the new system appeared to be far too restrictive as the stock of gold was too narrow to support the economic activity. The Peel Act accordingly resulted in a series of credit crises in 1847, 1857, and 1866 (when the 1844 Act even had to be suspended for a time). These crises in turn promoted the development of the bank's role—as described by Bagehot—of "lender of last resort" with its bank rate becoming the "great regulator." Some flexibility was introduced over time (we have already noted that bank deposits were omitted from regulation; as a result they expanded more rapidly than the official money supply composed of notes and coins), but the Act itself was suspended only in 1931.

To sum up, this system applied the principles of the bullionists and currency school proponents to the banking practice of advanced commercial countries *under normal conditions* (Silberling 1924b: 439). But inasmuch as the key principle was the separation of money from credit markets, the system proved leaky since the operation of credit markets affected monetary conditions (rather than, according to the principles of the currency school, merely being determined by the rule-based monetary regime that became known as the gold standard). When conditions became abnormal after the 1929 stock market crash and ensuing Great Depression, just as in response to the economic shocks experienced in Britain in the first half of the nineteenth century, experts and policymakers rediscovered interest in more rigorous ring fencing of banks and credit from the money supply.

Narrow versus Free Banking

This twentieth-century version of the currency school was centered on a group of economists at the University of Chicago including Frank Knight, Lloyd Mints, and Henry Simons, who in March 1933 circulated their proposal on the banking system.

This proposal, which became known as the Chicago Plan, consisted in abolishing the fractional reserve system and replacing it with a 100 percent reserve requirement on demand deposits. The idea was that by separating money creation from credit creation, the money supply and hence the price level could be more easily controlled. While the 100 percent reserve requirement was never adopted and the fractional reserve banking system survived, the Chicago Plan was and is highly influential. Its influence is reflected in the Banking Act of 1933 (known as the Glass–Steagall Act, repealed in 1999), whereby commercial and investment banking were segregated, and in subsequent advocacy of the merits of "narrow banking."

There is a long list of eminent economists who have taken up ideas from the Chicago Plan, starting with Irving Fisher and his 1935 book *100% Money* and later including Milton Friedman (1960) in *A Program for Monetary Stability*. Friedman's program modified the Chicago Plan by including paying an interest rate on reserves to overcome the distortions (such as incentives for avoidance of compulsory reserve requirements imposed by banking regulators) stemming from the alternative of imposing an effective tax on reserves. Johnson (1968: 976) worded this concern as follows:

The convention of non payment of interest by the central bank on commercial bank reserves constitutes in effect a tax on the creation and use of deposit money, which militates against the efficient provision of a payments mechanism.

Sargent (2011: 203) remarked that the way that this school of thought envisages remunerating banks' compulsory reserves "either through taxation [i.e., by using tax revenues for the purpose] or through earnings on the central bank's portfolio" highlights "how monetary and fiscal policies are inextricably linked" (Sargent, 2011: 203n20).

Fundamentally, paying interest on reserves eradicates the separation between money and credit markets recommended by the Chicago Plan. This happens by making reserves

> as good an investment for banks as are the alternative assets that earn that interest rate, rendering the demand for reserves indeterminate. When the demand for reserves becomes indeterminate, so do the taxes that have to be raised to pay interest on reserves. (Sargent, 2011: 204)

The reason why the bullionist/anti-bullionist, currency/banking school, and Chicago Plan (i.e., narrow banking versus free banking) controversies interest us here is that exerting strict control over the monetary base has always had its supporters and detractors. The detractors emphasize the urgency of providing liquidity to distressed institutions whose fall may threaten the entire financial system (and with it monetary stability), while supporters warn of the moral hazard whereby the next crisis may be even more damaging, having let rogue institutions off the hook too easily. These issues were never more vivid than in the period starting from the 1990s onward. The historical controversies reviewed above were echoed in the heated discussions that erupted in the wake of the financial crisis that began in 2007. These debates boil down once again to the real bills doctrine or free banking versus the quantity theory or narrow banking.

Monetary policy cannot be effective without a sound financial system: but regulating the financial services sector is a formidable challenge. The extent of the difficulties was given thorough airings in reports such as the LSE report *The Future of Finance* (2010) and *The Squam Lake Report* (French et al., 2010). These multiauthor surveys pointed to the major issues at stake: the conflict of interest due to a misalignment of incentives between the management and shareholders of financial institutions, whereby the losses and profits are not shared evenly; and the difficulty of bankrupting large financial institutions on which so much economic activity depends. This last problem—of systemically important institutions that are "too big to fail" (TBTF)—creates expectations that after potentially fatal losses from excessive borrowing and risky lending these institutions will always be rescued. Some commentators warn that the resulting cycle of crises cannot be averted through incremental regulation:

> Having worked for many years in formerly communist countries, this [adding regulations] reminds us of the repeated attempts by central planners to rescue their systems with additional regulations until it became all too apparent that collapse was imminent. (Boone and Johnson, 2010: 246)

And in a future crisis coming after a series of preceding bank bailouts, national authorities may be so financially drained that they would no longer be able to bail out TBTF institutions—except in a way that could cause inflation to get out of control. From our point of view—that is from the inflation perspective—the issue is always that the liability side of central banks' balance sheets should not get unsustainably burdened by "unsafe" bank assets, which in a world where bank deposits are insured (and other senior creditors of banks are also reckoned to be too important—for future financial and economic activity—to be allowed to lose their money) means that the tab is left to be picked up by central banks and governments, that is, by the taxpayer.

In the face of this profound lack of security, both doctrines—real bills/free banking and narrow banking—share the same goals of providing a safe payment system and limiting the risk engendered by moral hazard and TBTF financial institutions of the taxpayer having to pay for the losses when things go wrong. Their approaches however are fundamentally different, one relying on free markets—the real bills—while narrow banking calls on the tradition of the currency school and believes that only by separating depository and lending services will the financial system be safe while still being innovative.

In other words, proponents of narrow banking view risk as stemming from the fact that banks have the discretion to invest their deposits in both safe and risky assets. The years since 2007 saw the publication of a series of new policy studies and proposals attempting to adapt the principles of narrow banking to acute contemporary difficulties. One approach would involve ring-fencing deposits. On this view, banks would be allowed to invest deposits only in safe assets—a change that would remove the moral hazard problem. Risky investments would instead be carried on by different institutions, where the shareholders would monitor closely their performance and whose capital would have been raised in full knowledge that some of the money would be invested in high risk–high reward projects, some of which will always fail (Phillips and Roselli, 2009).

The twenty-first-century adapters of narrow banking ideas and critics of the real bills doctrine also focused on the fact that under a fiat money regime, the money supply and hence the price level are susceptible to much wider fluctuations than under a reserve-based system. One plausible argument runs that under paper money there is no justification for the fractional reserve banking system to survive since its aim is to economize on costly reserves (gold) under commodity-based money:

> The central logic of leverage banking, of any sort, is absent under the operation of a pure fiat money system. Buchanan (2010: 255)

This idea of the removal of leverage is taken to its logical conclusion in the most thoroughgoing of all fresh narrow banking proposals—"limited purpose banking" (LPB)—as presented by Laurence Kotlikoff in his 2010 book *Jimmy Stewart Is Dead: Ending the World's Ongoing Financial Plague with Limited Purpose Banking*. Kotlikoff's (2010: xviii) motto is "limit banks to their legitimate purpose—connecting lenders to borrowers and savers to investors—and *don't let them gamble*." The central feature of LPB compared to other suggested variants of narrow banking is the replacement of limited liability banking with the compulsory adherence to a mutual society form of organization:

> *all banks*—all financial and insurance companies with limited liability (e.g., C-corps, S-corps, LLPs) that are engaged in financial intermediation— would operate as pass-through mutual fund companies, which sell mutual funds—safe as well as risky collections of securities. (Kotlikoff, 2010: 123)

As such, financial companies would be prohibited from borrowing short to lend long, and the losses or gains would go straight to their clients, not to the banks themselves.

The reasoning underlying all these "narrow banking" plans is that in a system determined by the real bills doctrine, the quantity of money issued and thus the price level are not anchored since they depend purely on the quantity of bills coming for discount. This view in effect presupposes that it is impossible in modern conditions to realize Adam Smith's vision of the benefits of the banking system:

> The judicious operations of banking, by providing, if I may be allowed so violent a metaphor, a sort of wagon-way through the air, enable the

country to convert, as it were, a great part of its highways into good pastures and corn-fields, and thereby to increase very considerably the annual produce of its land and labour. (Smith, [1776] 1986: 420)

But, as we have already seen, establishing a system of 100 percent reserve cover and then assuming that those reserves would have to be remunerated ends up producing no less indeterminacy than could be expected under a free banking regime. Sargent highlights the irony that the difference between the Chicago Plan and free banking is thereby eliminated: both plans end up as efficient with credit and money markets integrated but with the price level as indeterminate or infinite in both cases. If the interest on reserves is paid out of central bank earnings, the result is basically the same, equivalent to the real bills doctrine, the main difference being when the interest paid on reserves is financed out of taxes. In the latter case, the distinction between fiscal and monetary policy is further blurred—raising "substantial issues about central bank independence" (Sargent, 2011: 205).

This brings us back once again to the practical difficulty of separating money and credit markets into watertight compartments in line with narrow banking principles. Yet, as acknowledged by Sargent and Wallace (1982: 1232), such arrangements are better at producing price stability than a real bills regime, under which "both the price level and the money supply fluctuate more than they do under restrictions that isolate the money market from the market for private credit." The problem, however, is that this gain comes at the price of reduced efficiency:

[T]he restrictions that separate money and credit markets achieve price level stability at a cost in terms of economic efficiency. Because different agents face different rates of return on assets with identical risks, the equilibrium allocation of resources is not Pareto optimal. (Sargent, 2011: 202)

One way to restore Pareto optimal allocation (that is to make sure that no one is made worse off) is to adopt free banking in line with Becker's ([1956] 1993) "A Proposal for Free Banking." And the trade-offs involved here look balanced:

Even so for the sample economy that we have analysed it is not possible to argue that the real bills regime is worse than the regime with restrictions. Some agents are better off under one regime, whereas others are better off under the other. (Sargent and Wallace, 1982: 1232)

This debate would have been less heated in the absence of the questions of lender of last resort and deposit insurance. We have already noted how central banks' LLR function underpins the motto of the financial system: profits go to our private pockets and losses to the taxpayers' purse. As for deposit insurance, when the U.S. Banking Act of 1933 adopted "temporary federal deposit insurance," this opened the way to moral hazard and bailouts:

> Deposit insurance made banks "safe" not by direct restrictions on their assets, but rather by the promise that the government would guarantee all banks, both good and bad. (Phillips, 1992: 11)

The fundamental difficulty of applying the real bills doctrine in the modern financial environment is that the existence of the LLR function and deposit insurance makes it difficult to define what should be seen as a real bill. To what extent, for example, can we attach the real bill label to "products that rely on statistical averaging and censoring to transform bundles of risky assets of various durations into less risky assets that can back short-term risk free deposits [i.e., triple-A-rated CDOs based on subprime mortgages]"? Such products are not inherently malign: on the contrary, they are "efficiency improving." The problem arises rather when institutions protected by deposit insurance and LLR bailout cover are allowed to "purchase or create . . . such assets and use them to back putatively risk-free liabilities" (Sargent, 2011: 209).

What started out as a pragmatic analysis of the interrelation between monetary and financial system stability has led us into some of the deepest questions about the nature of money—and an attempt to grasp these issues with the help of historical perspectives. We should not be surprised at having to confront first principles in this way. The property of money as the necessary facilitator of real economic activity—Adam Smith's "wagonway through the air"—engenders an objective tension with price stability. But we have seen how attempts to ring fence money markets from banking and credit for the sake of monetary stability fell short even in their own terms—as a result of the suboptimal effects on the wider economy of obstructing the action of money in promoting trade and production as intuited three hundred years ago by John Law.

The equivalent modern-day intuition might involve combining the advantages of allowing financial intermediation to serve the economy (the "real bills") while minimizing inflation risks. This could be achieved by requiring the players in a free banking system to take on some of the characteristics of financial institutions advocated by the proponents of narrow banking. That might mean that all the institutions are mutual societies rather than limited liability companies, channeling their own more or less unlevered capital to borrowers with a risk profile of their own choice, and above all with balance sheets that do not grow larger than a defined limit.

Despite the long-term benefits of such arrangements, many governments would be reluctant to accept the shorter-term pain caused by the contraction of oversize financial sectors. The reasons for such reluctance might include loss of certain benefits to which governments have become accustomed. These include political control over credit allocation and the loss of revenues from taxing current large profits of systemically hazardous institutions (or taxing the incomes of those institutions' managers and employees who habitually appropriate most of the profits). A still more important deterrent is the fear of systemic collapse if taxpayer-funded LLR and deposit insurance were renounced. But Sargent (2011: 207) asks "If not now, when?" referring to the advice given by Lawrence Summers to Mervyn King when Northern Rock failed in 2007: "Now is not the time to bring out the moral hazard police." As for deposit insurance, in a healthy "real bills" environment any such insurance would be funded only or mainly by premiums paid in by deposit-taking institutions participating in any such scheme. King (2010: 17) himself formulated a powerful summary of the precondition for combining monetary and financial stability:

> Ultimately, we need a system whereby the suppliers of funds to risky activities, whether intermediated via banks or any other entity, must understand that they will not be protected from loss by taxpayer bailouts. Creditors should know that they will bear losses in the event of failure.

Inflation in an Open World
Does That Change the Rules?

> The question was: what is the quantity of money that a
> given country needs? Hume ("Of Money" in Political
> Discourses, 1752) seems to have been the first to show
> clearly and explicitly that on the level of pure logic this
> question has no meaning—on the one hand any quantity
> of money, however small, will do in an isolated country; on
> the other hand, with perfect gold currency all round, every
> country will always tend to have the amount appropriate to
> its relative position in international trade.
> —Schumpeter ([1954] 1997: 316)

PAUL KRUGMAN WROTE in 1999, "We live in the Age of Central Banker. . . .
Through much of the world, quasi independent central banks are now entrusted with the job of steering economies between the rocks of inflation
and the whirlpool of deflation. Their judgment is often questioned, but
their power is not."

The responsibilities and expectations which thus bear down on central
bankers must have weighed particularly heavily on Mervyn King, the governor of the Bank of England when, one evening in June 2008, he carried
out his legal obligation to send a public letter to the chancellor of the Exchequer with an explanation of the sharp increases in the consumer price
index (CPI). Under the Bank of England Act 1998, this embarrassing epistolary task falls to the governor when the underlying inflation rate (measured by the twelve-month increase in the CPI) diverges by more than 1
percentage point from its operational target approved by Parliament (since
2003, this target has been 2 percent). Governor King blamed this failure on
external inflationary pressures, writing in particular that

> [i]nflation has risen sharply this year, from 2.1% in December [2007] to
> 3.3% in May [2008]. That rise can be accounted for by large and, until

recently, unanticipated increases in the prices of food, fuel, gas and electricity. . . . Those sharp price changes reflect developments in the global balance of demand and supply for food and energy. . . . The global nature of these price changes is evident in inflation rates not only in the UK, but also overseas, although the timing of their impact on consumer prices differs across countries. In May, HICP inflation in the euro area was 3.7% and US CPI inflation was 4.2%.

This self-exculpatory approach prompted much criticism of the governor on the grounds that, despite his previous career as a prominent academic macroeconomist, he had preferred political expediency to communicating a proper economic understanding. One of his academic colleagues from the London School of Economics put a satirical gloss on the economics of King's letter:

[T]here must be interplanetary trade: the world is importing inflation.[1]

An essential component in the understanding of inflation established by economists since Milton Friedman has been to show that changes in relative prices (even the prices of basic inputs like food and energy referred to by Governor King) can occur at any given level of inflation. Inflation is defined as a persistent increase in the general price level as measured by a price index. A specific price may rise dramatically as in the case of wheat or oil, but if the specific price is offset by declines in other prices, the general price level may not rise at all.

From another perspective, this episode with the Bank of England in mid-2008 captured an important question for economists and economic policymakers alike. Does the force of upward and downward pressures on prices being felt throughout the world as a result of contemporary globalization justify any revisions to the fundamental understanding of inflation mechanisms and/or to counterinflationary policy practice?

For most of the first decade of the twenty-first century, the world economy enjoyed a combination of strong growth and relatively low inflation rates—despite accommodative monetary policies in the United States, Japan, and Europe. Laurence Ball (2006: 1) quotes Alan Greenspan as saying in 2005 that globalization "would appear to be [an] essential element of any paradigm capable of explaining the events of the past ten years," including low inflation. The implied argument reflected by both statements is that the integration into the global economy of giant emerging

---

[1] Willem Buiter, *FT* blog, June 18, 2008, http://blogs.ft.com/maverecon/2008/06/.

economies led by China creates new external (downward) pressures on the price level and that these pressures make traditional thinking on inflation weaker.

Proponents of this view—that globalization has changed the behavior of inflation and the ability of central banks to control inflation—have identified two main channels through which this effect might work: increasing financial openness and international trade. Under those two broad headings, a number of economists (Romer, 1993; Rogoff, 2004, 2006; Chen, Imbs, and Scott, 2004; Wynne and Kersting, 2007; Ahmed, Levin, and Wilson, 2004; Stock and Watson, 2002) have identified more specific factors at work here, including central banks' incentives, increasing competition coming from globalization, technological change, acceleration of productivity, and luck (smaller shocks to productivity and low commodity prices), as having a determining impact on price stability.

If such suggestions were substantiated, this would mean that globalization interferes with the task of monetary authorities to preserve price stability and hence calls into question the principles determining inflation established in the previous chapters. Consequently, domestic monetary strategy and the components of credible domestic inflation targeting may have to be revised. One economist in an investment bank titled his contribution to this debate thus: "An Inflation Model from a Bygone Era."[2]

This chapter argues that the principles underlying the problem of inflation and how to contain it have not been superseded by globalization, and that the notion that globalization calls for a complete rethinking of the ideas presented in the previous chapters of this book is misconceived.

The following sections examine the case that various changes in external conditions—that is, the results of globalization—call for a changed understanding of the causes and cure of inflation. Three different aspects of globalization that have been held to bring about these changes to the inflation picture are considered in turn: the expansion of international trade, the effects of increased competition and productivity, in particular as regards capacity utilization constraints, and the implications of financial openness and integration (cross-border financial flows) for domestic monetary policy.

---

[2] Larry Hatheway, "An Inflation Model from a Bygone Era," UBS, August 24, 2008.

Effect of Greater Price Flexibility and Increased Competition on Inflation

Much discussion of the supposed transformative impact of globalization on inflation starts with the rapid expansion of global trade, which quadrupled during the two decades from the late 1980s. International trade is seen by some economists as a direct channel through which price shocks can be transmitted. Proponents of this view fasten on two particular trends associated with the growth of global trade.

The first trend is the downward pressure on import prices. The debate therefore hinges on whether changes in real import prices have any impact on inflation. The argument that they do runs as follows: sharply varying import prices affect the overall price level by generating lower/higher costs and lower/higher nominal wage demands in the domestic (importing) economy. The second way that the huge expansion in international trade has been thought to affect inflation comes through the downward pressure on producer prices from the increased competition generated by growing cross-border trade.

References to more flexible prices arising from the increasing volumes of international trade and cross-border financial flows take insufficient account of the way in which these features of globalization have had contrary effects on price movements. A deflationary effect stems from growing supplies of cheap manufactured goods stimulating demand in the countries importing those goods, and leading the manufacturing countries to increase supplies. This, in turn, results in rising demand for energy and other primary resources, generating inflationary pressures. Trends in import prices thus reflect the contrasting impact of the emerging world on supply and demand. Before 2008, when inflation was low, it was often heard that Chinese manufactured goods flooding into world markets capped global prices. But the years leading up to 2008 also saw increasing inflationary pressures stemming from the demand of China, and some other emerging giants such as India, for primary resources (not only hydrocarbons and minerals, but also agricultural commodities) and for capital goods to develop their infrastructure and industrial base. The deflationary effect coming from cheap manufactured goods and the inflationary effect coming from rising demand for energy and primary resources should neutralize each other—or at least any net impact resulting from one of those two effects outweighing the other will be modest (Mishkin, 2008c: 4).

Turning to the effect of competition, low production costs of exporters in China and other emerging countries have been the main cause of reductions in overall import prices. A study that I coauthored with Sushanta Mallick and Ning Zeng showed that specifically as regards China this factor—the low production cost of exported Chinese goods, due to structural factors such as high productivity, excess capacity in state-owned enterprises, distorted factor prices at the micro level (Rawski, 2002), plus a sizable surplus of labor in the rural sector and state-owned enterprises (Brooks and Tao, 2003)—was much more important than the managed exchange rate of the Chinese currency in driving down the price of G7 countries' imports. This much is clear from observing that the moderate renminbi appreciation from 2005 onward was not reflected in higher U.S. import prices—which is probably the result of Chinese firms "pricing to market" in the sense of decreasing their profit margins rather than letting export prices rise in line with the exchange rate (Granville, Mallick, and Zeng, 2011).

Observing and explaining the phenomenon of downward pressure on import prices does not, however, prove that changes in import prices affect the overall price level—that is, inflation. The same goes for cases where, in contrast to trade with China, exchange rates float more freely and increased external deficits on the back of competitively priced imports result in exchange rate depreciation and, in turn, upward moves in import prices. All such price shifts are relative, whereas inflation as measured by changes in the CPI is the result of nominal prices not relative price changes. As Ball (2006: 12) eloquently explains, there is no reason why import prices, which are relative prices, should affect inflation as long as monetary policy does not attempt to accommodate for any such relative price shifts rather than continuing to target the general price level. Put another way, while central banks may allow shifts in the terms of trade stemming from globalization to influence monetary policy decisions (Rogoff, 2006: 6), this does not mean that imports as a relative price directly affect the overall price level—that is, inflation. Any decrease or increase of one of the items in the consumer basket is automatically balanced by an increase/decrease of some other item as consumers will adjust their spending accordingly. We come back to Milton Friedman's (1992) famous summation: "inflation is always and everywhere a monetary phenomenon"—in other words it is determined by monetary policy.

Ball (2006: 13) remarks that there may be a gap between theory and practice stemming from some unknown mechanism by which relative prices affect inflation. For example, Ball and Mankiw (1995) take the case of the 1973 inflation caused by OPEC's decision to hike oil prices and conclude that relative price changes matter for inflation only if very large, while steady price changes have no effect.

Mishkin (2008c: 9) remarks that with increased openness, real import prices may have a greater impact on inflation. But the downward pressure on import prices resulting from globalization still lacks the magnitude of the 1970s oil price shock. IMF research heavily qualifies the impact of lower import prices. The IMF's *World Economic Outlook* (2006: 109) calculated that real import prices for a sample of eight advanced countries declined on average by 3.8 percent a year during 1997–98 compared to an average decline of 1 percent a year from 1960 to 2004.[3] In other words, the acceleration in import price deflation, although marked, has not been extreme. Given that the share of imports in their sample of eight countries ranged between 10 to 35 percent of GDP, the impact on inflation is small: one-tenth of an import price decline relative to the long-term trend passes through into inflation during the first year and the effect disappears after two years. A similar finding emerges when modeling an annual average 1 percent fall in real import prices (IMF, 2006: 110): the initial effect can be quite substantial (about 40–60 percent of average inflation), but the cumulative effects are small. In other words the impact is short term. I reproduce in table 7.1 the IMF's results.

The conclusion must therefore be that the appearance of globalization-driven changes in import prices affecting inflation are deceptive—or at least, that changes in the import prices of some goods will not result in large and, above all, lasting changes in the CPI.

EFFECT OF PRODUCTIVITY GROWTH ON INFLATION

A second suggestion is that globalization explains the decreasing response of inflation to domestic output gaps—that is, the difference between actual and full capacity utilization. One argument is that since households and businesses can shop more extensively outside the country, less upward pressure is put on domestic prices by full capacity utilization. Little evidence however has been found to support the suggestion that the more open to trade a country is, the less inflation it experiences.

A separate line of argument focuses on the effect of globalization in boosting productivity through increased competition—a theme already introduced. Sbordone (2007: 5) summarizes the argument as follows:

---

[3] These countries are Australia, Canada, France, Germany, Italy, Japan, the United Kingdom, and the United States.

TABLE 7.1

The cumulative impact of a 1 percent decrease in real
import prices on inflation (percentage points).

	Impact on inflation			
	First year	Second year	Third year	Import share[a]
Australia	−0.10	−0.07	−0.03	0.21
Canada	0.08	−0.07	−0.03	0.34
France	−0.07	−0.01	0.01	0.26
Germany	−0.07	−0.01		0.33
Italy	−0.01	−0.05	−0.02	0.26
Japan	−0.08			0.11
United Kingdom	0.19	−0.07	−0.03	0.28
United States	−0.15	−0.12	−0.06	0.15
Advanced economies[b]	−0.08	−0.07	−0.03	0.20

Source: IMF (2006: 109, table 3.2).

a. Share of imports in GDP.

b. PPP-weighted average of the sample countries.

Increased competition, the argument goes, creates two effects: a direct effect of containment of costs, by restraining increases in workers' compensations and reducing real import prices, and a second, indirect effect of creating pressure to innovate, which contributes to increasing productivity.

The "direct effect" was reviewed in the previous section. The "indirect effect" posits that in a stable monetary environment, rising productivity will lead to a decline in prices and facilitate the monetary authorities' task of controlling the inflation rate while output will be growing (Mishkin, 2008c: 2). Rogoff (2006: 8) argues that monetary authorities, assuming correct forecasting results, can take advantage of an increase in productivity growth by delivering lower inflation rates in the presence of strong real growth rates. In other words the literature has raised the question of whether globalization might have reduced the inflation output trade-off—in other words, whether it has affected "the slope of the Phillips curve—the overall response of inflation to output (or output gap)" (Sbordone, 2007: 3). The debate has focused on whether it has become easier for the monetary authorities to control inflation in periods of overheated economic activity. The literature seems to have reached a consensus that indeed during the period of intensifying globalization starting from the 1990s, the sensitivity of inflation to the domestic output gap has diminished (worded in economic jargon as a flattened Phillips curve) (Ball, 2006; Mishkin, 2008c; Sbordone, 2007). But whether this is due to globalization remains uncertain (Sbordone, 2007; Ihrig, Kamin, Lindner, and Marquez, 2010). It may be that by far the more important factor here was the improved performance of monetary policy in anchoring inflation expectations. The credibility of central banks' pursuit of greater price stability—particularly by means of inflation targets—is more likely to be the reason for the low inflation in the past decade than globalization (Ball, 2006: 8).

Central Banks' Incentives

The third aspect of globalization that has been posited as a modifier of previous assumptions about inflation is financial integration, fueled by deregulation (both of the financial services industry and through the easing or lifting of exchange controls) and manifest in rapidly rising volumes of cross-border financial flows. The suggestion here is that this phenomenon may have affected the incentives faced by central banks and, specifically, has compromised central banks' ability to control inflation because domestic interest rates come to depend on external factors. On this view, domestic nominal interest rates are influenced by the global rather than the domestic supply of liquid assets, and real interest rates by balances between savings and investments on a global rather than domestic scale.

This suggestion is not convincing. For one thing, the premise—namely, global financial integration—is, in reality, partial and patchy. For example, Hsiao, Hsiao, and Yamashita (2003) examine the financial interdependence of the United States and the Asia-Pacific region through stock markets. They show that severe reductions in U.S. stock indices produce similar equity price drops in Japan, but not China, mainly because the lack of full currency convertibility. But the main counterargument must be that even in case of close financial integration—such as between the United States and the EU—central banks remain in the driving seat as regards domestic monetary policy. This is because they always retain power over short-term interest rates, which drive the domestic cost of credit and long-term interest rates—and also, therefore, consumer spending and business investment, hence inflation and output.

The straightforward answer to the question of whether globalization changed the way inflation should be controlled is no. Woodford (2007) analyzed systematically the effect of three types of increases in international integration—financial, goods, and factor markets—on the transmission links between monetary policy actions and goals, and reached the following conclusion:

> Above all, there is little reason to expect that globalization should eliminate, or even substantially weaken, the influence of domestic monetary policy over domestic inflation. Whatever the pace of globalization and however great its eventual extent may be, it should remain possible for a central bank with a consistent strategy directed to the achievement of a clearly formulated inflation target to achieve that goal, without any need for coordination of policy with other central banks. Hence it remains appropriate for central banks to be assigned responsibility for stabilizing a suitably chosen index of domestic prices, despite continuing changes in the real economy, whether domestic or foreign in origin. (Woodford, 2007: 73)

What has changed as a result of globalization is that the all-important credibility of central banks in controlling inflation—or, put another way, the credibility of the chosen nominal anchor (which in most countries these days is an inflation target)—has become subject to fresh challenges and opportunities coming from outside. For example, some monetary authorities have attempted to take advantage of growing integration of trade and financial flows by importing credibility from abroad by means of exchange rate pegs adopted as a nominal anchor. Yet, as emphasized by Ferguson and Schularick (2008: 28), "the market is unlikely to find the promise of 'tough' policies equally credible in all circumstances." In other words, a commitment to a currency board or a fixed exchange rate may appear unsustainable to investors because of the destabilizing social and political effects of the associated policies. International financial history offers many examples of fixed exchange rate regimes leading to financial crisis, including Argentina's default of 2001 and, a decade later, the Eurozone crisis. In this sense, international capital flows are a vehicle for transmitting monetary shocks, which in turn affect real incomes. But the root cause remains the lack of credibility of national monetary authorities. In another perspective, international financial integration may often create positive incentives to enhance that credibility. The competition for investment capital in a world where exchange controls are rare can have a disciplinary effect on monetary policy, since one driver of the investment decisions that set the direction of freely moving capital flows will be the credibility of monetary and broader macroeconomic policies. Greater openness to financial capital might therefore lead to lower inflation by exerting a disciplinary influence on monetary policy (Wagner, 2001; Tytell and Wei, 2004) and perhaps also on efforts to implement structural reforms designed to make the financial system more stable (Mishkin, 2006).

Another way in which globalization has created fresh challenges for domestic monetary authorities' task of establishing credibility stems from the extent to which capital deregulation, increasing countries' openness to financial and trade flows, may have increased the sensitivity of exchange rates to monetary policy and of the economy as a whole to exchange rates (Mishkin, 2008c: 11). For Taylor (2009a) the influence of the exchange rate on inflation is seen as one explanation for the trend of central banks (the ECB and the Fed) shadowing each other's interest rate decisions. Reviewing the same set of issues, Rogoff (2006: 21) wondered whether central banks should include in their monetary rules, the exchange rate, the terms of trade, or the current account.

All such discussions lead to the conclusion not that global financial integration has put inflation beyond the control of domestic monetary authorities but rather that the effects of globalization can necessitate additional efforts to maintain monetary policy on a steady and credible course. If monetary authorities are distracted by the impact of exchange rate trends on the domestic economy, this could affect their policy decisions and their focus on the inflation target (or other chosen nominal anchor), and globalization may end up affecting inflation. Conversely, a key factor in breaking the link between currency depreciation and rising inflation (or between currency appreciation and rising unemployment) is the preservation of a stable monetary policy environment (Mishkin, 2008b).

These questions came into sharp focus in the debate about the causes of the global financial crisis that began in 2007. The preceding discussion supports the view of Taylor (2009a) and Obstfeld (2010) that the credit bubble was created by loose monetary policy and excessive risk taking rather than excess saving by emerging markets, especially as the bulk of the U.S. credit boom was largely financed by European banks.[4] But this is not to dismiss the relevance of excess savings—or the "savings glut" as it was called by Ben Bernanke (2005), the most prominent advocate of the importance of this factor. The U.S. Treasury bond market was the most attractive investment destination for the bulk of the international reserves which were accumulated after the 1997–98 financial crisis and then the 2000 dot-com crash (if not, in the case of China, with its uniquely large-scale savings, the *only* practical destination). Warnock and Warnock's (2009) study of the period January 1984

---

[4] See Borio and Disyatat (2011) for a review and critic of the excess savings view.

to May 2005 found that large foreign capital flows into the United States combined with the reduction in long-term inflation expectations and the volatility of long-term interest rates contributed to the decline in the ten-year U.S. government bond yield. In other words, globalization trends helped create the conditions for the unprecedented credit expansion that ended in the subprime mortgage disaster, but they did not somehow emasculate the Federal Reserve. Obstfeld (2010: 608) observes that large-scale international reserve hoarding continued unabated after 2005, when interest rates in the United States and most other countries began to rise. In short, the chain of cause and effect linking global imbalances to the financial crash of 2007–8 runs through the failings of domestic monetary and financial policies.

NEW AND OLD INFLATION THREATS: MERCANTILISM IN MANY FORMS

That last point was framed by Obstfeld and Rogoff (2009) in a way that opens new horizons: while global imbalances and the financial crisis were interconnected, their respective sources were to be found in domestic economic policies. The global imbalances, or excess savings reflected in the huge accumulation of international reserves by China and several other emerging countries, have emerged as a central feature and effect of contemporary globalization. But an important distinction needs to be made here. On the one hand, and as we have argued, the core symptoms of globalization—that is, expanding international trade and capital flows—cannot in themselves be reckoned to result in some conceptual transformation of inflation and monetary policy. On the other hand, the "savings glut" stems from a policy choice of China and other developing countries, and the results pose a serious practical challenge to the maintenance of monetary and financial stability in the global economy. The most important policy driver giving rise to this challenge is the preoccupation of central banks and governments with the effects of exchange rate movements.

From the 1990s onward, when choosing an anchor for their anti-inflationary efforts, most central banks chose, or were mandated, to use the inflation rate itself as the anchor, as opposed to alternatives such as exchange rate pegs or money supply targets. As we saw in chapter 3, this approach is known as inflation targeting (IT), and for the "strict" inflation targeters—such as the Eurozone, Chile, and Israel—the exchange rate matters only to the extent that it affects inflation. Such monetary authorities rarely intervene in the foreign exchange market. And as observed by Rose (2006: 18),

[I]t is striking that no country has ever been forced to abandon an inflation-targeting regime. But the domestic focus of inflation targeting does not seem to have observable international costs. Countries that target inflation experience lower exchange rate volatility and fewer "sudden stops" of capital flows than their counterparts, nor do they have different current account imbalances, or reserve levels.

Other countries, including some self-declared inflation targeters, opted in practice for a hybrid system where both inflation and exchange rates are targeted. In most such cases, especially from 2000 onward, the concern was not the risk of exchange rate depreciation and the resulting stimulus to inflation through higher import prices, but, on the contrary, the upward pressure on the nominal exchange rate leading to the appreciation of the real exchange rate which in turn affected the competitiveness of their firms (exporters most obviously, but also import substituting sectors). These countries' central banks often intervened in the foreign exchange markets—especially to impede the natural appreciation of their domestic currencies' exchange rates against the background of current account surpluses and/or capital inflows.

This challenge of exchange rate appreciation in emerging market countries has its origins, as we saw in chapter 3, in the search for attractive returns that led international investors to direct capital massively to those countries in the 1990s. The same happened after the bursting of the dot-com bubble in 2000 and again after the 2007 subprime mortgage crisis in the United States (during the remaining months until the financial crash went global in 2008). Low interest rates and growth prospects in the United States and other mature economies resulted in large capital flows into emerging market countries, many of which had little room for maneuver by way of policy response since lowering interest rates to deter capital inflows would have been inappropriate given already quite high inflation rates.

Capital inflows mean that the domestic currency is purchased in exchange for foreign currency creating a supply of foreign currency. In daily operations, the total supply of foreign currency generated by trade transactions and capital inflows is matched by the total demand for foreign currency by domestic banks. If the total supply of foreign currency is in excess of the total demand, this affects the spot exchange rate which will appreciate. Under a floating exchange rate regime, the overall supply and demand for foreign currency should be brought into equilibrium through movements in the exchange rate. If, however, the affected countries are under a pegged exchange rate regime, the monetary authorities have to intervene to absorb the excess supply to keep the exchange rate inside the target band. In practice, whatever the official exchange rate regime, many countries intervene to stem capital inflows lest those inflows feed asset price bubbles, or expose the economy to great risks through the appreciation of the domestic currency in the short run and, further down the road, through a sudden reversal in the direction of these capital flows as a result of some shock. According to the IMF (2010b) the annual volume of global net private capital flows to emerging markets increased from $90 billion in 2002 to $600 billion in 2007.

Thus, many countries such as the Middle East oil-producing economies, Russia, and China, but also those with more flexible exchange rate regimes such as Japan, Korea, and India, have limited the changes in the value of their domestic currencies to the dollar and built large stocks of international foreign exchange reserves. Inflationary pressures result from this accumulation of reserves if the monetary expansion is not fully sterilized and is in excess of money demand growth (Aizenman, Chinn, and Ito, 2008). International reserve accumulation, mainly concentrated in U.S. dollars, reached 13 percent of world GDP by 2009—a threefold increase since the beginning of that decade (IMF, 2010b).

Two motives can be identified for amassing reserves: precautionary and mercantilist.

The precautionary motive entails insurance against future shocks—such as an oil price collapse in the case of economies that are highly dependent on oil exports. Aizenman (2007: 13) remarks that after 2000 reserve hoarding could no longer be explained solely in terms of hedging against such external shocks—as had been the case in the aftermath of the emerging market crises of 1997–98—but rather by a multiplicity of reasons such as "self insurance against latent domestic and external instability, and exposure to instability associated with growing weaknesses of banks' balance sheets."

Such "insurance" was recommended to emerging market countries by various authors such as Feldstein (1999c). The kind of cushion envisaged was close to the "Guidotti-Greenspan" rule that is "a country's liquid foreign exchange reserves should at all times cover its foreign-currency debt repayable within one year" (Obstfeld, 2009: 42). But it was never envisaged that the amount of international reserves held would reach the astronomic levels seen in Asia by the end of the decade—and especially in China, where reserves stood at about 50 percent GDP in 2009. China's foreign exchange reserves (mostly held in U.S. dollar assets) increased from less than 1 percent of China's GDP (about $2 billion) in 1978—the beginning year of economic reform—to $2.4 trillion in 2009 (about 50 percent of GDP), a more than thousandfold expansion, "making China the world's largest holder of foreign exchange reserves" (Wen, 2011: 2). The IMF (2010b:13) noted that since there are only two sources for "self-insurance"—importing capital and running current account surpluses—it is rather difficult to assess what portion of those reserves had been accumulated for precautionary purposes.

A related concern is to enhance sovereign self-sufficiency—as opposed, for example, to relying on the collective insurance offered by the IMF and other international financial institutions, which are controlled by the United States and other high-income countries and are therefore perceived by many other countries as unreliable. This desire to reduce risk accounts for the most common decision on how to invest the reserves—not in a range of instruments and asset classes (equity, fixed income, real estate, and so on), but rather in risk-free government bonds.

Turning to the mercantilist motive for increasing international reserves, the main contrast with the precautionary agenda consists in reserve accumulation ceasing to be an end in itself. The main goal rather is exchange rate management—which means preventing the strengthening of the national currency against trading partners' currencies, thereby protecting competitiveness and boosting output and employment. Increases in official foreign exchange reserves are an incidental side effect of this strategy.

This distinction between precautionary and mercantilist motives is useful for understanding China's massive holding of foreign reserves. Wen (2011) argues that this reserves accumulation is driven by the precautionary rather than the mercantilist motive given that the Chinese economy, despite its high growth rate, still exhibits many characteristics of a developing country—namely, underdeveloped insurance and financial markets and the absence of social safety nets. Chinese households hedge against uncertainties by saving an increasingly larger portion of their income including dollars earned from international trade to guarantee themselves a certain level of safety net and self-insurance. One way to reduce Chinese foreign reserves given that household consumption and income have not grown in line with GDP would therefore be to encourage consumer spending. To this end Feldstein (2008) recommends

> a better mortgage market and a consumer credit market would allow individuals to pay for durable products as they consume them instead of having to save in advance. A better health insurance market would reduce the need for individuals to accumulate funds in anticipation of potential medical expenditures. An expanded Social Security retirement system would reduce household retirement saving.

But whatever the motives, amassing reserves has consequences for monetary policy. The central bank must choose between two broad alternative means of funding the acquisition of foreign reserve assets—unsterilized or sterilized intervention.

The first option consists in the sale by the central bank of domestic currency to buy foreign assets in the foreign exchange markets. This causes an equal increase in its foreign reserves and monetary base. The increase in the reserve money base (often referred to as "printing money") is potentially inflationary. Financing reserves accumulation without sterilization has a direct inflationary effect on the countries which adopt this practice. Russia, for instance, managed only very partial sterilization of its reserves accumulation by transferring its fiscal surpluses into a sovereign fund invested abroad. The price it paid for largely unsterilized accumulation was successive years of inflation rates well above its targeted level. In the first decade of the century, Russia experienced persistently high inflation, both in absolute terms and relative to the peer group of former Soviet economies. This failure to control inflation was all the more striking in a strongly deflationary global environment where single-digit inflation has prevailed for more than a decade even among Eastern Europe and Latin America countries with histories of high inflation.

The second funding option for a central bank intent on accumulating foreign reserves is to reduce its net domestic assets (NDA). This is known as "sterilization" and entails for the monetary authorities intervening in foreign exchange markets with matching open market operations that keep the monetary base—and, by extension, the rate of inflation—relatively stable. This operation frequently takes the form of selling low-yielding debt instruments to captive domestic investors. Other instruments include foreign exchange swaps and repurchase operations.

Sterilization may at first sight seem positive in delaying inflation and real exchange rate adjustment. In practice, however, sterilization has costs. The first of these is fiscal costs (the difference between the returns paid to domestic investors on sterilization instruments and the returns on the foreign government bonds into which the reserves are then invested). As mentioned by the IMF (2010b) there are also opportunity costs in terms of lost consumption and investment. By investing these reserves into safe assets—that is, government bonds mainly in the United States—the effect has been both to divert resources from the domestic economy and to soften the budget constraint of the receiving country namely the United States.

If sterilization is done through open market operations, this increases the level of domestic debt. For Steiner (2010: 10), policy makers might be tempted to reduce the nominal value of the debt through surprise inflation. Hence, increasing domestic debt aggravates the commitment problem of the central bank and inflation expectations.

Moreover, most of the countries practicing sterilization and reserve accumulation have relatively underdeveloped financial systems. In these conditions, central banks' preferred monetary policy instruments are to vary the level of compulsory reserves, which banks must hold against their deposits and to impose direct credit controls—rather than conducting open market operations, which require precisely the kind of mature domestic bond markets that are lacking in such countries. A vicious circle results in which this style of monetary policy further hinders the development of domestic financial markets, which in turn would enable the authorities in these countries to conduct more flexible and sophisticated monetary policies.

Aizenman and Glick (2008) found that in the 2000s the degree of international reserves sterilization considerably increased in emerging market countries, reflecting growing concerns about inflation. Obstfeld (2009: 47) notes that since 1997 local-currency bond markets not only have grown substantially but also have become more open to international investors. He quotes the World Bank (2008: 66) as reporting that "East Asian bond markets grew from $400 billion in 1997 to $1.6 trillion by end-September 2005." Obstfeld (2009: 54) remarks that when an emerging market country with an open capital account intervenes to prevent the appreciation of its currency by selling central bank domestic assets, this results in even more capital inflows and buildup of external reserves. Various countries have attempted to inhibit short-term capital inflows by means of tax and other administrative measures, but with limited successes (a good example being Brazil).

Aizenman and Glick (2008: 13) observe that in the period 2000–2006 in Asia reserve accumulation "primarily reflected current account surpluses, rather than large capital inflows." Equally countries with current account deficits but concerned by the effect of capital inflows on their currency have accumulated large external reserves. To illustrate this weak relation between the current account and reserve position, Borio and Disyatat (2011: 12) mentioned some examples from the previous decade:

> [T]he monetary authorities of Australia, Turkey and South Africa have accumulated foreign reserves in substantial amounts in the second half of the past decade in the context of persistent and sizeable current account deficits. Brazil's substantial accumulation of reserves since 2005 has taken place against the backdrop of both deficits and surpluses in its current account.

The incidental negative effects of accumulating foreign exchange reserves were well summarized by Dorrucci and McKay (2011: 24, table 3), and may be broken down into global, regional, and domestic effects, as set out in table 7.2.

Our concern here has to do with the effect of this accumulation of reserves on world inflation. In the 1970s following the breakup of the Bretton Woods system, a large literature emerged on the interrelationship between floating exchange rates, international reserves accumulation, and inflation. For instance Keran (1975) found that a 1 percent increase in world reserves translates over a three-year period into a 1 percent increase in world prices (his study was based on a survey of developed countries over the period 1962 to 1974). Heller (1976), with a larger country sample and survey period than Keran, found that a 10 percent increase in world reserves leads to a 5 percent increase in world prices with a lag of 2.5 to 4 years. Striking a more cautious note, Crockett and Goldstein (1976: 520) warn that the result magnitudes are uncertain as various variables are omitted such as inflationary expectations. Recent studies on the accumulation of reserves and its effect on inflation include Steiner's (2010) econometric analysis. His sample covers between 66 and 116 countries depending on the specification including both mature and developing economies (excluding small countries with populations of less than three million in 2000) for the period 1970 to 2006. Steiner's (2010: 20) results warned that dramatic increases in international reserves constitute a threat for monetary stability as sterilization instruments seem to have become less effective:

> The observation that sterilization is relatively low during the 2000s allows two concluding remarks. First, sterilization policies of central banks might be increasingly offset by private capital flows in a financially integrated world. Therefore the instrument of sterilization has become less effective. As a result, central banks might engage less in sterilization policies. Second since the recent accumulation of reserves is sterilized to a lower extent than in previous periods, its inflationary impact in the future might be larger.

Steiner further inquires whether the relation changes according to the level of inflation. Therefore running a new regression this time with a smaller sample disregarding all countries with an inflation level above 50 percent per year, he found that at this level of inflation the growth of international reserves significantly contributes to higher moderate inflation rates.

Accumulating large external reserves means seeking out safe financial assets. Starting in about 2000, the search for sound financial instruments led

TABLE 7.2

Medium-term distortions, costs, and risks of reserve accumulation beyond optimality thresholds.

	Distortions, costs, and risks
Global level	Reserve accumulation corresponds to a large-scale reallocation of capital flows organized by the public sector of the accumulating countries. This produces major distortions in the global economy and international financial markets and can have financial implications for: *Global liquidity conditions*, by possibly contributing to an artificially low yield environment *The potential for buildup of asset price bubbles*, to the extent that reserve accumulation is not sufficiently sterilized *Global exchange rate configurations*, including the risk of misalignments *Trade flows*, to the extent that reserve accumulation becomes the equivalent of a protectionist policy subsidizing exports and imposing a tariff on imports
Regional level	Reserve accumulation by a major economy in one region may contain currency appreciation in competitor countries in the same region when this is needed. This: *Constrains the degree of flexibility of the other currencies* in the region *May magnify capital flow volatility* in the region's other economies in a context of misaligned exchange rates
Domestic level	Reserve accumulation can: *Undermine a stability-oriented monetary policy* if the monetary policy of the anchor country is more expansionary than domestically required *Hamper the market-based transmission of monetary policy impulses* and *the development of the domestic financial market* Be *costly* as reserves have a relatively lower return and involve sterilization costs *Distort resource allocation, impede service sector development, and constrain consumption and employment* by unduly favoring the tradable sector to the detriment of the nontradable sector Affect *income distribution and consumption growth* by unduly damaging the household sector as a result of artificially low interest rates on deposits in a financially underdeveloped economy

Source: Dorrucci and McKay (2011: 24, table 3).

naturally to government bonds of the major high-income trading partners. In the long run, the recycling by exporting countries of sterilized reserve accumulations into the apparently risk-free instruments of consuming countries can create both inflationary and stabilization risks on a global scale stemming first from demand pressures (especially for primary resources) and from the acute fiscal problems discussed in chapter 4. Governments issuing international reserve currencies like the United States are able to borrow more cheaply than would otherwise be the case. But this privilege can easily lead to over-indebtedness. In the case of the United Kingdom and sterling, the trigger for this was the First World War. An obvious contemporary example is the euro, which—as the Harvard economist Kenneth Rogoff has noted—was conceived by its instigators as a competing reserve currency for the dollar and "succeeded" only too well in the sense that it facilitated excessive credit expansion in the currency area's peripheral countries without the discipline of a "single" fiscal authority, which the Eurozone notoriously lacks. This absence of a central fiscal authority for all Eurozone countries was supposed to be corrected by the introduction of stringent fiscal rules in the Maastricht Treaty, but Sargent (2010: 36) points out that these fiscal rules lost all credibility when France and Germany failed to respect them; they "lost the moral authority to say that they were leading by example."

Since the dollar succeeded the pound sterling as the international reserve currency, many central banks and institutions hold U.S. debt as backing for their currencies. Like the United Kingdom before the First World War, the United States is financing many countries' trade surpluses. But what at first might seem a gift to the United States —the exchange of real goods for government bonds—revealed itself to be poisoned. The great bust of 2007–8 and ensuing recession caused the government budget deficit to explode. This situation was made worse by the previous Bush administration's "money-no-object" attitude to foreign wars and domestic entitlements—an attitude made possible by the dollar's "safe haven" status. As for the countries practicing various form of mercantilism—that is, accumulating the store of value rather than the goods—these countries could end up finding that the store of value gets debased.

Chapter 1 gave a historical perspective on the decline of sterling and its replacement as the global reserve currency by the dollar. In the pre–World War I heyday of the sterling-centered gold standard, not only did large numbers of countries use sterling as a means of payment and reserve asset, but their central banks had a strong interest in assisting the Bank of England in the running of the gold standard by providing liquidity and bullion in times of crisis. It follows that a well-established reserve asset will not be lightly forsaken—and then only when a credible alternative reserve currency is available. This is relevant for the present prospect of the dollar losing the dominant share of the global reserve currency business, which it has had since the mid-twentieth century.

The interwar experience of sterling suggests that the shift to short-term indebtedness from being a global creditor (with the shock of WWI also impairing the United Kingdom's net external asset position) was the single most important factor in the currency's loss of reserve asset status—a process that culminated in the further increase in U.K. indebtedness to the United States as a result of WWII.

A second factor was the loss of dominance in global trade and trade finance, which was both cause and effect of the erosion of sterling's reserve currency status. This development was aggravated by the U.K. authorities' key postwar economic policy decision—in 1925—to return to the gold standard and sterling's prewar parity with the dollar. The loss of external competitiveness and domestic economic weakness brought about by this highly deflationary move was in turn exacerbated by the mercantilist policies of the United States (and other key trading partners such as France) of hoarding gold and sterilizing balance of payments surpluses.

The parallels with the predicament of the United States in the early twenty-first century are not difficult to spot: a loss of competitiveness relative to large new global economic players pursuing mercantilist policies (China above all, of course) and dire government indebtedness. These two problems are closely linked. China's relentless accumulation of international reserves is heavily concentrated in U.S. government debt (reflecting the depth and liquidity of the market in U.S. Treasuries—another key factor in the dollar's attraction as a reserve asset).

Just as the shock of WWI fundamentally altered financial linkages between countries and led to the eclipse of sterling as the global reserve asset, so a U.S. government debt crisis would remove the risk-free benchmark at the heart of the present global financial system and cast the whole world financially adrift. It is worth recalling that it took over three decades and the shocks of two world wars to complete the process of replacing one global reserve currency with another—and this despite the availability of a credible replacement in the form of the dollar. The ability of China to provide a replacement reserve currency in the twenty-first century depends on utterly imponderable political change in that country while the credentials of other candidates—in particular the euro—would themselves be impaired by the financial and economic fallout from a crisis in the U.S. Treasury market (even on the ambitious assumption that the Eurozone meanwhile succeeds in resolving its own internal structural flaws).

RESERVE CURRENCY AND INTERNATIONAL MONETARY COOPERATION

The global financial crisis of 2007–8 highlighted the price to be paid for neglect of external equilibrium—or, put another way, toleration of ballooning global imbalances, which, in turn, led to such acute financial stresses borne of surging credit-fueled consumption. That price could extend well beyond undermining price stability—the immediate subject of this book—to bring down the entire international monetary and financial system.

Managing and minimizing this risk requires much more intense and effective international cooperation. In the precrisis good times, governments had no incentive to pursue such cooperation. As pointed out by Dorrucci and McKay (2011), the incentive was weakest of all in those countries that were running the largest external deficits and surpluses since an agreeable by-product of those imbalances was an economic expansion that exceeded trend rates of growth while not being accompanied by rising inflation.

This outcome seems like an instance of the familiar phenomenon of political short-termism. In other words, governments are unlikely to trade off the short-term domestic outcomes (price stability and buoyant employment) that generate the greatest political dividends against international arrangements designed to sustain such positive trends in the long run by stabilizing savings and investment (current account) positions and capital flows. Only when crisis hits will the incentive for international cooperation improve. This could be seen in the aftermath of the events of the autumn of 2008 (centered on the failure of Lehman Brothers). Even as world leaders played the blame game, with most claiming that the crisis had been "made in America" while U.S. politicians pointed the finger at Chinese exchange rate manipulation, international cooperation was enhanced—notably through the G20 Forum.

Yet national leaders signing communiqués on pursuing desirable policies is sham cooperation. Commitments to new approaches—for example, to the regulation of banks and financial markets—are worthless unless countries back such declarations by willingness to submit to multilateral enforcement mechanisms.

Of course, such mechanisms already exist—principally, the WTO for resolving trade disputes and, in the sphere of finance and economics, which is now the main area of crisis management, the Articles of Agreement of the

IMF. But in the years leading up to 2007–8 crisis, the IMF's Articles were in effect sidelined and the IMF itself (especially in its surveillance role) made redundant by the policies of its major member countries. As Rajan (2008: 114) emphasized, before the "phoenix rebirth" of the IMF in the midst of the unfolding euro crisis, only poor countries were listening to the IMF as mature economies saw "themselves as more sovereign than others, and their politicians brook no interference in their own domestic policies, while being fully prepared to use multilateral agencies to intervene in the domestic policies of others," while at the same time reserve accumulation by emerging market countries was designed at least in part to avoid having to submit themselves to IMF conditionality.

The original Bretton Woods architecture was designed to reconcile economic security (for which national governments are accountable to their citizens) with the opportunities and risks of economic activity across borders. But countries have in practice retreated from the insurance against those risks provided by the IMF's policy surveillance capacity and, above all, by the pooling of reserves in the IMF which the IMF can then lend to its members facing external financing crunches. Insurance has been replaced by self-insurance.

In the case of the mature economies—the United States, Japan, and EU member states—this has taken the form of ignoring or censoring the IMF's policy recommendations, with the Bush administration going as far as refusing to allow the U.S. financial sector to be scrutinized by the IMF under procedures devised in the light of the Asian and Russian crises of 1997–98. Such behavior, which contained an implicit claim of immunity against future crises, was emulated by China and several other emerging countries—which also took this self-insurance approach one crucial step further by accumulating vast international reserve holdings.

This strategy began as a response to the "Asian crisis." As we saw, piling up foreign exchange reserves is a way of insuring against the risk of the kind of sudden reversal of capital flows and huge exchange rate volatility seen in 1997. Reserves hoarding by China and the commodity-exporting countries has been preferred to the more efficient alternative of relying on the collective insurance offered by the IMF for reasons of sovereign self-sufficiency: while quotas and voting shares were (very modestly) amended (2008 Amendment on Voice and Participation effective on March 3, 2011), the IMF remained controlled by the so-called advanced countries, namely the G7 countries (see table 7.3).

Rajan (2008: 114) noted that more governance reform would be needed for international collaboration to resume using the IMF as a vehicle, and

TABLE 7.3

Quota and voting shares before and after implementation of reforms agreed in 2008 and 2010 (in percentage shares of total IMF quota).

	Quota shares		Voting shares	
	Pre-Singapore[a]	Post–2010 Reform[b]	Pre-Singapore[a]	Post–2010 Reform[b]
I. Advanced economies	61.6	57.7	60.6	55.3
G7 advanced economies	46.0	43.4	45.1	41.2
United States	17.4	17.4	17.0	16.5
Japan	6.2	6.5	6.1	6.1
Germany	6.1	5.6	6.0	5.3
France	5.0	4.2	5.0	4.0
United Kingdom	5.0	4.2	5.0	4.0
II. Emerging market and developing countries	38.4	42.3	39.4	44.7
Brazil	1.4	2.3	1.4	2.2
China	3.0	6.4	2.9	6.0
India	2.0	2.8	1.9	2.6
Russia	2.8	2.7	2.7	2.6
Total (I + II)	100.0	100.0	100.0	100.0

Source: IMF Finance Department.

a. Shares prior to the first round of ad hoc quota increased for China, Korea, Mexico, and Turkey, which was agreed during the annual meetings in Singapore in September 2006.

b. Projected shares that reflect quota increases agreed at the conclusion of the 14th General Review of Quotas. Basic votes are calculated as a fixed percentage (5.502 percent) of total votes (provided there are no fractional votes) in the Voice and Participation amendment.

in particular the removal of the "archaic prerogatives" of its American and European members:

> The IMF and the World Bank will need substantial governance reform—not just a realignment of voting quotas with economic importance today, but also the free and transparent selection of their heads from the community of nations (rather than the World Bank being headed by an American and the IMF by an European, as is the custom today)—in order to truly be seen as an honest broker.

In the aftermath of the financial crash of 2008, this "substantial reform" started to be addressed—as related by Chwieroth (2010). G20 summits have replaced the G8, and this broader participation combined with the euro crisis to bring the issue of IMF governance reform to the fore. However, improving the legitimacy of the IMF is a necessary but not sufficient condition for avoiding dangerous imbalances. It would not in itself remove the underlying drive for export-led growth fueled by managed exchange rates to maintain competitiveness. That drive hinged on China's providing "vendor finance"—above all to the United States, not only because of the importance of the United States as a market for its exports, but mainly given that the United States issues the most credible reserve currency. Events have shown, however, that the sustainability of this international monetary system depends also on the borrowers (i.e., reserve currency issuers) preventing the consequent domestic financial imbalances—i.e., excess debt—from becoming unsustainable.

In other words, as long as the United States and other reserve-issuing countries are willing and able to take on more debt to finance imports from the lending country, the "show can go on"—that is, the export-led growth strategy can be continued, resulting in current account surpluses. But what if the debt of the reserve issuer becomes unsustainable? This is not such a far-fetched scenario. Warnock (2010) in "How Dangerous Is U.S. Government Debt?" describes the pressures on US long-term interest rates and how the Eurozone crisis provided a short-term reprieve.

Default—whether explicit or (through inflation) implicit—could take place, resulting in the reserve currency countries being at the center of large shocks with dire consequences for the entire international monetary and financial system. Since the initial path of least resistance after the crash was to offset private-sector deleveraging with fiscal loosening, sovereign debt became the epicenter of the global crisis. The resulting imperative of fiscal adjustment, even if pulled off (very uncertain at time of writing), is not the same as a cure—without which the calamitous cycle will sooner or later resume. Successive crises—quite apart from their individual ravages—could easily end up discrediting altogether the free flow of goods and capital. As extensively analyzed by Obstfeld and Taylor (2004: 259), "open capital markets allow countries to exploit the opportunities for risk-sharing and intertemporal smoothing that would be closed off under autarky"; but they also involve the risk of crisis, the costs of which—unemployment, foregone growth, social instability—may be perceived as excessive compared to the benefits (Bhagwati, 1998; Rodrik, 2006).

From self-insurance to autarky is but a small step. While the literature is still debating on the benefits of financial openness for growth, most empirical studies agree on having found a positive effect of trade openness on economic growth. Moreover as pointed out by Obstfeld and Taylor (2004: 271),

> [F]oreign capital inflows, should broaden the financial market, open up a large pool of foreign savings to fund domestic investment, and ease provision of the trade credit needed to grease the wheels of commerce. In turn, many studies have shown that incomes and growth rates are improved by higher levels of financial development, higher levels of investment, and higher levels of trade.

Therefore imposing widespread protectionism and capital controls are like the cure that kills the patient—the patient in question being the world economy and the prospect for spreading prosperity and lifting millions out of poverty.

A first practical step to prevent this outcome—while also remedying the situation where foreign exchange reserve accumulation has resulted in an extremely hazardous soft budget constraint for the United States and other mature economies while volatile cross-border capital flows have created havoc in several emerging market countries—would be an international agreement on reserves management.

We have already noted two motives for building international reserves: precautionary and nonprecautionary ("mercantilist"). As far as the precautionary motive is concerned, the IMF (2010b) has proposed approaches to temper the volatility of cross-border capital flows by monitoring capital movements and reinforcing transparency and clarity of data on gross capital flows as well as developing a multilateral framework for managing capital flows. As for the nonprecautionary motive, the IMF (2010b:16) rightly pointed out that "protracted one sided intervention does impose a negative externality on the International Monetary System, and solutions are needed to induce countries to internalize this cost." Solutions whether voluntary and/or involving penalties therefore should be sought, but the task seems enormous as it would require a common understanding of the risks for the world economy and an international consensus.

It follows that to have any chance of success, any new arrangements for international monetary cooperation should not run counter to governments' natural priority to pursue domestic growth agendas. Hence the specific features of my own conclusion—that the best way forward would be a binding new rule on the management of countries' foreign exchange reserves. The problem is that no countries—and especially the principal actors, the United States and China—will in practice bow to the international rule of financial law in preference to what they reckon to be their domestic economic and social priorities. The key therefore is to go with the grain of countries' existing preferences and incentives, while in the process equipping the IMF to deal better with future economic imbalances.

An even more important detail than how reserves are invested is how their acquisition is funded—either by naked money printing or, as in the central case of China, by so-called sterilization. The first option, with Russia being a notable practitioner, is internationally responsible (even if unwittingly so) since imbalances are corrected by the resulting inflation—which, however, makes this approach domestically irresponsible (in this perspective, the credit bust of 2008 looked like a blessing in disguise for the millions of poor people in Russia in that it induced the authorities to focus much more seriously on controlling inflation). The opposite holds for the Chinese way of sterilization, which, because it controls inflation benefiting the poor, also prevents the exchange rate from appreciating in real terms, thereby entrenching external imbalances.

One approach might be to say that the solution is to be found not in the ideas of macroeconomists or the related macroeconomic policies, but rather in better "micro" regulation of financial institutions and markets to prevent the recurrence of bubbles. Regulatory improvements, however, will have the desired effects only if bolstered by a sound macroeconomic foundation. The optimal solution might be that the whole world should adopt inflation targeting regimes operated by independent central banks with freely floating currencies.

But instead of ending there and suggesting that we should simply wait for the day when China and other surplus countries are ready to embrace such an approach (having at last improved their fiscal, financial, and monetary institutions), we should consider how the insights studied in the previous chapters could be used to help overcome the hesitations of surplus countries or, most interesting of all, give rise to new strategies for achieving a more balanced world economy.

The "regime change" concept could be realized in a new way. There would be a new global economic compact. Like its predecessor at Bretton Woods, originally based on agreements between the United States and the United Kingdom—at that time the two most important countries in the global economy and finance (apart from the defeated powers)—the new Bretton Woods would hinge on an agreement between the United States and China, backed by the EU, Japan, and major emerging economies besides China itself.

Many scholars including Bordo and James (2010), Eichengreen (2009), and Schularick (2011) see the IMF's "new" job as being that of "reserves manager." Various options are considered such as transferring foreign reserves to the IMF if the current account surplus is in excess of 3 percent of GDP for three years or taxing foreign exchange reserves if they have been increasing for 3 years and the increase in the current years exceeded 3 percent of GDP. Most of these options, while easy to use, involve some "rules of thumb" based on arbitrary measures of percentages of GDP or foreign currency short-term liabilities, or the persistence of so-called dangerously large trade surpluses. Lately attempts have been made to provide a measure assessing the "optimal" level of reserves (Becker, Jeanne, Mauro, Ostry, and Ranciere, 2006). New metrics have been developed at the IMF to assess reserve adequacy attempting to encompass a maximum of factors allowing an assessment of the costs and benefits of holding reserves according to a country's level of economic development (IMF, 2011).

Once an "optimal" measure of international reserves is established and weighted to take into account each country's level of financial development, the rule should be automatic: when official foreign exchange reserves increase above the preagreed threshold, countries should automatically have to transfer the reserves surplus to the IMF, as highlighted by Eichengreen (2009: 8):

> This approach would have the advantage that it would not be necessary for IMF staff or anyone else to decide whether a surplus country was "manipulating" its currency or whether that currency was "fundamentally undervalued." The country would not have to be cited as in violation of its obligations as an IMF member.

The beauty of this scheme is that it would not threaten countries' sovereignty: they could continue to pursue the monetary and exchange rate regime of their choice. Without this feature, there would be zero chance of it being accepted by China or anyone else. The agreement would leave countries free to choose between the conventional inflation targeting regime and some alternative to their taste (such as the hybrid approach where both inflation and exchange rate are targeted)—but with a condition: if and when an agreed international reserves threshold had been passed, countries would have to transfer the reserves surplus to the IMF, now turned into a "reserves manager." Of course this assumes that all precautionary reserves countries trust the IMF to intervene to defend their exchange rate in situation of turbulence. It follows that for such a scheme to have any chance of getting off the ground, there would have to be changes in governance at the IMF (and to the extent relevant, in other international financial institutions) to give the surplus, reserve-accumulating countries like China a greater say in the lending of pooled reserves to assist countries experiencing payments difficulties—with accompanying inflationary risks—as a result of global imbalances.

But even after essential changes in IMF governance had given reserve-accumulating countries like China more influence over IMF decisions, this would not make them enthusiastic reserve sharers. The approach of the reserve-sharing threshold would therefore strengthen their incentive to boost domestic demand relative to export demand—something that is both in their own interest and in that of a more balanced and sustainable world economy. At the same time, this approach would be consistent with the recommendations of Wen (2011: 34) that the solution to the massive hoarding of China foreign reserves is to "(i) facilitate financial development in China and (ii) encourage Chinese firms to increase investment spending on capital goods both domestically and abroad." It might therefore be possible to secure the agreement of surplus countries like China to such a discipline.

Agreements and rules are not, however, the same as practical application. That was shown by the experience of the Scarce Currency Clause (SCC) in the IMF's Articles of Agreement, reflecting Keynes's concept of an international monetary system, which would discipline both surplus and deficit. The SCC proved inoperable for reasons well summed up by Eichengreen (2009: 7):

> Authorizing other members to invoke the SCC against a country running chronic surpluses and to impose tariffs and other restrictions on its exports would be politically charged and difficult for the Executive Board. Reflecting the difficulties of doing so in a collegial institution, the SCC has never been invoked.

All such difficulties arising from the enforcement of mutually agreed obligations would be more easily overcome if the agreements in question were inherently cooperative rather than disciplinary. This proposal to pool "excess" reserves would meet that test. Above all, the resulting incentive for surplus governments would be to avoid the reserve pooling commitment going live by accelerating the implementation of their own declared strategy of expanding investment targeting domestic demand. And to the extent that some additional reserve pooling did occur, this would equip a reformed IMF to cushion the fallout from future crises.

Adapting to Expectations

The toilers in academe are uniquely placed to develop
analyses of institutions and to educate the public and
policymakers about economic trade-offs. The essence
of our argument is that, at least in macroeconomics,
these toilers have delivered large returns to society
over the last several decades.
—Chari and Kehoe (2006: 26)

THE PRECEDING CHAPTERS have covered a wide variety of topics, perspectives, and debates surrounding inflation. It will be clear from this mosaic that I hold to a holistic understanding of monetary economics—in the sense that I see the phenomenon of inflation as arising out of a confluence of economic policies. Inflation is not the sole result of expansionary monetary policy, so cannot be controlled solely by running a tight monetary policy. The role of fiscal policy is central. Most important of all is the authorities' credibility, as this is the key to anchoring the public's expectations about the price level.

The economic researchers and thinkers who forged a new analytical synthesis of those factors created a foundation for the developments in practical policymaking that put an end to the Great Inflation of the 1970s. There is no facile assumption here that the research and ideas of academic economists have been the sole or decisive influence on more effective counter-inflationary policies as opposed to luck, timing, natural economic historical development, and improving productivity. Several senior monetary policy practitioners such as Laurence Meyer (2004) have downplayed the influence of contemporary economic research.[1] At the same time, it is beyond reasonable doubt that important changes in monetary policy preferences and design were informed, however indirectly or even unconsciously, by the

---

[1] Meyer was chairman of the President's Council of Economic Advisers from 2003 to 2005 and a governor of the Federal Reserve from 1996 to 2002.

research and reflection of a number of outstanding contemporary economists. The background contribution of academic research to policymaking was well captured in the account that the distinguished economist Alan Blinder (1997: 17) gave of his experience as a vice chairman of the Federal Reserve:

> Having looked at monetary policy from both sides now, I can testify that central banking in practice is as much art as science. Nonetheless, while practising this dark art, I have always found the science quite useful.

In this light, it is natural and urgent to consider how far those same economic insights could be applied to address the dire predicament of balance sheet recession and chronic stagnation characterizing large parts of the world economy since 2007. Contemporary policymakers have striven to stimulate demand despite huge debt overhangs and without undermining confidence in the future value of money or sustainability of the public finances and debt. As we have seen from several different angles, excess public debt is fraught with future inflation risk.

A good starting point for assessing possible applications to the contemporary Great Recession of the advances in macroeconomics associated with a past Great Inflation is to highlight two characteristics underlying the best thinking about inflation. These features are adaptation and remembering, and they operate in two related senses.

The first, and more straightforward, is that breakthroughs in monetary economics have been shaped by analysis of major historical episodes of inflation and revisiting classical monetary thought from the eighteenth century (Hume, Law, Cantillon, Smith) to the twentieth century (Keynes, Hayek, Friedman). Such creative adaptation of past wisdom and the lessons of experience is important for research in many other disciplines. A distinguishing feature of the learning trajectory of monetary economists and policymakers is its tendency to thrive in a nonlinear dynamic environment in which experiments occur at irregular intervals—and at considerable human cost, since the experiments in question are called hyper- or high inflations and financial crises. "Remembering" such episodes of inflation means recalling the economic thinking that underlay the policy response for the purpose of reapplying those lessons to different circumstances, times, and states of knowledge.

The insight that can be gained from real-life experiences of inflation and monetary policy responses is of course a far cry from the product of specially designed experiments in controlled laboratory conditions. As Robert Solow (1988: 311) remarked, "That [laboratory] option is not available to economists." As a result, economists have often relied instead on a priori reasoning:

> Hume derived his theoretical belief of neutrality from a priori reasoning, frequently presented in the form of thought experiments that Lucas finds "a little magical." (Velde, 2009b: 591)

This "magical" element can often lead to misspecified models and therefore to misguided policy. In general, there have been some notable advances in the use of experimentation in economics—as set out by List (2011) in his historical survey of social experiments dating back to the 1960s, and also as shown more recently by the application in certain fields of economics such as development economics of randomized controlled trials where various "interventions" or treatments are randomly applied to groups of people with the results compared to those for similar "control" groups that did not receive the intervention (Banerjee and Duflo, 2011). In monetary economics, however, only on rare occasions have economists had opportunities to make what might be recognized as experimental observations.

One such monetary experiment brings us to the second, and more subtle, way in which adaptation and remembering matter for monetary economics. The episode in question was related by Francois Velde (2009b) in "Chronicle of a Deflation Unforetold." In France in 1724, the monetary authorities decreased unexpectedly the money supply by 45 percent in order to reduce the price level. Velde (2009b: 592) described how this almost "real-world" experiment "did not support the neutrality of money." The analysis of this experiment underlines the role played by expectations in shaping future monetary policy:

> Alone they [expectations] cannot account for non-neutrality but could be important in combination with some other factor, and they were thought important by contemporary observers, including the government. A feature of the 1724 experiment is that the timing and magnitude of the reductions in money supply were not announced in advance, but the prior history of monetary policy must have shaped agents' expectations. (Velde, 2009b: 593)

In other words, what matters is not just economic researchers and policymakers recalling past inflationary experiences but also the active recollection—"remembering"—of the public, as this determines expectations about the likely future level of prices. It follows that monetary policy must be shaped in the light of those expectations. The literature on learning, and Evans and Honkapohja (2011: 43) in particular, emphasize "adaptive learning approaches, in which agents revise their forecasting model, or their choice of models, over time as new data become available." Monetary authorities learn over time how monetary systems based on fiat rather than commodity money work. Imperfect knowledge and understanding of events and structures result in conceptual flaws in economic models and consequently in monetary policies. This was well illustrated by Sargent's (2008: 16) account of the how the U.S. monetary authorities gradually "learned about inflation-unemployment dynamics after World War II."

For Marimon (2000: 406), the importance of Sargent's (1999) *The Conquest of American Inflation* lay in the way he made use of the rise and fall of U.S. inflation in the 1970s to the 1990s "for an exploration in dynamic economic theory" integrating the work of

> Sims (1988) and Chung (1990), who suggest how a government that adaptively learns from its Phillips curve experience may end up discovering a version of the natural rate theory.... King and Watson (1994), who show how different specifications of the unemployment-inflation trade-off (i.e., alternative pattern recognition procedures) can lead to different policy recommendations.... Kreps, who ... asks: "How should we (as economists) model dynamic choice behaviour, where the dynamics involve a process of adaptative learning?" (Kreps, 1999: 264). (Marimon, 2000: 406)

This "dynamic"—of expectations being adapted in the light of the lessons learned from experience—allows Sargent to show how regime shifts can hinge on rational expectations and therefore do not have to owe their existence to the invention of new policies or "changes in ... states of the system, underlying parameters, or exogenous changes in beliefs (sunspots)" (Marimon, 2000: 406).

Inflation targeting emerged from this process as the most widely used and effective regime—that is, a "working" nominal anchor for a rules-based monetary policy framework. By being defined "directly in terms of inflation, [this anchor] avoids the potential instability problems associated with alternatives such as money growth that are only indirectly linked to inflation" (Clarida, Gali, and Gertler, 1999: 1700). Sargent (2008: 25) reckoned that the adoption of an inflation target as the nominal anchor was justified "as a device that compensates for model misspecification."

How might inflation targeting be usefully applied to the post-2007 problems of recession and stagnation against a background of excessive indebtedness? The most conspicuous monetary policy development in this period aimed to overcome the so-called zero bound of nominal interest rates by means of direct central bank purchases of the domestic government's bonds and other domestic securities. The huge expansion of central bank balance sheets entailed by this policy of "quantitative easing" was designed to create a stimulatory monetary environment offsetting the contractionary effect of tighter fiscal policy. This fiscal tightening was necessitated, in turn, by the surge in public debt that resulted mainly as the mirror image of private-sector deleveraging but was also aggravated by the socialization of bank losses—and all this against a background of imprudent procyclical loosening of fiscal positions during the preceding boom years owing to hikes in discretionary spending on items such as welfare and defense.

"Debt reduction ultimately requires primary budget surpluses": this was the unsurprising conclusion of an IMF (2012) review of six historical cases of highly indebted countries—the United Kingdom (1918), the United States (1946), Belgium (1983), Canada (1995), Italy (1992), and Japan (1997). Shifting to a primary surplus requires some combination of lower expenditure or higher revenue. Increased tax revenue can, in turn, be achieved either by tax rises or faster growth. The ideal result in this situation would be an "expansionary fiscal adjustment." Research in this area based on a study of twenty-one OECD countries from 1970 to 2010 has shown that adjustments based on spending cuts (as opposed to tax rises) are

> less contractionary and are more likely to lead to a permanent stabilization or a reduction of the debt to GDP ratio; second, in some cases spending based adjustments have been associated with no recession at all, even in the short run, thus producing an expansionary fiscal adjustment. (Alesina and Ardagna, 2012: 2)

These authors emphasize that this is especially true if the fiscal adjustment is carried out in parallel with other reforms such as labor market liberalization:

> These accompanying reforms may signal a "change of regime," that is a policy switch towards a more market friendly policy stance, less taxation, liberalizations etc., perhaps in some cases agreed upon with the unions. These results would be consistent with what we also find, namely a very different reaction of business confidence during spending-based and tax-based adjustments, much more negative in the latter. (Alesina, Favero, and Giavazzi, 2012: 5)

This combination of fiscal tightening and growth proved elusive in reality. In most cases, fiscal tightening was self-defeating by undermining growth and causing, in turn, a further deterioration in the public finances. Given the increasing size of both central banks' balance sheets and government' indebtedness, it will be only a matter of time before inflationary expectations rise. The specific expectation is that the mutually reinforcing "doom loop" of high indebtedness and falling or stagnant output will induce authorities to inflate the debt away. At that point, the fiscal limit to monetary policy would have been reached. As for what could trigger a buyers' strike in the government debt market of mature economies, Reinhart and Rogoff (2009: x) provided this warning:

> Highly indebted governments, banks or corporations can seem to be merrily rolling along for an extended period, when *bang!*—confidence collapses, lenders disappear, and a crisis hits.

In other words, the *bang* can happen any time, and once that moment is reached, the road to deficit bond financing will be closed, leaving no alternative to inflating the debt away. In that same celebrated historical study of financial crises, Reinhart and Rogoff (2009: 189) presciently remarked,

> [W]e will see if inflation resurfaces again in the years following the financial crisis of the late 2000s, particularly as government debt stocks mount, fiscal "space" (the capacity to engage in fiscal stimulus) erodes, and particularly if a rash of sovereign defaults in emerging markets eventually follows.

This reference to possible sovereign defaults by emerging market countries reflected the assumption that developed country governments borrow in their own currencies, giving them the last-resort option of avoiding explicit default by inflating away their debt—an option not open to developing countries whose sovereign bonds are often denominated in foreign currency, or for that matter to countries that use the euro and thereby have given up monetary sovereignty.

The best defense against such a disaster is inflationary expectations remaining low. In addition to the deflationary realities of persistent deleveraging, high unemployment, and spare capacity, the key to restrained inflationary expectations is the track record of successful inflation targeting—or, at least, stably low inflation—during previous years. The U.K. authorities tried to take advantage of this stock of credibility by engineering an inflation surprise: while sticking to the official inflation target of 2 percent, much higher inflation was tolerated. With the BOE's policy rate kept at 0.5 percent, interest rates remained deeply negative in real terms. The resulting transfer from savers to debtors was tacitly justified on the grounds that the latter were in a large majority and only by supporting demand by limiting borrowers' debt service costs—and by the gradual effect of this inflation in reducing the real value of the their obligations—could growth resume for the benefit of all.

The risk of this approach—namely, of maintaining an inflation targeting regime under false pretences—lies in the consequences of failure. That is, were inflationary expectations to become unanchored, the BOE would be wanting to reverse QE and put up interest rates just at the time when the government would be seeking new buyers for its bonds (including more QE purchases) to replace those investors who had started to flee the gilts market. This scenario would in effect mean that the previous stealth policy had been exposed; and, as a result, it would be that much more difficult to restore credibility thereafter. A vicious bout of stagflation would be in the cards.

It follows that for the sake of credibility, it would be more advisable to announce an explicit increase in the inflation target. As argued in chapter 4, increasing the inflation target as a way of preserving a monetary policy framework oriented toward long-term price stability in the face of a fiscal shock would amount to an expedient to ease government budget constraints while reducing the consequent risks by incorporating this strategy into a transparent IT regime rather than through the back door.

The central objection to this approach is that the credibility of inflation targeting depends on never altering the target. For, on this view, after a first change in the target, the public would assume that other changes could come in quick and unpredictable succession. This is not, however, the way in which credibility is understood by the best thinkers on monetary economics. Alan Blinder (2000: 1422), while pointing that there is "no generally agreed-upon definition" of credibility, offers his "own definition [that] involves matching deeds to words: A central bank is credible if people believe it will do what it says."

The lesson of the monetary thinking and policy practice that we have seen in this book is that inflation targeting can be used to anchor expectations. It seems far more dangerous to continue proclaiming a target while in reality ignoring it than to make a single alteration in that target—and in so doing, preserving transparency and credibility. By making a conditional commitment to keep interest rates low on a two- to three-year horizon, Ben Bernanke at the U.S. Fed implicitly signaled an increase in the level of inflation that the Fed would tolerate until unemployment fell. The fact that the Fed does not have a mandate to target inflation prevented it from following to the letter the excellent advice offered by Michael Woodford ahead of the Fed's annual Jackson Hole retreat in 2011:

Mr Bernanke can and should use his speech today to explain how his policy intentions are conditional upon future developments. A clarification could help the economy in two ways. First he could signal that a temporary increase in inflation will be allowed, before policy tightening is warranted. This would stimulate spending by lowering real interest rates. Second, specifying the size of any permanent price level increase would avoid an increase in uncertainty about the long run price level. This in turn would ward off an increase in inflation risk premiums that might otherwise counteract the desirable effect of the increase in near term inflation expectations.

The most serious danger of all stems from the reality that QE has weakened central bank independence from the fiscal authorities (Allen, 2012) while also failing to deliver the desired effect of reigniting economic growth. This is not surprising as

> when dealing with major financial busts monetary policy addresses the symptoms rather than the underlying causes of the slow recovery. It alleviates the pain, but masks the illness. It gains time, but makes it easier for policymakers to waste it. (Borio, 2011: 6)

As a result, central banks may come under irresistible political pressure to take QE a step further by, for example, cancelling some or all of the government bonds purchased by the central bank or direct central bank financing of fiscal expenditure. Until that point is reached, central banks could always attempt to reverse QE once inflationary pressures were felt. That process may be fraught—as the central bank would be selling government bonds into a falling market—but, to repeat, the attempt could be made (and, in any case, the bonds could simply be held to maturity, at which point the government would have to repay without any central bank refinancing). Put another way, QE in its initial form represented only a temporary increase in the monetary base. Were this to become a permanent increase, then the Rubicon would have been definitively crossed. In that case, the unanchoring of inflationary expectations would only be a matter of "when," not "if."

In a system of fiat money, credibility—that is, the principle that "a promise is a promise"—is the anchor. Credibility could not long survive straightforward monetary financing of the public debt. In that environment, governments will be caught, before they have time to realize it, in the spiral of higher and higher inflation, as the "hot potato" of inflated currency will be passed from hand to hand at an ever faster pace, while the "barbarous relic"—gold—in parallel with other durable assets will be seen once again as the safe haven against the profligacy of extravagant government spending.

In the midst of the Great Recession political necessity justified the introduction of discretionary measures—so-called unconventional monetary policy that "temporarily" replaced the monetary policy rule. This has created an uncertain world where large and snowballing levels of public debt might soon, under political expediency, force the central bank to act as the banker of the government. There is nothing new about central banks being called to the rescue in times of profound crisis. The problem occurs only when the expectations are that monetary policy will

> manage the economy, restore full employment, ensure strong growth and preserve price stability. This, in fact, is a taller order than many believe, and one that central banks alone cannot deliver. To pretend otherwise risks undermining their credibility and public support in the longer run. Borio (2011: 11)

Indeed, monetary policy on its own can do nothing in the long term to bring order to the public finances and to increase real income; but high public debt can seriously increase inflation expectations. In other words, and to repeat the formulation put on display in chapter 2, money is the *droit du seigneur*, but the *seigneur* should not put his hand in the till. No sleight of hand can prevent the loss of credibility, and from this flows great distress.

Lest this should seem like scaremongering, I would maintain that the worst dangers should be vigilantly kept in the clearest possible view, for which the reward may be the consolation and relief of the dawn that follows a troubled night:

> If we shadows have offended,
> Think but this, and all is mended,
> That you have but slumber'd here
> While these visions did appear.
> And this weak and idle theme,
> No more yielding but a dream,
> Gentles do not reprehend.
> If you pardon, we will mend.
> —Shakespeare, *A Midsummer Night's Dream*, Act 5, Scene 2

References

Acemoglu, D., S. Johnson, P. Querubin, and J. A. Robinson (2008). "When does policy reform work? The case of central bank independence." *NBER Working Paper Series* 14033 (May).

Aggarwal, V. and B. Granville (2003). *Sovereign Debt: Origins, Management, and Restructuring.* London, RIIA.

Ahmed, S., A. Levin, and B. A. Wilson (2004). "Recent US macroeconomic stability: Good policies, good practices, or good luck?" *Review of Economics and Statistics* 86(3): 824–32.

Aizenman, J. (2007). "Large hoarding of international reserves and the emerging global economic architecture." *NBER Working Paper Series* 13277 (July).

Aizenman, J., M. D. Chinn, and H. Ito (2008). "Assessing the emerging global financial architecture: Measuring the trilemma's configurations over time." *NBER Working Paper Series* 14533 (December).

Aizenman, J. and R. Glick (2008). "Sterilization, monetary policy, and global financial integration." *NBER Working Paper Series* 13902 (March).

Aizenman, J. and Y. Jinjarak (2008). "The US as the 'demander of last resort' and its implications on China's current account." *NBER Working Paper Series* 14453 (October).

Aizenman, J. and N. Marion (2009). "Using inflation to erode the US public debt." *NBER Working Paper Series* 15562 (December).

Alesina, A. (1988). "Macroeconomics and politics." *NBER Macroeconomics Annual* 3: 13–52.

——— (1989). *Why Are Stabilizations Delayed?* Cambridge, Mass., National Bureau of Economic Research.

Alesina, A. and S. Ardagna (2012). "The design of fiscal adjustments." *NBER Working Paper Series* 18423 (September).

Alesina, A. and A. Drazen (1991). "Why are stabilizations delayed?" *American Economic Review* 81 (December): 1170–88.

Alesina, A., C. Favero, and F. Giavazzi (2012). "The output effect of fiscal consolidations." *NBER Working Paper Series* 18336 (August).

Alesina, A. and L. H. Summers (1993). "Central bank independence and macroeconomic performance: Some comparative evidence." *Journal of Money, Credit and Banking* 25 (May): 151–62.

Allais, M. (1975). "Le Concept de Monnaie, la Création de la Monnaie et de Pouvoir d'Achat par le Mécanisme de Crédit et ses Implications." *Essais en l'Honneur de Jean Marchal*, tome 2. Paris, Editions Cujas: 106–45.

Allen, W. A. (1999). *Inflation Targeting: The British Experience.* Handbooks in Central Banking Lecture Series No. 1. London, Centre for Central Banking Studies, Bank of England.

——— (2012). "Government debt management and monetary policy in Britain since 1919." *Threat of Fiscal Dominance? BIS Papers* 65 (May): 15–50. http://www.bis.org /publ/bppdf/bispap65b_rh.pdf.

Allen, W. A. and G. E. Wood (2006). "Defining and achieving financial stability." *Journal of Financial Stability* 2: 152–72.

Ames, B., W. Brown, S. Devarajan, and A. Izquierdo (2001). "Macroeconomic policy and poverty reduction." Washington, D.C., IMF.

Andersen, P. and D. Gruen (1995). "Macroeconomics policies and growth." *Research Discussion Paper, Reserve Bank of Australia* 9507 (October).

Andres, J. and I. Hernando (1999). "Does inflation harm economic growth." *The Costs and Benefits of Price Stability.* M. S. Feldstein, ed. Chicago, University of Chicago Press: 315–41.

Åslund, A. (1995). *How Russia Became a Market Economy.* Washington, D.C., Brookings Institution.

——— (1997). *Russia's Economic Transformation in the 1990s.* London, Pinter.

Athukorala, P. and J. Menon (1994). "Pricing to market behaviour and exchange rate pass through in Japanese exports." *The Economic Journal* 104 (423): 271–81.

Auerbach, A. J., J. Gokhale, and L. J. Kotlikoff (1991). "Generational accounting: A meaningful alternative to deficit accounting." *NBER Book Series Tax Policy and the Economy*, 5. D. Bradford, ed. Cambridge, Mass., MIT Press: 55–110.

Averbug, A. (2002). "The Brazilian economy in 1994–1999: From the real plan to inflation targets." *The World Economy* 25(7): 925–44.

Backus, D. and J. Driffill (1985). "Rational expectations and policy credibility following a change in regime." *Review of Economic Studies* 52(2): 211–21.

Bagehot, W. (1876). *Lombard Street.* New York, Scribner.

Bailey, M. (1956). "The welfare costs of inflationary finance." *Journal of Political Economy* 64(2): 93–110.

Baldacci, E. and M. S. Kumar (2010). "Fiscal deficits, public debt and sovereign bond yields." *IMF Working Paper* WP/10/184 (August).

Ball, L. (1992). "Why does high inflation raise inflation uncertainty." *Journal of Monetary Economics* 29: 371–88.

——— (1993). "The dynamics of high inflation." *NBER Working Paper Series* 4578 (December).

——— (1994). "What determines the sacrifice ratio?" *Monetary Policy.* G. N. Mankiw, ed. Chicago, University of Chicago Press: 155–93.

——— (2006). "Has globalization changed inflation?" *NBER Working Paper Series* 12687 (November).

Ball, L. and S. Cecchetti (1990). "Inflation and uncertainty at long and short horizons." *Brookings Papers on Economic Activity* 21: 215–54.

Ball, L. and G. N. Mankiw (1995). "Relative-price changes as aggregate supply shocks." *Quarterly Journal of Economics* 110 (February): 161–93.

Ball, L., G. N. Mankiw, and R. Reiss (2005). "Monetary policy for inattentive economies." *Journal of Monetary Economics* 52(4): 703–25.

Ball, L., G. N. Mankiw, and D. Romer (1988). "The New Keynesian economics and the output-inflation trade off." *Brookings Papers on Economic Activity* 1: 1–65.

Ball, L. and N. Sheridan (2005). "Does inflation targeting matter?" *The Inflation-Targeting Debate*, 32. B. Bernanke and M. Woodford, eds. Chicago, University of Chicago Press: 249–82.

Banerjee, A. and E. Duflo (2011). *Poor Economics: A Radical Rethinking of the Way to Fight Global Poverty*. New York, PublicAffairs.

Bank for International Settlements (BIS) (1998, June 8). "68th annual report, 1st April 1997–31st March 1998." Basel.

———— (1999, May). "Central Bank Survey of Foreign Exchange and Derivatives Market Activity, 1998." Basel.

———— (2000, June 5). "70th Annual Report, 1st April 1999–31st March 2000." Basel.

Barro, R. J. (1974). "Are government bonds net wealth?" *Journal of Political Economy* 82(6): 1095–1117.

———— (1979). "On the determination of the public debt." *Journal of Political Economy* 87(5): 940–71.

———— (1995). "Inflation and economic growth." *NBER Working Paper Series* 5326 (October).

———— (2002). *Nothing Is Sacred: Economic Ideas for the New Millennium*. Cambridge, Mass., MIT Press.

Barro, R. J. and S. Fischer (1976). "Recent developments in monetary theory." *Journal of Monetary Economics* 2 (April): 133–67.

Barro, R. J. and D. B. Gordon (1983). "A positive theory of monetary-policy in a natural rate model." *Journal of Political Economy* 91(4): 589–610.

Barsky, R. B. and J. Bradford DeLong (1991). "Forecasting pre–World War I inflation: The Fisher effect and the gold standard." *Quarterly Journal of Economics* 106(3): 815–36.

Basevi, G. and F. Giavazzi (1986). "Stabilization policies in an explosive economy." *European Economic Review* 30: 43–55.

Bass, K. (2010). "Testimony, hearing on the financial crisis." Financial Crisis Inquiry Commission. http://fcic-static.law.stanford.edu/cdn_media/fcic-testimony/2010-0113-Bass.pdf.

Batini, N. and A. Yates (2003). "Hybrid inflation and price level targeting." *Journal of Money, Credit, and Banking* 35(3): 283–300.

Bean, C. (2003). "Inflation targeting: The UK experience." *Bank of England Quarterly Bulletin* (Winter).

Becker, G. S. ([1956] 1993). "A proposal for free banking." *Free Banking*. L. H. White, ed. Aldershot, Elgar: 20–25.

Becker, T., O. Jeanne, P. Mauro, J. D. Ostry, and R. Ranciere (2006). "Country insurance: The role of domestic policies." *Discussion Paper, International Monetary Fund* (June).

Benjamin, D. K. and L. A. Kochin (1984). "War, prices, and interest rates: A martial solution to Gibson's paradox." In *A Retrospective on the Classical Gold Standard,*

1821–1931. M. D. Bordo and A. J. Schwartz, eds. Chicago, University of Chicago Press: 587–612.

Berg, C. and L. Jonung (1999). "Pioneering price level targeting: The Swedish experience 1931–1937." *Journal of Monetary Economics* 43: 525–51.

Berk, J. M., B. Bierut, and E. E. Meade (2011). "Member type and tenure effects in the Bank of England's MPC." Paper presented at the Conference of the Allied Social Science Associations, January 5–8, Chicago.

Bernanke, B. (2000). *Essays on the Great Depression*. Princeton, N.J., Princeton University Press.

——— (2005). "The global saving glut and the U.S. current account deficit." Sandridge Lecture at the Virginia Association of Economists, March 10, Richmond. www .federalreserve.gov/boarddocs/speeches/2005/200503102/default.htm.

Bernanke, B., M. Gertler, and S. Gilchrist (1998). "The financial accelerator in a quantitative business cycle framework." *NBER Working Paper Series* 6455 (March).

Bernanke, B. and H. James (1990). "The gold standard, inflation, and financial crisis in the great depression: An international comparison." *NBER Working Paper Series* 3488 (October).

Bernanke, B. S. and K. N. Kuttner (2005). "What explains the stock market's reaction to Federal Reserve policy?" *Journal of Finance* 60(3): 1221–57.

Bernanke, B., T. Laubach, F. S. Mishkin, and A. S. Posen (1999). *Inflation Targeting: Lessons from the International Experience*. Princeton, N.J., Princeton University Press.

Bernanke, B. and F. S. Mishkin (2007). "Inflation targeting: A new framework for monetary policy?" *Monetary Policy Strategy*. F. S. Mishkin, ed. Cambridge, Mass., MIT Press: 207–26.

Bernholz, P. (2003). *Monetary Regimes and Inflation: History, Economic and Political Relationships*. Cheltenham, UK, Edward Elgar.

Bhagwati, J. N. (1998). "Why free capital mobility may be hazardous to your health: Lessons from the latest financial crisis." Paper presented at the NBER Conference on Capital Controls, November 7, 1998, Cambridge, Mass. http://hdl.handle .net/10022/AC:P:8151.

Bhatia, R. J. (1960). "Inflation, deflation and economic development." *IMF Staff Papers* 8 (November): 101–14.

Black, F. (1970). "Banking in a world without money: The effects of uncontrolled banking." *Journal of Bank Research* 1: 9–20.

Blanchard, O., G. Dell'Ariccia, and P. Mauro (2010). "Rethinking macroeconomic policy." *IMF Staff Position Note* SPN/10/03.

Blank, R. and A. Blinder (1986). "Macroeconomics, income distribution, and poverty." *Fighting Poverty: What Works and What Doesn't*. S. Danziger and D. Weinberg, eds. Cambridge, Mass., Harvard University Press: 180–208.

Blank, R. and D. Card (1993). "Poverty, income distribution and growth: Are they still connected?" *Brookings Papers on Economic Activity* 2: 285–339.

Blinder, A. S. (1997). "What central bankers can learn from academics—and vice-versa." *Journal of Economic Perspectives* 11(2): 3–19.

—— (2000). "Central bank credibility: Why do we care? How do we build it?" *American Economic Review* 90: 1421–31.

—— (2010). "How central should the central bank be?" *Journal of Economic Literature* 48(1): 123–33.

Bloomfield, A. I. (1959). *Monetary Policy under the International Gold Standard*. New York, Federal Reserve Bank of New York.

Boke, J. (1996). "The foreign exchange management system in China, 1978–95." *China's Opening Door*. D. Wall, J. Boke, and Y. Xiangshuo, eds. London, Royal Institute of International Affairs: 61–91.

Bomfim, A. and G. D. Rudebusch (2000). "Opportunistic and deliberate disinflation under imperfect credibility." *Journal of Money, Credit, and Banking* 32(4): 707–21.

Boone, P. and S. Johnson (2010). "Will the politics of global moral hazard sink us again?" *The Future of Finance. The LSE Report*. London, London School of Economics and Political Science: 238–74.

Booth, A. (1987). "Britain in the 1930s: A managed economy?" *Economic History Review* 40(4): 499–522.

Bordo, M. D. (1981). "The classical gold standard: Some lessons for today." *Federal Reserve Bank of St. Louis Review* 64(5): 2–17.

—— (1983). "Some aspects of the monetary economics of Richard Cantillon." *Journal of Monetary Economics* 12: 235–58.

—— (2008). "An historical perspective on the crisis of 2007–2008." *NBER Working Paper Series* WP14569 (December).

Bordo, M. D. and T. A. Bayoumi (1996). "Getting pegged: Comparing the 1879 and 1925 gold resumptions." *NBER Working Paper Series* WP5497 (March).

Bordo, M. D., M. J. Dueker, and D. C. Wheelock (2008). "Inflation, monetary policy and stock market conditions." *NBER Working Paper Series* 14019 (May).

Bordo, M. D. and H. James (2010). "The past and future of IMF reform—A proposal." *The New International Monetary System*. C. Wyplosz, ed. London, Routledge: 9–28.

Bordo, M. D. and F. E. Kydland (1992). "The gold standard as a rule." *Federal Reserve Bank of Cleveland Working Paper* 9205.

Bordo, M. D. and J. S. Landon-Lane (2010). "The global financial crisis of 2007–08: Is it unprecedented?" *NBER Working Paper Series* 16589 (December).

Bordo, M. D. and H. Rockoff (1996). "The gold standard as a 'good housekeeping seal of approval.'" *Journal of Economic History* 56(2): 389–428.

Bordo, M. D. and A. J. Schwartz (1984) *A Retrospective on the Classical Gold Standard, 1821–1931*. Chicago, University of Chicago Press.

Borio, C. (2006). "Monetary and financial stability: Here to stay?" *Journal of Banking and Finance* 30(12): 3407–14.

—— (2011). "Central banking post-crisis: What compass for uncharted waters?" *BIS Working Papers* 353.

Borio, C. and P. Disyatat (2011). "Global imbalances and the financial crisis: Link or no link?" *BIS Working Papers* 346.

Borio, C., B. English, and A. Filardo (2003). "A tale of two perspectives: Old or new challenges for monetary policy?" *BIS Working Papers* 127.

Borio, C. and P. Lowe (2002). "Asset prices, financial and monetary stability: Exploring the nexus." *BIS Working Papers* 114.

Bowles, P. and B. Wang (2006). "Flowers and criticism: The political economy of the renminbi debate." *Review of International Political Economy* 13(2): 233–57.

Boycko, M. and A. Shleifer (1994). "The Russian restructuring and social assets." Paper presented at Russian Economic Reforms in Jeopardy, June 15–16, Stockholm School of Economics, Stockholm, Sweden.

Briault, C. (1995). "The costs of inflation." *Bank of England Quarterly Bulletin* 35 (February): 33–45.

Brock, P. L. (1984). "Inflationary finance in an open economy." *Journal of Monetary Economics* 14 (July): 37–53.

Brooks, R. and R. Tao (2003). "China's labor market performance and challenges." *IMF Working Paper* 210 (November).

Bruno, M. (1990). "High inflation and the nominal anchors of an open economy." *NBER Working Paper Series* 3518 (November).

——— (1993). *Crisis, Stabilization and Economic Reforms: Therapy by Consensus.* Oxford, Oxford University Press.

——— (1995). "Does inflation really lower growth." *Finance and Development* 32 (September): 35–38.

Bruno, M., G. Di Tella, R. Dornbusch, and S. Fischer, eds. (1988). *Inflation Stabilization: The Experience of Israel, Argentina, Brazil, Bolivia and Mexico.* Cambridge, Mass., MIT Press.

Bruno, M. and W. Easterly (1998). "Inflation crises and long-run growth." *Journal of Monetary Economics* 41: 3–26.

Bryant, J. (1980). "A model of reserves, bank runs, and deposit insurance." *Journal of Banking and Finance* 4(4): 335–44.

Buchanan, J. H. (2010). "The constitutionalization of money." *Cato Journal* 30(2): 251–58.

Buiter, W. (2002). "The fiscal theory of the price level: A critique." *The Economic Journal* 112(481): 459–80.

——— (2010). "Don't raise the inflation target, remove the zero bound on nominal interest rates instead." *Global Macro View Citigroup Global Markets* (March 5).

Bulir, A. (2001). "Income inequality: Does inflation matter." *IMF Staff Papers* 48(1).

Bullard, J. and J. W. Keating (1995). "The long run relationship between inflation and output in post war economies." *Journal of Monetary Economics* 36(3): 477–96.

Burdekin, R. C. K., A. T. Denzau, M. W. Keil, T. Sitthiyot, and T. Willett (2004). "When does inflation hurt economic growth? Different nonlinearities for different economies." *Journal of Macroeconomics* 26(3): 519–32.

Cagan, P. (1956). "The monetary dynamics of hyperinflation." *Studies in the Quantity Theory of Money.* M. Friedman, ed. Chicago, University of Chicago Press: 25–117.

Cagan, P. and W. J. Fellner (1983). "Tentative lessons from the disinflationary effort." *Brookings Papers on Economic Activity* 2: 603–8.

Calvo, G. A. (1978). "Optimal seigniorage from money creation: An analysis in terms of the optimum balance of payments deficit problem." *Journal of Monetary Economics* 4: 503–17.

——— (1998). "Varieties of capital-market crises." *The Debt Burden and Its Consequences for Monetary Policy.* G. Calvo and M. King, eds. London, Macmillan: 181–202.

Calvo, G. and L. Leiderman (1992). "Optimal inflation tax under precommitment: Theory and evidence." *American Economic Review* 82(1): 179–94.

Calvo, G., L. Leiderman, and C. Reinhart (1996). "Inflows of capital to developing countries in the 1990s." *Journal of Economic Perspectives* 10(2): 123–29.

Campbell, J. Y. and T. Vuolteenaho (2004). "Inflation illusion and stock prices." *American Economic Review* 94(2): 19–23.

Canzoneri, M., R. Cumby, and B. Diba (2011). "The interaction of monetary and fiscal policy." *Handbook of Monetary Economics.* B. M. Friedman and M. Woodford, eds. Amsterdam, North Holland: 935–99.

Cardoso, E. (1992). "Inflation and poverty." *NBER Working Paper Series* 4006 (March).

Cardoso, E. and A. Fishlow (1989). "Latin American economic development: 1950–1980." *NBER Working Paper* W3161 (November).

Cardoso, E. and A. Helwege (1995). *Latin America's Economy, Diversity, Trends and Conflicts.* Cambridge, Mass., MIT Press.

Cargill, T. F. and E. Parker (2004). "Price deflation, money demand, and monetary policy discontinuity: A comparative view of Japan, China, and the United States." *North American Journal of Economics and Finance* 15: 125–47.

Casella, A. and J. S. Feinstein (1990). "Economic exchange under hyperinflation." *Journal of Political Economy* 98(11): 1–27.

Cassel, G. (1932). "Monetary reconstruction." *International Affairs* 11(5): 658–77.

——— (1936). *The Downfall of the Gold Standard.* Oxford, Clarendon.

Congressional Budget Office (CBO) (2010a). "Federal debt and interest costs." U.S. Congress (December).

——— (2010b). "The long term budget outlook, federal debt held by the public under two budget scenarios." U.S. Congress (June, revised August).

——— (2011). "Budget and economic outlook: Fiscal years 2011 to 2021." U.S. Congress (January).

Cebula, R., K. Bates, and A. Roth (1988). "Financial market effects of federal government budget deficits." *Welwirtschaftliches Archiv* 124(729–33).

Cecchetti, S. G. (1995). "Inflation indicators and inflation policy." *NBER Working Paper Series* 5161 (February).

Cecchetti, S. (2008a). "Monetary policy and the financial crisis of 2007–2008." *Centre for Economic Policy Research, Policy Insight* 21 (April).

——— (2008b). *Money, Banking and Financial Markets.* 2nd ed. New York, McGraw-Hill Irwin.

Cecchetti, S. G., A. Flores-Lagunes, and S. Krause (2006). "Has monetary policy become more efficient? A cross-country analysis." *The Economic Journal* 116 (April): 408–33.

Cecchetti, S., P. Hooper, B. C. Kasman, K. L. Schoenholtz, and M. W. Watson (2007). "Understanding the evolving inflation process." Paper presented at the US Monetary Policy Forum, July, Washington, D.C.

Cecchetti, S. and J. Kim (2005). "Inflation targeting, price path targeting and output variability." *The Inflation Targeting Debate: National Bureau of Economic Research Studies in Business Cycles*, 32. B. Bernanke and M. Woodford, eds. Chicago, University of Chicago Press: 173–95.

Chari, V. V. (1998). "Nobel Laureate Robert E. Lucas, Jr.: Architect of modern macroeconomics." *Journal of Economic Perspectives* 12(1): 171–86.

Chari, V. V. and P. J. Kehoe (2006). "Modern macroeconomics in practice: How theory is shaping policy." *Journal of Economic Perspectives* 20(4): 3–28.

Chen, N., J. M. Imbs, and A. Scott (2004). "Competition, globalization and the decline of inflation." *CEPR Discussion Paper* 4695.

Chenery, H. B., S. Robinson, and M. Syrquin (1986). *Industrialization and Growth: A Comparative Study*. New York, Oxford University Press.

Chenery, H. B. and M. Syrquin (1975). *Patterns of Development, 1950–1970*. London, Oxford University Press.

Christiano, L. J. and T. J. Fitzgerald (2000). "Understanding the fiscal theory of the price level." *NBER Working Paper Series* 7668 (April).

——— (2003). "Inflation and monetary policy in the 20th century." *Federal Reserve Bank of Chicago* 27: 22–45.

Chung, H. (1990). "Did policy makers really believe in the Phillips curve? An econometric test." PhD dissertation, University of Minnesota.

Chwieroth, J. M. (2010). *Capital Ideas, the IMF and the Rise of Financial Liberalization*. Princeton, N.J., Princeton University Press.

Clarida, R. and B. M. Friedman (1983). "Why have short term interest rates been so high." *Brookings Papers on Economic Activity* 2: 553–78.

Clarida, R., J. Gali, and M. Gertler (1999). "The science of monetary policy: A new Keynesian perspective." *Journal of Economic Literature* 37(4): 1661–1707.

Cochrane, J. H. (1998). "A frictionless view of U.S. inflation." *NBER Working Paper Series* 6646 (July).

——— (2001). "Long term debt and optimal policy in the fiscal theory of the price level." *Econometrica* 69: 69–116.

——— (2011). "Understanding policy in the Great Recession: Some unpleasant fiscal arithmetic." *European Economic Review* 55: 2–30.

Cogley, T., G. E. Primiceri, and T. J. Sargent (2008). "Inflation-gap persistence in the US." *NBER Working Paper Series* 13749 (January). Published in *American Economic Journal: Macroeconomics* 2(1, January 2010): 43–69.

Cogley, T. and T. Sargent (2001). "Evolving post–World War II U.S. inflation dynamics." *Department of Economics, W. P. Carey School of Business, Arizona State University Working Papers* 2132872. Published in *NBER Macroeconomics Annual* 16(2001): 331–88.

——— (2005). "The conquest of US inflation: Learning and robustness to model uncertainty." *Review of Economic Dynamics* 8(2): 262–302.

Colander, D. C. (2007). *The Making of an Economist, Redux*. Princeton, N.J., Princeton University Press.

Coleman, W. (2001). "Is it possible that an independent central bank is impossible? The case of the Australian Notes Issue Board, 1920–1924." *Journal of Money, Credit, and Banking* 33(3): 729–48.

Coletti, D., R. Lalonde, and D. Muir (2008). "Inflation targeting and price level path targeting in the global economy model: some open economy considerations." *IMF Staff Papers* 55(2).

Crockett, A. and M. Goldstein (1976). "Inflation under fixed and flexible exchange rates." *IMF Staff Papers* 23(3): 509–44.

Crowe, C. and E. E. Meade (2007). "The evolution of central bank governance around the world." *Journal of Economic Perspectives* 21(4): 69–90.

Cukierman, A., S. Edwards, and G. Tabellini (1989). "Seignorage and political instability." *NBER Working Paper Series* 3199 (December).

Cukierman, A., G. P. Miller, and B. Neyapti (2002). "Central bank reform, liberalization and inflation in transition economies-an international perspective." *Journal of Monetary Economics* 49: 237–64.

Cukierman, A., S. Webb, and B. Neyapti (1992). "Measuring the independence of central banks and its effect on policy outcomes." *World Bank Economic Review* 6(3): 353–98.

Cutler, D. M. and L. Katz (1991). "Macroeconomic performance and the disadvantaged." *Brookings Papers on Economic Activity* 2: 1–74.

Da Fonseca, M. A. (1998). "Brazil's real plan." *Journal of Latin American Studies* 30(3): 619–39.

Dale, S. (2010). "Inflation, inflation, inflation." Remarks at Cardiff Business School, September 22. http://www.bankofengland.co.uk/publications/speeches/2010/speech448.pdf.

Danthine, J. P., J. B. Donaldson, and L. Smith (1987). "On the superneutrality of money in a stochastic dynamic macroeconomic model." *Journal of Monetary Economics* 20: 475–99.

Datt, G. and M. Ravallion (1996). "Macroeconomic crises and poverty monitoring: A case study for India." *World Bank Policy Research Working Paper* 1685 (November).

Davidson, P. (2007). "Keynes's serious monetary theory." econ.as.nyu.edu/docs/IO/8801/DavidsonKeynesMonetary.pdf.

De Graeve, F., T. K. Kick, and M. Koetter (2007). "Monetary policy and financial (in)stability: An integrated micro-macro approach." http://papers.ssrn.com/sol3/papers.cfm?abstract_id=966252.

De Gregorio, J. (1991a). "Economic growth in Latin America." *IMF Working Paper* WP/91/71.

——— (1991b). "The effects of inflation on economic growth: Lessons from Latin America." *IMF Working Paper* WP/91/95.

———— (1993). "Inflation taxation and long run growth." *Journal of Monetary Economics* 31: 271–98.

Deininger, K. and L. Squire (1996). "A new data set measuring income inequality." *World Bank Economic Review* 10(3): 565–91.

Del Mar, A. (1969). *History of Monetary Systems: A History of Actual Experiments in Money Made by Various States of the Ancient and Modern World.* New York, A. M. Kelley.

Del Negro, M., G. B. Eggertsson, A. Ferrero, and N. Kiyotaki (2010). "The great escape? A quantitative evaluation of the Fed's non standard policies." Federal Reserve Bank of New York and Princeton University. http://www.frbsf.org/economics/conferences/1003/delnegro_eggertsson_ferrero_kiyotaki.pdf.

DeLong, B. J. (1997). "America's Only Peacetime Inflation: The 1970s." *Reducing Inflation: Motivation and Strategy. NBER Studies in Business Cycles*, 30. C. D. Romer and D. Romer, eds. Chicago, University of Chicago Press: 247–76.

Demertzis, M., M. Marcellino, and N. Viegi (2008). "A measure for credibility: Tracking US monetary developments." *Working Paper, De Nederlandsche Bank* 187 (November).

Demopoulos, G. D., G. M. Katsimbris, and S. M. Miller (1987). "Monetary policy and central-bank financing of government budget deficits: A cross-country comparison." *European Economic Review* 31(5): 1023–50.

Diamond, D. and P. Dybvig (1983). "Bank runs: Deposit insurance and liquidity." *Journal of Political Economy* 91: 401–19.

Dornbusch, R. (1998). "Debt and monetary policy: The policy issues." *The Debt Burden and Its Consequences for Monetary Policy.* G. Calvo and M. King, eds. London, Macmillan: 3–22.

Dornbusch, R. and S. Edwards, eds. (1991). *The Macroeconomics of Populism in Latin America.* Chicago, University of Chicago Press.

Dornbusch, R., F. Sturzenegger, and H. Wolf (1990). "Extreme inflation: Dynamics and stabilization." *Brookings Papers on Economic Activity* 2: 1–84.

Dorrance, G. S. (1963). "The effects of inflation on economic development." *IMF Staff Papers* 10 (March): 1–47.

———— (1966). "Inflation and growth." *IMF Staff Papers* 13 (March): 82–102.

Dorrucci, E. and J. McKay (2011). "The international monetary system after the financial crisis." *European Central Bank, Occasional Paper Series* 123 (February).

Dutton, J. (1984). "The bank of England and the rules of the game under the international gold standard: New evidence." *A Retrospective on the Classical Gold Standard, 1821–1931.* M. D. Bordo and A. J. Schwartz, eds. Chicago, University of Chicago Press: 173–202.

Easterly, W. and S. Fischer (2001). "Inflation and the poor." *Journal of Money, Credit and Banking* 33(2): 160–78.

Easterly, W., P. Mauro, and K. Schmidt-Hebbel (1995). "Money demand and seigniorage-maximising inflation." *World Bank Policy Research Working Paper* WPS 1049.

Eggertsson, G. B. and M. Woodford (2003). "The zero bound on interest rates and optimal monetary policy." *Brookings Papers on Economic Activity* 1: 139–211.

Eichengreen, B. (1995). *Golden Fetters: The Gold Standard and the Great Depression, 1919–1939*. New York, Oxford University Press.

———— (1996). *Globalizing Capital: A History of the International Monetary System*. Princeton, N.J., Princeton University Press.

———— (2009). "Out of the box thoughts about the international financial architecture." *IMF Working Paper* 116 (May).

Eichengreen, B. and P. Masson, with H. Bredenkamp, B. Johnston, J. Hamann, E. Jadresic, and I. Otker (1998). "Exit strategies, policy options for countries seeking greater exchange rate flexibility." *IMF Occasional Paper* 168.

Eichengreen, B., P. Masson, M. Savastano, and S. Sharma (1999). "Transition strategies and nominal anchors on the road to greater exchange-rate flexibility." *Princeton University Essays in International Finance* N.213.

Ellison, M. and T. J. Sargent (2009). "A defence of the FOMC." *Discussion Paper Series, Department of Economics, University of Oxford* 457 (October).

Eltis, W. (2001). "Lord Overstone and the establishment of British nineteenth-century monetary orthodoxy." *Discussion Papers in Economic and Social History* 42 (December).

Engle, R. F. (1983). "Estimates of the variance of U.S. inflation based upon the ARCH model." *Journal of Money, Credit, and Banking* 15: 286–301.

English, W. B. (1996). "Inflation and financial sector size." *Board of Governors of the Federal Reserve System, Finance and Economics Discussion Series* 96-16 (April).

Ericsson, N. R., J. S. Irons, and R. W. Tryon (2000). "Output and inflation in the long run." *FRB International Finance Discussion Paper* 687 (November). http://ssrn.com/abstract=255462.

Eurostat (2010). "Taxation trends in the European Union." Publications Office of the European Union. http://ec.europa.eu/taxation_customs/resources/documents/taxation/gen_info/economic_analysis/tax_structures/2010/2010_full_text_en.pdf.

Evans, G. W. and S. Honkapohja (2011). "Learning as a rational foundation for macroeconomics and finance." *Bank of Finland Research Discussion Papers* 8/2011.

Evans, P. (1985). "Do large deficits produce high interest rates?" *American Economic Review* 75 (March): 68–87.

———— (1987). "Interest rates and expected future budget deficits in the United States." *Journal of Political Economy* 95(1): 34–58.

Fama, E. (1980). "Banking in the theory of finance." *Journal of Monetary Economics* 6(1): 39–57.

Feinstein, C. H. (1972). *Statistical Tables of National Income, Expenditure and Output in the UK, 1855–1965*. Cambridge, Cambridge University Press.

Feldstein, M. S. (1997). "Price stability." *Achieving Price Stability*. Kansas City, Federal Reserve Bank of Kansas City.

———— (1999a). "Capital income taxes and the benefit of price stability." *The Costs and Benefits of Price Stability*. M. Feldstein, ed. Chicago, University of Chicago Press: 9–40.

———— (1999b). "Introduction." *The Costs and Benefits of Price Stability*. M. Feldstein, ed. Chicago, University of Chicago Press: 1–7.

—— (1999c). "A self-help guide for emerging markets." *Foreign Affairs* 78 (March/April): 93–109.

—— (2008). "Resolving the global imbalance: The dollar and the U.S. saving rate." *Journal of Economic Perspectives* 22(3): 113–25.

Fellner, W. J. (1976). *Towards a Reconstruction of Macroeconomics: Problems of Theory and Policy.* Washington, D.C., American Enterprise Institute for Public Policy Research.

—— (1979). "The credibility effect and rational expectations: Implications of the Gramlich study." *Brookings Papers on Economic Activity* 1: 167–78.

—— (1982). "In defense of the credibility hypothesis." *American Economic Review* 72(2): 90–91.

Ferguson, N. (2001). *The Cash Nexus: Money and Power in the Modern World, 1700–2000.* London, Allen Lane.

—— (2008). *The Ascent of Money: A Financial History of the World.* New York, Penguin.

Ferguson, N. and B. Granville (2000). "Weimar on the Volga: Causes and consequences of inflation in 1990s Russia compared with 1920s Germany." *Journal of Economic History* 60(4): 1061–87.

Ferguson, N. and L. J. Kotlikoff (2003). "Going critical: American power and the consequences of fiscal overstretch." *The National Interest* 73 (Fall): 21–32.

Ferguson, N. and M. Schularick (2008). "The 'thin film of gold': Monetary rules and policy credibility in developing countries." *NBER Working Paper Series* 13918 (April).

Ferreira, F., P. Leite, and J. A. Litchfield (2006). "The rise and fall of Brazilian inequality: 1981–2004." *World Bank Policy Research Working Paper* 3867 (March).

Ferreira, F., P. Leite, and M. Ravallion (2010). "Poverty reduction without economic growth? Explaining Brazil's poverty dynamics, 1985–2004." *Journal of Development Economics* 93: 20–36.

Ferreira, F. and J. A. Litchfield (1998). "Education or inflation? The roles of structural factors and macro-economic instability in explaining Brazilian inequality in the 1980s." *Discussion Paper, DARP, LSE, STICERD* 41 (July).

Feyzioglu, T. and L. Willard (2006). "Does inflation in China affect the United States and Japan?" *IMF Working Paper* WP/06/36 (February).

Fischer, S. (1979). "Anticipations and the non-neutrality of money." *Journal of Political Economy* April: 225–52.

—— (1981). "Towards an understanding of the costs of inflation: II." *Carnegie-Rochester Conference Series on Public Policy* 15: 5–42.

—— (1984a). "The benefits of price stability." Paper presented at the Price Stability and Public Policy symposium, Jackson Hole, Wyo.

—— (1984b). "Contracts, credibility and disinflation." *NBER Working Paper Series* 1339 (April).

—— (1991). "Growth, marcoeconomics, and development." *NBER Working Paper Series* 3702 (May).

—— (1993). "The role of macroeconomic factors in growth." *Journal of Monetary Economics* 32: 485–512.

———— (1994). "Modern central banking." *The Future of Central Banking: The Tercentenary Symposium of the Bank of England*. F. Capie, C. Goodhart, S. Fischer, and N. Schnadt, eds. Cambridge, Cambridge University Press: 262–308.

———— (1998). "The Asian crises. A view from the IMF." Speech delivered at the IMF, January 22, Washington, D.C.

Fischer, S. and F. Modigliani (1978). "Towards an understanding of the real effects and costs of inflation." *Weltwirtschaftliches Archiv* 114(4): 811–33.

Fischer, S., R. Sahay, and C. A. Vegh (1996). "Stabilization and growth in transition economies: The early experience." *Journal of Economic Perspectives* 10: 45–66.

———— (2002). "Modern hyper- and high inflations." *IMF Working Paper* WP/02/197.

Fisher, I. (1935). *100% Money; Designed to Keep Checking Banks 100% Liquid; to Prevent Inflation and Deflation; Largely to Cure or Prevent Depressions; and to Wipe Out Much of the National Debt*. New York, Adelphi.

Fishlow, A. and J. Friedman (1994). "Tax Evasion, Inflation and Stabilization." *Journal of Development Economics* 43: 105–23.

Frankel, H. (1953). "The price of gold and the purchasing power of the pound sterling." *Journal of the Royal Statistical Society* 116(1): 35–46.

Frankel, J. (2006). "On the yuan: The choice between adjustment under a fixed exchange rate and adjustment under a flexible rate." *CESifo Economic Studies* 52(2): 246–75.

French, K. R., M. N. Baily, J. Y. Campbell, et al. (2010). *The Squam Lake Report: Fixing the Financial System*. Princeton, N.J., Princeton University Press.

Friedman, B. M. (1983). "Perspectives in and on macroeconomics." *NBER Working Paper Series* 1208 (September).

———— (1984). "Lessons from the 1979–82 monetary policy experiment." *American Economic Review* 74 (May): 382–87.

Friedman, M. (1960). *A Program for Monetary Stability*. New York, Fordham University Press.

———— (1962). "Should there be an independent monetary authority?" *In Search of a Monetary Constitution*. L. B. Yeager, ed. Cambridge, Mass., Harvard University Press: 219–43.

———— (1966). "Comments on 'The case against the case against the guideposts' by Robert M. Solow." *Guidelines, Informal Controls and the Market Place*. G. P. Shulz and R. Z. Aliber, eds. Chicago, University of Chicago Press: 55–61.

———— (1968). "The role of monetary policy." *American Economic Review* 58(1): 1–17.

———— (1969). "The optimum quantity of money." *The Optimum Quantity of Money and Other Essays*. M. Friedman, ed. Chicago, Aldine: 1–50.

———— (1970a). *The Counter-Revolution in Monetary Theory: First Wincott Memorial Lecture, Delivered at Senate House, University of London, 16 September*. London, Institute of Economic Affairs.

———— (1970b). "A theoretical framework for monetary analysis." *Journal of Political Economy* 78(2): 192–238.

——— (1977). "Nobel lecture: Inflation and unemployment." *Journal of Political Economy* 85: 451–72.

——— (1984). "Monetary policy in the 1980s." *To Promote Prosperity*. J. Moore, ed. Stanford, Calif., Hoover Institution: 23–60.

——— (1992). *Money Mischief: Episodes in Monetary History*. New York, Harcourt Brace Jovanovich.

——— (2001). "An interview." *Macroeconomic Dynamics* 5: 101–31.

Friedman, M. and A. J. Schwartz (1963). *A Monetary History of the United States, 1867–1960*. Princeton, N.J., Princeton University Press.

Fuhrer, J. C. (1997). "The (un)importance of forward looking behavior in price specifications." *Journal of Money, Credit, and Banking* 29(3): 338–50.

Fuhrer, J. C. and G. R. Moore (1995). "Forward-looking behavior and the stability of a conventional monetary policy rule." *Journal of Money Credit and Banking* 27(4): 1060–70.

Furman, J. and J. Stiglitz (1998). "Economic crises: Evidence and insights from East Asia." *Brookings Papers on Economic Activity* 2.

Galbis, V. (1979). "Money, investment and growth in Latin America, 1961–73." *Economic Development and Cultural Change* 27 (April): 423–43.

Galbraith, J. K. (1975). *Money: Whence It Came, Where It Went*. London, Deutsch.

Gali, J. (2008). *Monetary Policy, Inflation and the Business Cycle: An Introduction to the New Keynesian Framework*. Princeton, N.J., Princeton University Press.

Garber, P. (1998). "Derivatives in international capital flow." *NBER Working Paper Series* 6623 (June).

Garber, P. and M. Spencer (1995). "Foreign exchange hedging and the interest rate defence." *IMF Staff Papers* 42(3): 490–515.

Garside, W. R. (1990). *British Unemployment, 1919–1939: A Study in Public Policy*. Cambridge, Cambridge University Press.

Gaspar, V. and F. Smets (2000). "Price level stability: Some issues." *National Institute Economic Review* 174 (October): 68–79.

Gerlach-Kristen, P. (2003). "Insiders and outsiders at the Bank of England." *Central Banking* 14(1): 96–102.

——— (2009). "Outsiders at the Bank of England's MPC." *Journal of Money, Credit and Banking* 41(6): 1099–1116.

Gertler, M. (1988). "Financial structure and aggregate economic activity: An overview." *Journal of Money, Credit, and Banking* 20(2): 559–88.

——— (2005). "Comment on 'Does inflation targeting matter' by Laurence Ball and Niamh Sheridan." *The Inflation-Targeting Debate*, 32. B. Bernanke and M. Woodford, eds. Chicago, University of Chicago Press: 276–82.

Geweke, J. (1986). "The superneutrality of money in the United States: An interpretation of the evidence." *Econometrica* 54(1): 1–22.

Ghosh, A. R. (2000). "Inflation and growth." *IMF Research Bulletin* 1: 1–3.

Ghosh, A. R. and S. Phillips (1998). "Inflation, disinflation, and growth." *IMF Working Paper* 68 (May).

Goh, M. H. and Y. Kim (2006). "Is the Chinese renminbi undervalued?" *Contemporary Economic Policy* 24(1): 116–26.

Goodfriend, M. (2005). "Inflation targeting in the United States." *The Inflation-Targeting Debate*, 32. B. S. Bernanke and M. Woodford, eds. Chicago, University of Chicago Press: 311–37.

——— (2007). "How the world achieved consensus on monetary policy." *Journal of Economic Perspectives* 21(4): 47–68.

——— (2009). "Central banking in the economic turmoil: An assessment of Federal Reserve practice." Paper presented at the Monetary-Fiscal Policy Interactions, Expectations and Dynamics in the Current Economic Crisis conference, May 22–23, Princeton University, Princeton, N.J.

Goodfriend, M. and R. G. King (2005). "The incredible Volcker disinflation." *Journal of Monetary Economics* 52(5): 981–1015.

Goodhart, C. (2006). "A framework for assessing financial stability?" *Journal of Banking and Finance* 30: 3415–22.

Goodhart, C., P. Sunirand, and D. Tsomocos (2006). "A model to analyse financial fragility." *Economic Theory* 27: 107–42.

Gordon, R. and S. King (1982). "The output cost of disinflation in traditional and vector autoregression models." *Brookings Papers on Economic Activity* 2: 205–42.

Granville, B. (1995). *The Success of Russian Economic Reforms*. London, Royal Institute of International Affairs, International Economic Programme.

——— (1999). "Bingo or fiasco: The global financial situation is not guaranteed." *International Affairs* 75(4): 713–28. Reprinted in *The International Library of Writings on the New Global Economy: The Political Economy of Financial Crises*. R. E. Allen, ed. Cheltenham, UK, Edward Elgar, 2004: 79–94.

——— (2001). "The problem of monetary stabilisation." *Russia's Post-Communist Economy*. B. Granville and P. Oppenheimer, eds. Oxford, Oxford University Press: 93–130.

——— (2003). "Taxation of financial intermediaries as a source of budget revenue: Russia in the 1990s." *Taxation of Financial Intermediation: Theory and Practice for Emerging Economies*. P. Honohan, ed. Washington, D.C., World Bank: 269–88. http://siteresources.worldbank.org/DEC/Resources/23658_chap_8_taxation.pdf.

Granville, B. and S. K. Mallick (2009). "Monetary and financial stability in the Euro area: Pro-cyclicality versus trade-off." *Journal of International Financial Markets, Institutions & Money* 19(4): 662–74.

——— (2010). "Monetary policy in Russia: Identifying exchange rate shocks." *Economic Modelling* 27(1): 432–44.

Granville, B., S. Mallick, and N. Zeng (2011). "Chinese exchange rate and price effects on G3 import prices." *Journal of Asian Economics* 22(6): 427–40.

Granville, B., J. Shapiro, and O. Dynnikova (1996). "Less inflation, less poverty: First results for Russia." *Discussion Paper, Royal Institute of International Affairs, International Economics Programme* 68.

Greenspan, A. (1999). Testimony before the Committee on Banking and Financial Services, U.S. House of Representatives, July 22.

——— (2002). *Economic Volatility*. Jackson Hole, Wyo., Federal Reserve Bank of Kansas City.

Grilli, V., D. Masciandaro, and G. Tabellini (1991). "Political and monetary institutions and public financial policies in the industrial countries." *Economic Policy* 13: 341–92.

Grimes, A. (1991). "The effects of inflation on growth: Some international evidence." *Weltwirtschaftliches Archiv* 127: 631–44.

Guitian, M. (1998). "Monetary policy: Equity issues in IMF policy advice." *Income Distribution and High-Quality Growth*. V. Tanzi and K. Y. Chu, eds. Cambridge, Mass., MIT Press: 333–50.

Guttman, W. and P. Meehan (1975). *The Great Inflation, Germany 1919–23*. Farnborough, UK, Saxon House.

Gylfason, T. and T. T. Herbertsson (2001). "Does inflation matter for growth?" *Japan and the World Economy* 13(4): 405–28.

Haldane, A. G. and C. K. Salmon (1995). *Three Issues in Inflation Targets: Targeting Inflation*. London, Bank of England.

Hall, G. J. and T. J. Sargent (2010). "Interest rate risk and other determinants of post WWII US government debt/GDP dynamics." *NBER Working Paper Series* 15702 (January).

Hansen, S. and M. McMahon (2010). "What do outside experts bring to a committee? Evidence from the Bank of England." *Working Paper, Economics Department, University of Warwick* 946. http://www2.warwick.ac.uk/fac/soc/economics/research/working papers/2010/twerp_946.pdf.

Harris, M. and C. Spencer (2008). "Decade of dissent: Explaining the dissent voting behavior of Bank of England MPC members." *MPRA Papers* 9100.

Hardouvelis, G. and S. Barnhart (1989). "The evolution of federal reserve credibility: 1978–1984." *Review of Economics and Statistics* 71(3): 385–93.

Hawtrey, R. G. (1918). "The bank restriction of 1797." *The Economic Journal* 28(109): 52–65.

Heller, R. H. (1976). "International reserves and world wide inflation." *IMF Staff Papers* 23 (March): 61–87.

Heymann, D. and A. Leijonhufvud (1995). *High Inflation*. Oxford, Clarendon.

Hicks, J. R. (1937). "Mr. Keynes and the 'classics': A suggested interpretation." *Econometrica* 5(2): 147–59.

Hines, J. R., Jr. (1999). "Three sides of Harberger triangles." *Journal of Economic Perspectives* 13(2): 167–88.

Hoelscher, G. (1986). "New evidence on deficits and interest rates." *Journal of Money, Credit, and Banking* 18 (February): 1–17.

Hoenig, T. M. (2010). "The Federal Reserve's mandate: Long run." Paper presented at the National Association of Business Economists annual meeting, Denver, Colo.

Honda, Y. and Y. Kuroki (2006). "Financial and capital markets' responses to changes in the central bank's target interest rate: The case of Japan." *The Economic Journal* 116 (July): 812–42.

Hooper, P., K. Johnson, and J. Marquez (2000). "Trade elasticities for the G-7 countries." *Princeton Studies in International Economics* 87 (August).

Hoover, K. D. (1988). *The New Classical Macroeconomics: A Sceptical Inquiry*. Oxford, Basil Blackwell.

——— (2008). "New Classical Macroeconomics." *The Concise Encyclopedia of Economics*. http://www.econlib.org/library/Enc/NewClassicalMacroeconomics.html.

Houben, A., J. Kakes, and G. J. Schinasi (2004). "Toward a framework for safeguarding financial stability." *IMF Working Paper* WP/04/101.

Hsiao, F. S. T., M. W. Hsiao, and A. Yamashita (2003). "The impact of the US economy on the Asia-Pacific region: Does it matter?" *Journal of Asian Economics* 14(2): 219–41.

Hume, D. (1752). "Of the balance of trade." *Essays, Moral, Political and Literary*. London, Longmans, Green: 330–45.

Hume, L. J. (1970). "The gold standard and deflation: Issues and attitudes in the 1920s." *The Gold Standard and Employment Policies between the Wars*. S. Pollard, ed. London, Methuen: 122–45.

Husain, A. M., A. Mody, and K. S. Rogoff (2004). "Exchange rate regime durability and performance in developing versus advanced economies." *NBER Working Paper Series* 10673 (August).

Ihrig, J., S. B. Kamin, D. Lindner, and J. Marquez. (2010). "Some Simple Tests of the Globalization and Inflation Hypothesis." *International Finance* 13: 343–75.

International Energy Agency (IEA) (2007). *World Energy Outlook 2007, Executive Summary, China and India Insights*. Paris, OECD/IEA.

International Monetary Fund (IMF) (1998a). *World Economic Outlook* (May).

——— (1998b). *World Economic Outlook and International Capital Markets, Interim Assessment* (December).

——— (2006). "How Has Globalization Affected Inflation?" *World Economic Outlook* (Spring): 97–134.

——— (2010a). *Central Banking Lessons from the Crisis: Monetary and Capital Markets Department*. Washington, D.C.

——— (2010b). *Reserve Accumulation and International Monetary Stability: Strategy, Policy and Review Department*.

——— (2010c). "United States: 2010 Article IV Consultation-Staff Report; Staff Statement; and Public Information Notice on the Executive Board Discussion." *IMF Country Report* 10/249 (July).

——— (2011). *Assessing Reserve Adequacy. Monetary and Capital Markets, Research, and Strategy, Policy and Review Department* (February 14).

——— (2012). "Coping with High Debt and Sluggish Growth." *World Economic Outlook* (October). http://www.imf.org/external/pubs/ft/weo/2012/02/pdf/text.pdf.

Issing, O. (2003). "Monetary and financial stability: Is there a trade-off?" *BIS paper* 18 (September).

———— (2011). "Lessons for monetary policy: What should the consensus be?" *IMF Working Paper* 97 (April)

James, H. (2001). *The End of Globalization: Lessons from the Great Depression.* Cambridge, Mass., Harvard University Press.

Johnson, H. G. (1968). "Problems of efficiency in monetary management." *Journal of Political Economy* 76(September/October): 971–90.

———— (1969). "Is inflation the inevitable price of rapid development or retarding factor in economic growth?" *Essays in Monetary Economics.* H. G. Johnson, ed. London, Allen & Unwin: 281–91.

———— (1970). "Is There an Optimal Money Supply," *Journal of Finance* 25(2): 435–42.

———— (1976). "Keynes's general theory: Revolution or war of independence?" *Canadian Journal of Economics* 9(4): 580–94.

Jonas, J. and F. S. Mishkin (2003). "Inflation targeting in transition countries: Experience and prospects." *NBER Working Paper Series* 9667 (April).

Jones, D. H. (1985). "Deficits and money growth in the United States, 1872–1983." *Journal of Monetary Economics* 16(3): 329–51.

Jones, L. E. and R. E. Manuelli (1993). "Growth and the effects of inflation." *NBER Working Paper Series* 4523 (December).

Jones, M. T. and M. Obstfeld (2001). "Saving, investment, and gold: A reassessment of historical current account data." *Money, Capital Mobility, and Trade: Essays in Honor of Robert Mundell.* G. A. Calvo, R. Dornbusch, and M. Obstfeld, eds. Cambridge, Mass., MIT Press: 303–64.

Kahn, G. A. (2009). "Beyond inflation targeting: Should central banks target the price level?" *Economic Review, Federal Reserve Bank of Kansas City* Third Quarter.

Kamin, S. B., M. Marazzi, and J. W. Schindler (2006). "The impact of Chinese exports on global import prices." *Review of International Economics* 14 (May): 179–201.

Kane, C. and J. Morisett (1993). "Who would vote for inflation in Brazil? An integrated framework approach to inflation and income distribution." *World Bank Policy Research Working Paper* 1183 (September).

Kareken, J. H. and N. Wallace (1978). "Deposit insurance and bank regulation: A partial-equilibrium exposition." *Journal of Business* 51(3): 413–38.

Karras, G. (1993). "Money, inflation and output growth: Does the aggregate demand–aggregate supply model explain the international evidence?" *Weltwirtschaftliches Archiv* 129(4): 662–74.

Kaufman, R. R. and B. Stallings (1991). "The political economy of Latin American populism." *The Macroeconomics of Populism in Latin America.* R. Dornbusch and S. Edwards, eds. Chicago, University of Chicago Press: 15–34.

Kay, J. (2009). *Narrow Banking: The Reform of Banking Regulation.* London, Centre for the Study of Financial Innovation.

Kehoe, T. J. (2003). "What can we learn from the current crisis in Argentina?" *Scottish Journal of Political Economy* 50(5): 609–33.

Kenen, P. (1988). "Managing exchange rates." *Chatham House Papers, Royal Institute of International Affairs.*

Keran, M. W. (1975). "Towards an explanation of simultaneous inflation-recession." *Federal Reserve Bank of San Francisco, Business Review* Spring: 18–30.

Keynes, J. M. (1919). *The Economic Consequences of the Peace.* London, Macmillan.

———— (1923). *A Tract on Monetary Reform.* London, Macmillan.

———— (1924) "Does Unemployment Need a Drastic Remedy?" *Nation and Athenaeum,* May 24.

———— (1925). *The Economic Consequences of Mr. Churchill.* London, L. and V. Woolf.

———— (1933). "A monetary theory of production." *The Collected Writings of John Maynard Keynes,* 13. D. Moggridge, ed. London, Macmillan: 343, 411–12.

———— (1936). *The General Theory of Employment, Interest and Money.* London, Macmillan.

———— (1970). "The economic consequences of Mr Churchill." *The Gold Standard and Employment Policies between the Wars.* S. Pollard, ed. London, Methuen: 27–43.

———— (1979). "The general theory and after: A supplement (to vols XIII and XIV)." *The Collected Writings of John Maynard Keynes,* 29. D. Moggridge, ed. London, Macmillan: 73–76.

———— (1981). *Activities 1922–9: The Return to Gold and Industrial Policy.* Vol. 19, *The Collected Writings of John Maynard Keynes.* D. Moggridge, ed. London, Macmillan.

Keynes, J. M. and H. Henderson (1929). "Can Lloyd George do it? An examination of the Liberal pledge." *The Nation and Atheneum.*

Khan, M. S. and A. S. Senhadji (2001). "Threshold effects in the relationship between inflation and growth." *IMF Staff Papers* 48(1): 1–21.

Khan, M. S., A. S. Senhadji, and B. D. Smith (2001). "Inflation and financial depth." *IMF Working Paper* WP/01/44 (April).

Kimborough, K. P. (1986). "The optimum quantity of money rule in the theory of public finance." *Journal of Monetary Economics* 18(3): 277–84.

Kindleberger, C. P. (1973). *The World in Depression 1929–1939.* London, Penguin.

———— (1996). *Manias, Panics and Crashes: A History of Financial Crises.* 3rd ed. New York, John Wiley.

King, M. (1995). "Commentary: Monetary policy implications of greater fiscal discipline." *Budget Deficits and Debt: Issues and Options.* Federal Reserve Bank of Kansas City: 171–83.

———— (2005a). "Remarks to the central bank governors' panel." Remarks at the Jackson Hole Conference, Jackson Hole, Wyo. http://www.bankofengland.co.uk/publications/Documents/speeches/2005/speech253.pdf.

———— (2005b). "What Has Inflation Targeting Achieved." *The Inflation-Targeting Debate,* 32. B. Bernanke and M. Woodford, eds. Chicago, University of Chicago Press: 11–16.

———— (2010). "Banking: From Bagehot to Basel, and back again." Second Bagehot Lecture, Buttonwood Gathering, October 25, New York.

King, R. G. and M. W. Watson (1994). "The post-war U.S. Phillips curve: A revisionist econometric history." *Carnegie-Rochester Conference Series on Public Policy* 41(0): 157–219.

Klein, B. (1974). "The competitive supply of money." *Journal of Money, Credit and Banking* 6: 423–53.

Kohn, M. (1984). "The inflation tax and the value of equity." *Canadian Journal of Economics* 17(2): 312–26.

Kormendi, R. and P. Meguire (1984). "Cross-regime evidence of macroeconomic rationality." *Journal of Political Economy* 92(5): 875–908.

——— (1985). "Macroeconomic determinants of growth: Cross country evidence." *Journal of Monetary Economics* 16(2): 141–63.

Kotlikoff, L. J. (2010). *Jimmy Stewart Is Dead: Ending the World's Ongoing Financial Plague with Limited Purpose Banking*. Hoboken, N.J., John Wiley.

Kreps, D. M. (1999). "Anticipated utility and dynamic choice." *Frontiers of Research in Economic Theory: The Nancy L. Schwartz Memorial Lectures, 1983–1997*. D. P. Jacobs, E. Kalai, and M. I. Kamien, eds. Cambridge, Cambridge University Press: 242–74.

Krugman, P. (1999). "Thinking about the liquidity trap." Paper presented at the NBER/CEPR/TCER Conference, Tokyo. http://web.mit.edu/krugman/www/trioshrt.html.

Kuttner, K. N. (2001). "Monetary policy surprises and interest rates: Evidence from the Fed funds futures rate." *Journal of Monetary Economics* 47: 523–44.

Kydland, F. E. and E. C. Prescott (1977). "Rules rather than discretion: The inconsistency of optimal plans." *Journal of Political Economy* 85(3): 473–91.

Laidler, D. (1977). "The welfare cost of inflation in neo-classical theory: Some unsettled problems." *Inflation Theory and Anti-Inflation Policy*. E. Lundberg. London, Macmillan: 314–28.

Laopodis, N. T. (2004). "Monetary policy implications of comovements among long-term interest rates." *Journal of International Financial Markets, Institutions and Money* 14(2): 135–64.

Leeper, E. M. (1991). "Equilibria under 'active' and 'passive' monetary and fiscal policies." *Journal of Monetary Economics* 27 (February): 129–47.

Leeper, E. M. and T. Yun (2005). "Monetary-fiscal policy interactions and the price level: Background and beyond." *NBER Working Paper Series* 11646 (September).

Levine, R. and D. Renelt (1991). "Cross-country studies of growth and policy: Methodological, conceptual and statistical problems." *World Bank Policy Research Working Paper* 608.

Lin, G. and R. M. Schramm (2003). "China's foreign exchange policies since 1979: A review of developments and an assessment." *China Economic Review* 14(3): 246–80.

List, J. A. (2011). "Why economists should conduct field experiments and 14 tips for pulling one off." *Journal of Economic Perspectives* 25(3): 3–16.

Litan, R. E. (1987). *What Should Banks Do?* Washington, D.C., Brookings Institution.

Loyo, E. (1999). *Tight Money Paradox on the Loose: A Fiscalist Hyperinflation*. Cambridge, Mass., J. F. Kennedy School of Government, Harvard University.

LSE Report (2010). *The Future of Finance*. London, London School of Economics and Political Science.

Lucas, R. E. (1972). "Expectations and the neutrality of money." *Journal of Economic Theory* 4 (April): 103–24.

——— (1973). "Some international evidence on output-inflation tradeoffs." *American Economic Review* 63(3): 326–34.

——— (1976). "Econometric policy evaluation: A critique." *Carnegie Rochester Conference Series on Public Policy* 1: 19–46.

——— (1980). "Two illustrations of the quantity theory of money." *American Economic Review* 70: 1005–14.

——— (1996). "Nobel lecture: Monetary neutrality." *Journal of Political Economy* 104(4): 661–82.

——— (2000). "Inflation and welfare." *Econometrica* 68(2): 247–74.

Lupton, J. and D. Hensley (2010). "Government debt sustainability in the age of fiscal activism." *J.P. Morgan Global Issues* (June 10).

Lustig, N. (2011). "The knowledge bank and poverty reduction." *Tulane Economics Working Paper Series* 1111 (February).

Mackay, C. D. ([1848] 1852). *Memoirs of Extraordinary Popular Delusions and the Madness of Crowds*. London, Office of the National Illustrated Library. http://www.econlib.org/library/Mackay/macEx1.html.

Makin, J. H. (1983). "Real interest, money surprises, anticipated inflation and fiscal deficits." *Review of Economics and Statistics* 65(3): 374–84.

Mankiw, G. N. (1987). "The optimal collection of seigniorage: Theory and evidence." *Journal of Monetary Economics* 20(2): 327–41.

——— (2001a). "The inexorable and mysterious tradeoff between inflation and unemployment." *The Economic Journal* 111(471): C45–C61.

——— (2001b). "US monetary policy during the 1990s." *NBER Working Paper Series* 8471 (September).

——— (2006). "The macroeconomist as scientist and engineer." *Journal of Economic Perspectives* 20(4): 29–46.

Marcet, A. and J. P. Nicolini (2003). "Recurrent hyperinflations and learning." *American Economic Review* 93(5): 1476–98.

Marcuzzo, M. C. and A. Rosselli (1987). "Profitability in the international gold market in the early history of the gold standard." *Economica* 54(215): 367–80.

Marimon, R. (2000). "Review of Sargent's The conquest of American inflation." *Journal of Economic Literature* 38(2): 405–11.

Marty, A. (1969). "Notes on money and economic growth." *Journal of Money, Credit, and Banking* 1 (May): 252–56.

——— (1973). "Growth, satiety and the tax revenue from money." *Journal of Political Economy* 81 (September/October): 1136–52.

Mascaro, A. and A. H. Meltzer (1983). "Long and short-term interest rates in a risky world." *Journal of Monetary Economics* 12(4): 485–518.

McCallum, B. (1981). "Price level determinacy with an interest rate policy rule and rational expectations." *Journal of Monetary Economics* 8(3): 319–29.

——— (1985). "Credibility and monetary policy." *NBER Working Paper Series* W1490 (June).

——— (2001). "Indeterminacy, bubbles and the fiscal theory of price level determination." *Journal of Monetary Economics* 47: 19–30.

McKinnon, R. I. (1973). *Money and Capital in Economic Development*. Washington, D.C., Brookings Institution.

Meier, G. M. (1993). "The new political economy and policy reform." *Journal of International Development* 5(4): 381–89.

Meltzer, A. H. (2005). "Origins of the great inflation." *Federal Reserve Bank of St. Louis Review* 87 (2, pt. 2): 145–75.

Meyer, L. H. (2004). *A Term at the Fed: An Insider's View*. New York, HarperBusiness.

Mishkin, F. S. (1999). "Global financial instability: Framework, events, issues." *Journal of Economic Perspectives* 13(4): 3–20.

——— (2004). *The Economics of Money, Banking, and Financial Markets*. 7th ed. Upper Saddle River, N.J., Pearson, Addison-Wesley.

——— (2006). "Financial stability and globalization: Getting it right." Paper presented at the Bank of Spain Conference, Central Banks in the 21st Century, June 8–9, 2006, Madrid.

——— (2007a). "How did we get there." *Monetary Policy Strategy*. F. S. Mishkin, ed. Cambridge, Mass., MIT Press: 1–27.

——— (2007b). "Will monetary policy become more of a science?" *NBER Working Paper Series* 13566 (October).

——— (2008a). "Does stabilizing inflation contribute to stabilizing economic activity." *NBER Working Paper Series* 13970 (April).

——— (2008b). "Exchange rate pass-through and monetary policy." *NBER Working Paper Series* 13889 (May).

——— (2008c). "Globalization, macroeconomic performance and monetary policy." *NBER Working Paper Series* 13948 (April).

Mishkin, F. S. and K. Schmidt-Hebbel (2007). "Does inflation targeting make a difference?" *NBER Working Paper Series* 12876 (January).

Moggridge, D. E. (1993). *Keynes*. Houndmills, Macmillan.

——— (1995). *Maynard Keynes: An Economist's Biography*. London, Routledge.

Morales, J. A. (1988). "Inflation stabilization in Bolivia." *Inflation Stabilization: The Experience of Israel, Argentina, Brazil, Bolivia and Mexico*. M. Bruno, G. Di Tella, R. Dornbusch, and S. Fischer, eds. Cambridge, Mass., MIT Press: 307–46.

Morgan, E. V. (1952). *Studies in British Financial Policy, 1914–25*. London, Macmillan.

Morrell, J. (1981). *The Future of the Dollar and the World Reserve System*. London, Butterworths.

Münchau, W. (2011). "Time to get real on Europe's inflation target." *Financial Times*, January 30, 11.

Murphy, A. E. (1986). *Richard Cantillon, Entrepreneur and Economist*. Oxford, Oxford University Press.

——— (1997). *John Law: Economic Theorist and Policy-Maker*. Oxford, Oxford University Press.

——— (2006). "John Law: Financial innovator." *Pioneers of Financial Economics*, 1. G. Poitras, ed. Cheltenham, UK, Edward Elgar: 100–116.

Murrell, P. (1995). "The transition according to Cambridge, Mass." *Journal of Economic Literature* 33(1): 164–78.

Mussa, M., P. Masson, A. Swoboda, E. Jadresic, P. Mauro, and A. Berg (2000). "Exchange rate regimes in an increasingly integrated world economy." Advance copy, Washington, D.C., International Monetary Fund (April).

Muth, J. F. (1961). "Rational expectations and the theory of price movements." *Econometrica* 29: 315–35.

Nelson, E. and A. J. Schwartz (2007). "The impact of Milton Friedman on modern monetary economics: Setting the record straight on Paul Krugman's 'Who was Milton Friedman?'" *NBER Working Paper Series* 13546 (October).

Nessén, M. and D. Vestin (2005). "Average inflation targeting." *Journal of Money, Credit, and Banking* 37(5): 837–63.

Ng, G. (2007). "Greater China." *J.P. Morgan Economic Research, Global Data Watch* (May 18): 71–74.

Niebyl, K. H. (1940). "A reexamination of the Classical theory of inflation." *American Economic Review* 30(4): 759–73.

Niehans, J. (1978). "The optimal return on money." *The Theory of Money*." J. Niehans. Baltimore, Md., Johns Hopkins University Press: 93–98.

Obstfeld, M. (1998). "The global capital market: Benefactor or menace?" *NBER Working Paper Series* 6559 (May).

——— (2009). "International finance and growth in developing countries: What have we learned?" *NBER Working Paper Series* 14691 (January).

——— (2010). "The immoderate world economy." *Journal of International Money and Finance* 29(4): 603–14.

Obstfeld, M. and K. Rogoff (1995). "The mirage of fixed exchange rates." *Journal of Economic Perspectives* 9(Fall): 73–96.

——— (2009). "Global imbalances and the financial crisis: Products of common causes." *Proceedings*. San Francisco, Federal Reserve Bank of San Francisco: 131–72.

Obstfeld, M., J. Shambaugh, and A. Taylor (2003). "Monetary sovereignty, exchange rates, and capital controls: The trilemma in the interwar period." *IMF Staff Papers* 51 (Special Issue).

Obstfield, M. and A. M. Taylor (1998). "The Great Depression as a watershed: International capital mobility over the long run." *The Defining Moment: The Great Depression and the American Economy in the Twentieth century*. M. Bordo, C. Goldin, and E. White, eds. Chicago, University of Chicago Press: 353–402.

——— (2004). *Global Capital Markets, Integration, Crisis, and Growth*. Cambridge, Cambridge University Press.

Office of Management and Budget (OMB) (2009). "The management's discussion and analysis." http://www.gao.gov/financial/fy2009financialreport.html.

———— (2010). "Historical tables." http://www.whitehouse.gov/omb/budget/Historicals/.

Okun, A. M. (1971). "The mirage of steady inflation." *Brookings Papers on Economic Activity* 2: 485–98.

———— (1978). "Efficient disinflationary policies." *American Economic Review* 68: 348–52.

O'Reilly, G. and K. Whelan (2005). "Has EURO-area inflation persistence changed over time?" *Review of Economics and Statistics* 87(4): 709–20.

Organisation for Economic Co-operation and Development (OECD) (1999). *Economic Outlook* 65 (June).

Orphanides, A. (2000). "Activist stabilisation policy and inflation: The Taylor rule in the 1970s." *Finance and Economics Discussion Series, Division of Research and Statistics and Monetary Affairs* 13.

———— (2003). "Monetary policy evaluation with noisy information." *Journal of Monetary Economics* 50(3): 605–31.

———— (2004). "The decline of activist stabilization policy: Natural rate misperceptions, learning and expectations." *Board of Governors of the Federal Reserve System, International Finance Discussion Papers* 804 (April).

Orphanides, A. and R. Solow (1990). "Money, inflation and growth." *Handbook of Monetary Economics*. B. M. Friedman and F. H. Hahn, eds. Amsterdam, North Holland: 223–63.

Orphanides, A. and J. C. Williams (2005). "Imperfect knowledge, inflation expectations, and monetary policy." *The Inflation-Targeting Debate*, 32. B. Bernanke and M. Woodford, eds. Chicago, University of Chicago Press: 201–46.

Otker, I. and C. Pazarbasioglu (1995). "Speculative attacks and currency crises: The Mexican experience." *IMF Working Paper* 112 (November).

Palgrave, R. H. I. ([1903] 1968). *Bank Rate and the Money Market in England, France, Germany, Holland and Belgium, 1844–1900*. New York, Greenwood.

Pan, S., S. Mohanty, M. Welch, D. Ethridge, and M. Fadiga (2007). "Effects of Chinese currency revaluation on world fiber markets." *Contemporary Economic Policy* 25(2): 185–205.

Pazos, Felipe (1972). *Chronic Inflation in Latin America*. New York, Praeger.

Perry, G. L. (1983). "What have we learned about disinflation?" *Brookings Papers on Economic Activity* 2: 567–602.

Persson, M., T. Persson, and L. E. O. Svensson (1998). "Debt, cash flow and inflation incentives: A Swedish example." *The Debt Burden and Its Consequences for Monetary Policy*. G. Calvo and M. King, eds. London, Macmillan: 28–62.

Phelps, E. (1966). *Golden Rules of Economic Growth*. New York, Norton.

———— (1967). "Phillips curves, expectations of inflation and optimal unemployment over time." *Economica* 34: 254–81.

———— (1968). "Money-wage dynamics and labor-market equilibrium." *Journal of Political Economy* 76: 678–711.

———— (1973). "Inflation in theory of public finance." *Swedish Journal of Economics* 75(1): 67–82.

Phelps, E. S. and J. B. Taylor (1977). "Stabilizing powers of monetary policy under rational expectations." *Journal of Political Economy* 85(1): 163–90.

Phillips, A. W. (1958). "The relation between unemployment and the rate of change of money wage rates in the United Kingdom, 1861–1957." *Economica* 25 (November): 283–99.

Phillips, R. J. (1992). "The Chicago plan and New Deal banking reform." *Jerome Levy Economics Institute of Bard College Working Paper* 76 (June).

Phillips, R. J. and A. Roselli (2009). "Narrow banking: A proposal to avoid the next taxpayer bailout of the financial system." *Aperta Contrada* (October 12).

Piergallini, A. and G. Rodano (2009). "Public debt, distortionary taxation, and monetary policy." *MPRA Papers* 15348 (May).

Pivetta, F. and R. Reis (2007). "The persistence of inflation in the United States." *Journal of Economic Dynamics & Control* 31(4): 1326–58.

Poloz, S. S. (2006). "Financial stability: A worthy goal, but how feasible?" *Journal of Banking and Finance* 30: 3423–27.

Posen, A. (2010). "The case for doing more." Speech at the Hull and Humber Chamber of Commerce, Industry and Shipping, September 28, Hull. http://www.bankof england.co.uk/publications/speeches/2010/speech449.pdf.

Poterba, J. M. and J. J. Rotemberg (1990). "Inflation and taxation with optimizing governments." *Journal of Money, Credit, and Banking* 22(1): 1–18.

Powers, E. T. (1995). "Inflation, unemployment, and poverty revisited." *Economic Review, Federal Reserve Bank of Cleveland* Quarter 3: 2–13.

Primiceri, G. E. (2006). "Why inflation rose and fell: Policy makers' beliefs and U.S. postwar stabilization policy." *Quarterly Journal of Economics* 121 (August): 867–901.

Radelet, S. and J. Sachs (1998). "The East Asian financial crisis: Diagnosis remedies, prospects." *Brookings Papers on Economic Activity* 1: 1–90.

Rajan, R. G. (2005). "Has financial development made the world riskier?" Paper presented at the Jackson Hole Conference, Jackson Hole, Wyo.

———— (2008). "The future of the IMF and the World Bank." *American Economic Review* 98(2): 110–15.

———— (2010). *Fault Lines: How Hidden Fractures Still Threaten the World Economy.* Princeton, N.J., Princeton University Press.

Ravallion, M. (2011). "A comparative perspective on poverty reduction in Brazil, China and India." *World Bank Research Observer* 26(1): 71–103.

Ravallion, M. and G. Datt (1996). "How important to India's poor is the sectoral composition of economic growth?" *World Bank Economic Review* 10: 1–25.

Rawski, T. G. (2002). "Will investment behavior constrain China's growth?" *China Economic Review* 13(4): 361–72.

Reinhart, C. M. and V. R. Reinhart (2008). "Capital inflows and reserve accumulation, the recent evidence." *NBER Working Paper Series* 13842 (March).

Reinhart, C. M. and K. S. Rogoff (2009). *This Time Is Different: Eight Centuries of Financial Folly*. Princeton, N.J., Princeton University Press.

Ridgeway, R. H. (1929). "Summarized data of gold production." *U.S. Department of Commerce, Bureau of Mines, Economic Paper* 6.

Roberts, I. and R. Tyers (2003). "China's exchange rate policy: The case for greater flexibility." *Asian Economic Journal* 17(2): 155–84.

Robinson, J. (1962). *Economic Philosophy*. London, Pelican Books.

Rodrik, D. (2006). "Goodbye Washington consensus, hello Washington confusion? A review of the World Bank's economic growth in the 1990s: Learning from a decade of reform." *Journal of Economic Literature* 44(4): 973–87.

Roger, S. and M. Stone (2005). "On target? The international experience with achieving inflation targets." *IMF Working Paper* 163 (August).

Rogoff, K. (1985). "The optimal degree of commitment to an intermediate monetary target." *Quarterly Journal of Economics* 100(4): 1169–89.

——— (2004). "Globalization and global disinflation." Paper presented at the Monetary Policy and Uncertainty: Adopting to a Changing Economy symposium, August 28–30, Jackson Hole, Wyo.

——— (2006). "Impact of globalization on monetary policy." Paper presented at the New Economic Geography: Effects and Policy Implications symposium, August 24–26, Jackson Hole, Wyo.

Romer, C. (2009). *Lessons from the Great Depression for Economic Recovery in 2009*. Washington, D.C., Brookings Institution.

Romer, C. and D. Romer (1998). "Monetary policy and the well-being of the poor." *NBER Working Paper Series* 6793 (November).

——— (2008). "The FOMC versus the staff: Where can monetary policymakers add value?" *American Economic Review* 98: 230–35.

Romer, D. (1985). "Financial intermediation, reserve requirements and inside money: A general equilibrium analysis." *Journal of Monetary Economics* 16(2): 175–94.

——— (1993). "Openness and inflation—Theory and evidence." *Quarterly Journal of Economics* 108(4): 869–903.

Rose, A. K. (2006). "A stable international monetary system emerges: Inflation targeting is Bretton Woods reversed." *NBER Working Paper Series* 12711 (November).

Roubini, N. and X. Sala-i-Martin (1992). "A growth model of inflation, tax evasion and financial repression." *NBER Working Paper Series* 3702 (May).

——— (1995). "A growth-model of inflation, tax evasion, and financial repression." *Journal of Monetary Economics* 35(2): 275–301.

Rudd, J. and K. Whelan (2003). "Inflation targets, credibility, and persistence in a simple sticky-price framework." *Board of Governors of the Federal Reserve System, Finance and Economics Discussion Series* 2003-43.

Rudebusch, G. D. (1995). "Federal reserve interest rate targeting, rational expectations and the term structure." *Journal of Monetary Economics* 35: 245–74.

Sachs, J. (1987). "The Bolivian hyperinflation and stabilization." *American Economic Review* 77(2): 279–83.

———— (1989). "Social conflict and populist policies in Latin America." *NBER Working Paper Series* 2897 (March).

Sachs, J., A. Tornell, and A. Velasco (1996). "Financial crisis in emerging markets: The lessons from 1995." *Brookings Papers on Economic Activity* 1: 147–215.

Saint Simon (1985). *Memoires (1714–1716), Additions au Journal de Dangeau*. Paris, Gallimard.

Samuelson, P. A (1946). "Lord Keynes and the general theory." *Econometrica* 14(3): 187–200.

———— (1958). "An exact consumption-loan model of interest with or without the social contrivance of money." *Journal of Political Economy* 66: 467–82.

———— (1968). "What classical and neoclassical monetary theory really was." *Canadian Journal of Economics* 1 (February): 1–15.

Samuelson, P. A. and R. Solow (1960). "Analytical aspects of anti-inflation policy." *American Economic Review* 50(2): 177–94.

Samuelson, R. J. (2008). *The Great Inflation and Its Aftermath: The Past and Future of American Affluence*. New York, Random House.

Sandmo, A. (2011). *Economics Evolving: A History of Economic Thought*. Princeton, N.J., Princeton University Press.

Sarel, M. (1996). "Non-linear effects of inflation on economic growth." *IMF Staff Papers* 43(1).

Sargent, T. J. (1973). "Rational expectations, the real rate of interest and the natural rate of unemployment." *Brookings Papers on Economic Activity* 2: 429–72.

———— (1982). "The ends of four big inflations." *Inflation, Causes and Effects*. R. Hall, ed. Chicago, University of Chicago Press: 41–97.

———— (1983). "Stopping moderate inflations: The methods of Poincare and Thatcher. *Inflation, Debt and Indexation*. R. Dornbusch and M. Simonsen, eds. Cambridge, Mass., MIT Press: 54–96.

———— (1987). *Dynamic Macroeconomic Theory*. Cambridge, Mass., Harvard University Press.

———— (1993). "The ends of four big inflations." *Inflation, Causes and Effects*. R. E. Hall, ed. Chicago, University of Chicago Press: 41–97.

———— (1999). *The Conquest of American Inflation*. Princeton, N.J., Princeton University Press.

———— (2008). "Evolution and intelligent design." *American Economic Review* 98(1): 5–37.

———— (2010) "Interview with Thomas Sargent." *The Region* 24(3): 26–39. http://www.minneapolisfed.org/pubs/region/10-09/region_sept2010.pdf.

———— (2011). "Where to draw lines: Stability versus efficiency." *Economica* 78: 197–214.

Sargent, T. J. and F. Velde (1995). "Macroeconomic features of the French Revolution." *Journal of Political Economy* 103(3): 474–518.

———— (2002). *The Big Problem of Small Change*. Princeton, N.J., Princeton University Press.

Sargent, T. J. and N. Wallace (1975). "Rational expectations, the optimal monetary instrument, and the optimal money supply rule." *Journal of Political Economy* 83(2): 241–54.

——— (1981). "Some unpleasant monetarist arithmetic." *Federal Reserve Bank of Minneapolis Quarterly Review* 5(3): 1–17.

——— (1982). "The real-bills doctrine versus the quantity theory: A reconsideration." *Journal of Political Economy* 90(6): 1212–36.

Sargent, T. J., N. Williams, and T. Zha (2009). "The conquest of South American inflation." *Journal of Political Economy* 117(2): 211–56.

Sayers, R. S. (1953). "Ricardo's views on monetary questions." *Quarterly Journal of Economics* 67(1): 30–49.

——— (1970). "The return to gold, 1925." *The Gold Standard and Employment Policies between the Wars.* S. Pollard, ed. London, Methuen: 85–98.

——— (1976). *The Bank of England, 1891–1944.* Cambridge, Cambridge University Press.

Sbordone, A. M. (2007). "Globalization and inflation dynamics: The impact of increased competition." *NBER Working Paper Series* 13556 (October).

Schelde-Andersen, P. (1992). "OECD country experiences with disinflation." *Inflation, Disinflation and Monetary Policy.* A. Blundell-Wignell, ed. Sydney, Reserve Bank of Australia, Ambassador Press.

Scheve, K. (2004). "Public demand for low inflation and the political economy of macroeconomic policymaking." *International Organization* 58 (Winter): 1–34.

Schmitt-Grohé, S. and M. Uribe (2005). "Optimal inflation stabilization in a medium scale macroeconomic model." *NBER Working Paper Series* 11854 (December).

Schularick, M. (2011). "Managing the world's dollar dependency." *Council on Foreign Relations Policy Innovation Memorandum* 1 (February).

Schumpeter, J. A. ([1954] 1997). *History of Economic Analysis.* London, Routledge.

Seabright, P., ed. (2001). *The Vanishing Rouble, Barter Networks and Non-Monetary Transactions in Post-Soviet Societies.* Cambridge, Cambridge University Press.

Shiller, R. J. (1996). "Why do people dislike inflation?" *NBER Working Paper Series* 5539 (April).

Shleifer, A. and D. Treisman (2000). *Without a Map: Political Tactics and Economic Reform in Russia.* Cambridge, Mass., MIT Press.

Sidrausky, M. (1967). "Rational Choice and Patterns of Growth in a Monetary Economy." *American Economic Review* 57: 534–44.

Silber, W. L. (2012). *Volcker: The Triumph of Persistence.* New York, Bloomsbury Press.

Silberling, N. J. (1924a). "Financial and monetary policy of Great Britain during the Napoleonic Wars, financial policy." *Quarterly Journal of Economics* 38(2): 214–33.

——— (1924b). "Financial and monetary policy of Great Britain during the Napoleonic Wars, Ricardo and the Bullion Report." *Quarterly Journal of Economics* 38(3): 397–439.

Sims, C. A. (1988). "Projecting Policy Effects with Statistical Models." *Revista da Análysis Económico* 3: 3–20.

——— (1994). "Simple model for study of the determination of the price level and the interaction of monetary and fiscal policy." *Economic Theory* 4: 381–99.

——— (2001). "Comment on Sargent and Cogley's evolving post–World War II inflation dynamics." *NBER Macroeconomics Annual* 16: 373–79.

———— (2005). "Limits to inflation targeting." *The Inflation-Targeting Debate*, 32. B. S. Bernanke and M. Woodford, eds. Chicago, University of Chicago Press: 283–309.

Skidelsky, R. (1992). *John Maynard Keynes: The Economist as Saviour, 1920–1937*. London, Macmillan.

———— (2009). *The Return of the Master*. London, Allen Lane.

Smith, A. ([1776] 1986). *The Wealth of Nations, Books I–III*. A. Skinner, ed. London, Penguin.

Smyth, D. J. (1994). "Inflation and growth." *Journal of Macroeconomics* 16(2): 261–70.

Solow, R. (1980). "On theories of unemployment." *American Economic Review* 70 (March): 1–11.

———— (1988). "Growth theory and after." *American Economic Review* 78(3): 307–17.

Steiner, A. (2010). "Central banks' dilemma: Reserve accumulation, inflation and financial instability." *Institute of Empirical Economic Research Working Paper* 84 (September).

Stiglitz, J. E. (2000). *Globalisation and Its Discontents*. London, Allen Lane.

———— (2010). "New $600B Fed stimulus fuels fears of US currency war." *Democracy Now* (November 5). http://www.democracynow.org/2010/11/5/new_600b_fed_stimulus_fuels_fears.

Stock, J. H. (2001). "Discussion of Cogley and Sargent's evolving post–World War II US inflation dynamics." *NBER Macroeconomics Annual* 16: 379–87.

Stock, J. H. and M. W. Watson (1999). "Forecasting inflation." *Journal of Monetary Economics* 44(2): 293–335.

———— (2002). "Has the business cycle changed and why?" *NBER Working Paper Series* W9127 (August).

Stockman, A. C. (1981). "Anticipated inflation and the capital stock in cash-in-advance economy." *Journal of Monetary Economics* 8: 387–93.

Sturzenegger, F. (1992). "Inflation and social welfare in a model with endogeneous financial adaptation." *NBER Working Paper Series* 4103 (June).

Sturzenegger, F. and M. Tommasi (1998). *The Political Economy of Reform*. Cambridge, Mass., MIT Press.

Summers, L. H. (1981). "Optimal inflation policy." *Journal of Monetary Economics* 7: 175–94.

Svensson, L. E. O. (1999). "Price stability as a target for monetary policy: Defining and maintaining price stability." *CEPR Discussion Papers* 2196.

Tanzi, V. (1978). "Inflation, real tax revenue, and the case for inflationary finance—Theory with an application to Argentina." *IMF Staff Papers* 25(3): 417–51.

———— (1985). "Fiscal deficits and interest rates in the United States: An empirical analysis, 1960–84." *IMF Staff Papers* 32 (December): 551–76.

Taylor, J. B. (1993). "Discretion versus policy rules in practice." *Carnegie-Rochester Conference Series on Public Policy* 39: 195–214.

———— (1997). Comment on America's only peacetime inflation: The 1970s. *Reducing Inflation: Motivation and Strategy. NBER Studies in Business Cycles*, 30. C. D. Romer and D. Romer, eds. Chicago, University of Chicago Press: 276–80.

———— (1998). "Monetary policy guidelines for unemployment and inflation stability." *Inflation, Unemployment and Monetary Policy*. R. M. Solow and J. B. Taylor, eds. Cambridge, Mass., MIT Press: 29–54.

———— (2009a). "The financial crisis and the policy responses: An empirical analysis of what went wrong." *NBER Working Paper Series* 14631 (January).

———— (2009b). "The need to return to a monetary framework." *Business Economics* 44(2): 63–72.

———— (2010). "Does the crisis experience call for a new paradigm in monetary policy?" *CASE Network Studies and Analyses* 402.

Temin, P. (1989). *Lessons from the Great Depression*. Cambridge, Mass., MIT Press.

Tirole, J. (2010). "Lessons from the crisis." *Balancing the Banks: Global Lessons from the Financial Crisis*. M. Dewatripont, J.-C. Rochet, and J. Tirole, eds. Princeton, N.J., Princeton University Press: 10–77.

Tobin, J. (1965). "Money and Economic Growth." *Econometrica* 33 (October): 671–84.

———— (1969). "A general equilibrium approach to monetary theory." *Journal of Money, Credit and Banking* 1 (February): 15–29.

Tommasi, M. (1999). "On high inflation and the allocation of resources." *Journal of Monetary Economics* 14: 401–21.

Tornell, A. and A. Velasco (1995). "Money-based versus exchange rate-based stabilization with endogenous fiscal policy." *C.V. Starr Center for Applied Economics, New York University Working Papers* 95–21.

Trabandt, M. and H. Uhlig (2009). "How far are we from the slippery slope? The Laffer curve revisited." *NBER Working Paper Series* 15343 (September).

Trehan, B. and C. E. Walsh (1990). "Seigniorage and tax smoothing in the United States, 1914–1986." *Journal of Monetary Economics* 25(1): 97–112.

Triffin, R. (1946–47). "National central banking and the international economy." *Review of Economic Studies* 14(2): 53–75.

Turnovsky, S. J. (1980). "The choice of monetary instrument under alternative forms of price expectations." *Manchester School* 48: 39–62.

Tytell, I. and S.-J. Wei (2004). "Does financial globalization induce better macroeconomic policies?" *IMF Working Paper* 84 (May).

Uhlig, H. (2005). "What are the effects of monetary policy on output? Results from an agnostic identification procedure." *Journal of Monetary Economics* 52 (2): 381–419.

U.S. Department of the Treasury (2007). "The second U.S.–China strategic economic dialogue, May 22–23, Washington, joint fact sheet." http://www.ustreas.gov/press/releases/hp425.htm.

Vegh, C. (1992). "Stopping high inflation: An analytical overview." *IMF Staff Papers* 39(3): 626–95.

Velde, F. R. (2009a). "The case of the undying debt." *Federal Reserve Bank of Chicago Working Paper* 2009–12. http://ssrn.com/abstract=1514417.

Velde, F. R. (2009b). "Chronicle of a deflation unforetold." *Journal of Political Economy* 117(4): 591–634.

Vestin, D. (2006). "Price level versus inflation targeting." *Journal of Monetary Economics* 53(7): 1361–76.

Viner, J. (1937). *Studies in the Theory of International Trade.* Library of Economics and Liberty. http://www.econlib.org/library/NPDBooks/Viner/vnSTT5.html.

Wagner, H. (2001). "Implications of globalization for monetary policy." *IMF Working Paper* 184 (November).

Wai, U. T. (1959). "The relation between inflation and economic development: A statistical inductive study." *IMF Staff Papers* 17 (October).

Walsh, C. E. (1998). *Monetary Theory and Policy.* Cambridge, Mass., MIT Press.

Warburton, P. (1999). *Debt and Delusion: Central Bank Follies That Threaten Economic Disaster.* London, Allen Lane.

Warnock, F. E. (2010). "How dangerous is U.S. government debt? The risk of a sudden spike in U.S. interest rates." *Capital Flows Quarterly* (June).

Warnock, F. E. and V. C. Warnock (2009). "International capital flows and U.S. interest rates." *Journal of International Money and Finance* 28(6): 903–19.

Wen, Y. (2011). "Explaining China's trade imbalance puzzle." *Federal Reserve Bank of St. Louis Working Paper* 2011-018A (August). http://research.stlouisfed.org/wp/2011/2011-018.pdf.

Wennerlind, C. (2005). "David Hume's monetary theory revisited: Was he really a quantity theorist and an inflationist?" *Journal of Political Economy* 113(1): 223–37.

White, L. H. (2010). "The rule of law or the rule of central bankers?" *Cato Journal* 30(3): 451–63.

White, W. R. (2006). "Is price stability enough?" *BIS Monetary and Economic Department Working Papers* 205.

Wijnbergen, S. van (1991). "Fiscal deficits, exchange rate crises and inflation." *Review of Economic Studies* 58: 81–92.

Williams, D. (1963). "London and the 1931 financial crisis." *Economic History Review, New Series* 15(3): 513–28.

Wolman, A. L. (2005). "Real implications of the zero bound on nominal interest rates." *Journal of Money, Credit, and Banking* 37(2): 273–96.

Woodford, M. (1994). "Monetary policy and price level determinacy in a cash in advance economy." *Economic Theory* 4: 345–80.

——— (1995). "Price level determinacy without control of a monetary aggregate." *Carnegie Rochester Conference Series on Public Policy* 43.

——— (1996). "Control of the public debt: A requirement for price stability." *NBER Working Paper Series* 5684 (July).

——— (1999a). "Optimal monetary policy inertia." *NBER Working Paper Series* 7261 (July).

——— (1999b). "Revolution and evolution in twentieth-century macroeconomics." Paper presented at the Frontiers of the Mind in the Twenty-First Century conference, June, Library of Congress, Washington, D.C.

——— (2001). "Fiscal requirements for price stability." *Journal of Money, Credit, and Banking* 33: 669–728.

———— (2003). *Interest and Prices: Foundations of a Theory of Monetary Policy*. Princeton, N.J., Princeton University Press.

———— (2007). "How important is money in the conduct of monetary policy?" *NBER Working Paper Series* 13325 (August).

World Bank (2007). "Brazil: Measuring poverty using household consumption." Poverty Reduction and Economic Management Sector Unit, Latin America and the Caribbean Region, 36358-BR (January 10).

———— (2008). *Global Development Finance: The Role of International Banking*. Washington, D.C., World Bank.

Wynne, M. A. and E. K. Kersting (2007). "Openness and inflation." *Federal Reserve Bank of Dallas Staff Papers* 2 (April).

Zhang, C. S. (2007). "Low inflation, pass-through, and a discrete inflation-targeting framework for monetary policy in China." *China & World Economy* 15(2): 59–73.

Index

Page numbers in italics refer to figures and tables.